Clifford Hanley is something of a Scottish institution. His working life began in journalism, and branched into radio writing, the music hall, the legitimate theatre, songwriting and television. His first published book, *Dancing in the Streets*, an affectionate evocation of Glasgow childhood, was hailed as a classic, and in a score of novels and non-fiction works he has acquired a mass of happy readers. His thrillers under the pseudonym of Henry Calvin have a cult quality.

His lyric to the ancient pipe tune *Scotland the Brave*, written absentmindedly one Saturday morning, is the undoubted national anthem of Scotland – much to his surprise.

Hanley is married, with three adult children. His hobbies are talking, language, music and golf.

Also by Clifford Hanley

ANOTHER STREET, ANOTHER DANCE

and published by Corgi Books

Dancing in the Streets

Clifford Hanley

CORGI BOOKS

DANCING IN THE STREETS

A CORGI BOOK 0 552 12458 3

Originally published in Great Britain by
Hutchinson & Co. (Publishers) Ltd.

PRINTING HISTORY

Hutchinson edition published 1958
Grey Arrow edition published 1961
Mainstream edition published 1983
Corgi edition published 1984

Copyright © Clifford Hanley 1983

This book is set in 10/11 Times

Corgi Books are published by Transworld Publishers Ltd.,
Century House. 61-63 Uxbridge Road, Ealing, London W5 5SA

Printed and bound in Great Britain by
Hunt Barnard Printing Ltd, Aylesbury, Bucks.

*This book is for my mother,
without whom, after all,
it truly wouldn't be here*

Let there be dancing in the streets, drinking in the saloons and necking in the parlours.
Julius (Groucho) Marx

CONTENTS

Author's Foreword

Although I have not knowingly tampered with any essential truths in this book, I have taken the reasonable liberty of telescoping some events, reshuffling various bits of chronology, moving some individuals about and giving some of them false moustaches to save them possible embarrassment in a public appearance which they did not seek. A man who is bandying his friends about ought to bandy them gently. My bandy acquaintances will understand this, and forgive me.

There's Something Out There

My brother Jimmie used to tell me the Hanleys came to Glasgow on a banana boat, and it worried me. I liked bananas, but I could tell from the way he said it there was something declassé about travelling with them. When I was older, he changed his story to a potato-boat, and this seemed acceptable, and may even be true.

At any rate, when I think of Glasgow I can't imagine it without Hanleys in it, and it has ended with a fair number, although some fled the country at intervals and tried to forget the whole thing.

The first Hanley of our line came from Dublin some time around the turn of the century. This was Fred, my grandfather. Although I recollect him as a tall, gaunt figure, it seems he was quite a small man, a piece of hereditary carelessness which we have never forgiven him. He spoke with a liverish precision of manner and took a terrible bucket. Soon after reaching Glasgow he settled in the far east of the city, in what was still virtually the quiet little village of Shettleston, and spent the rest of his life there, most of it in the same house as far as I know.

Fred was a master shoemaker, so good at the trade that he picked up a good job with the Co-operative straight away. He would work away at this till he got thirsty, and then drink himself into a murderous state of grievance, or maybe work himself into the state without the thirst, and stamp out never to return. Then he would set up in his own shop in competition, till he had drunk the kitty, and go back to the Co-op. There was more room in Glasgow in those days for a good man with eccentric habits. All I know about him, apart from that, are that he was sometimes supposed to be related to O'Donovan Rossa, a hero of the Irish Fenians freedom movement, and he may well have been, since all Irishmen are related to the kings of Ireland; and that he was a man of uninhibited principle as shown in two family legends.

One winter morning when my father was a boy of about

fourteen, he got up with his father to go to work at some dauntingly early hour. As he was putting his boots on he dozed off gently in the chair by the fire, and Fred called him sharply to a sense of duty by throwing a shoemaker's last at his head. That last has been flying through my own head since I first heard of it.

The other thing happened many years later when my mother had taken her first few children to visit the old man, who was very strong on the inaudibility of well-behaved children. My sister Mary asked innocently what was the stuff in the jar that Grandpa spread on his meat. Before my mother could hush her or explain, Fred cried, 'If you're inquisitive, miss, you can find out!' And he filled a spoon with mustard and stuffed it into Mary's mouth.

What went before Fred I have never plucked up the courage to find out. Another legend suggests that there was an uncle, or a cousin, or perhaps even a neighbour or some sort, in Ireland, who emigrated to America and became rich with a silk mill in Pennsylvania so that he could send money home to help the Irish throw out the English. It all sounds too pat to be true. If it is, he is the smartest Hanley yet. None of us has ever been able to trace hair or hide of him, which makes him even smarter.

But it isn't only to parade the aristocratic blood I have mentioned this old history. The subsequent affairs of this immigrant breed are kind of symbolic of Glasgow itself, and if they aren't I'm still going to tell them.

Fred was not only a Southern Irishman but a good Catholic, and yet he married an English girl who was a Protestant. This is a thing that goes on and on happening in Glasgow, in spite of the tuts of the ministers and the thunderings of the priests, and every time it does happen, Glasgow people shake their heads as if it was an original catastrophe, the first of its kind and the beginning of the end of the world. His large family was brought up in the Catholic faith, but all his sons married Protestant girls too. The wives turned Catholic, and twice as Romish as any born Irishman, so it looked like the vindication of the glum Protestant prophesies that the Papes are overrunning

12

the country and will drive everybody else under in time. But my father did what he could to restore the balance by adopting Protestantism when he married his Protestant bride, and giving the city nine fresh Hanley children to keep things even. My mother's maiden name was Griffiths but her mother was a McLean from Tiree in the Inner Hebrides, so our branch of the Hanleys can claim a thorough mixture of Scots, Irish, English and Welsh, and it would be ungrateful to ask for more.

But that is Glasgow – a million people as mixed and unexpected as any Oriental bazaar, and they can stay mixed as far as I'm concerned. That's the way I like them. There are prettier cities, and it wouldn't be hard for a city to be prettier, but few of them that I know have the seething cauldron effect that Glasgow has always had for me. Out of its horrible smoke bleary streets it keeps throwing up jokes and songs and poetry as well as bloody murder. A dark jollity of life bubbles through it as if it were not a city at all but a monster, an enormous octopus of the kraken itself, except that this kraken has never slept. I can feel it around me as I write, and I can tell you, it fairly gives me the creeps.

A Breathless Hush in the Close Tonight

It is so ludicrous to imagine anybody actually building the things that I have always assumed that Glasgow's tenements have just always been there. Nobody could have put them up deliberately. When I first read about the ancient Picts running about in woad and scaring the life out of Caesar's legions, I took it for granted that they did their running about through the closes and back courts of Gallowgate where I was born.

The tenements are built extravagantly of good sandstone, so that they have outlasted all those generations of Picts and are still there, and there doesn't seem anything anybody can do about them. It's true that in George Street and over in Govan, on the south side of the Clyde, some of them have started falling down spontaneously during the past ten years, but this is probably because people left them and they got lonely, and not through any constitutional weakness.

Most of them run to four storeys, built in rectangles to enclose the back courts. The back courts are divided by brick walls and brick-built wash-houses built for climbing over. It was on one of these that I made my first acquaintance with the terror that lurks in the big city. I would be four years old at the time, a perilous age in Glasgow because in order to live a full rich life at four, you have to attach yourself to the bigger fry and they can always run faster and jump higher than you can. So I was at the tail end of the line one night on the run along the top of the back court wall in Gallowgate and on to the high wash-houses of Cubie Street, and I was good and far behind when I arrived at one of the obstacles of the course.

There was a turn in the wall, and in order to finish the run you had to dreep to the ground, stand on a dustbin to get astride the next bit of wall and then home to the roofs. The instant I lowered myself to dreep I knew it was too far. It was too dark to see the ground below, but I had heard enough about people breaking both legs. I had heard practically nothing else, in fact, from the time I could walk. But by this time I was hanging by my fingers and I couldn't climb back up either. I shouted, but nothing happened, so I screamed, and I had a good vibrant scream in those days. A Glasgow back court on a dark Tuesday night is the loneliest place in the world.

Some time later my sister Johanne, sitting in the house a hundred yards away and two storeys up, recognized the screams and bolted out to save me. She had to prise my fingers off the top of the wall before she could pick me down.

Danger and death were always familiar acquaintances. A few weeks later the boy downstairs, Tommy Mulholland, was playing on his rocking-horse on the first-floor landing when the whole thing overturned and carried him down a flight in a oner. It never seemed to cure him of riding facing the stairs, though it may seem odd that he was riding a rocking-horse on the landing at all.

The explanation is that the close in Glasgow is not just a hole in a building but a way of life. The close leads directly from the street to the back court, and the staircase to the flats above starts in the middle of it; and there is always something going on – somebody is always washing it or writing on the walls or hiding in it or giving a yell to test the echo.

After they wash it, the women give the stone flags a finish of wet pipeclay that dries bold and white and shows every footprint. Then, round the edges, they add a freehand border design drawn in pipeclay; sometimes a running loop like blanket-stitch, sometimes more tortuous key patterns, always mathematically accurate. It's a symptom of the unquenchable folk memory, or something, derived from long-buried Celtic eternity and fertility symbols.

By day the close and the stairs rang with the old cries and chants of Glasgow. Sonny Hillhouse (Sonny would be about twenty years old), always obliged with his own version of the popular hits on his way upstairs. I can still hear him:

> 'Am I wasting my time,
> By smoking Woodbine
> And wheezing the way that I do . . .'

Or another Gallowgate favourite:

> 'If you should see a big fat wummin
> Staunin' at the coarner bummin'
> That's my Mammy . . .'

Some cheery housewife on the top landing would join in the chorus with encouraging shouts of 'Nark it!' or 'Shut yer noisy jaw!'

The steady thud of a doormat being walloped against

15

the back wall of the close would counterpoint the descending clatter of Tommy Mulholland's rocking horse, and through the open stairhead window on the mid-landing my own voice would shrill up at our kitchen window from the back court, 'Haw Maw! Throw doon a jeely piece!' We had insatiable appetites for jeely pieces, cut thick from the loaf and spread thick, and at any moment of the day at least one kitchen window would be open and at least one slab of bread and jelly would be flying down to at least one ravenous wean in the back court. My mother, unlike some reckless parents, always wrapped it in a paper bag before she threw it. But the children of the non-wrapping parents picked their pieces out of the puddles and ate them all the same. We were all immune to earth and mud.

When young fry passed one another on the stairs, the close would clang to another two-part chant that gave us a deep sense of satisfaction.

'Honny-ne-naw, watch yer jaw!'

'Honny-ne-aye, watch yer eye!'

As night closed down, and in my recollection it closed down darker in Gallowgate, in spite of the street lamps and the lit shops, than it ever does in the unlit countryside, the close cries died too, but there were other noises for the dim hours. When it was really quiet, then was the hour of the curious yell, 'Who broke Singer's sewin' machine?' and the answering shout, 'It was me, it was me!' and the frantic clattering of feet on stone stairs.

Kicking other people's doors is a sport with its own added dimension when played in Glasgow tenements. The gang requires an innocent sucker, and explains to him that it's his turn to be het, and that he must go to the top landing of the close and running down answering 'It was me, it was me!' when he hears the question from the close. As soon as he gets up, the rest of the gang kick all the doors or ring all the doorbells on the lower landings so that the tenants will rush out in answer just as the victim passes with his innocent, damning cry. I don't believe anybody was ever taken in with this. The victim always knew what the game was, but he played it out anyway.

We always talked about getting bits of rope and tying door-handles together in the closes or the landings so that two families would be trapped in their houses, but bits of rope were hard to find. Everybody remembered what a great game this had been the last time he played it, but nobody ever actually got a piece of rope *this* time. Except once I was playing with two of the big yins, who let me come along to be 'het' in the Singer's sewing machine game, and we actually got some string. I was given one end and they took the other, and we went into a close in Cubie Street to tie the two facing doors together. The two of them were giggling between themselves, and looking back years later I realized they were probably planning some surprise trick, like kicking their door and escaping in time to leave me behind and trapped. But as I stretched up to tie my end of string round my door-handle, the door casually opened and a man looked out. I was out of the close and scuttling for safety in less than a second, but the two others were caught red-handed.

It was fine ringing doorbells in a gang, but lone children coming up their own stairs after sunset had another cry – 'O-pen! PN!' It penetrated through every house in the building, a merry ring. But under the mere expression of noisy high spirits was a thin undertone of fear. For a close at night, even your own familiar close, is a menacing thing, and there is nothing you want so much as the heartening sound of your mother opening the door for you upstairs before you even start climbing. There might be Anything lurking on one of the landings under the sputtering gaslight; in fact, there is, you know there is. But you can't linger at the foot of the stairs either, for there you are too close to the back court, and that's nothing but a rectangle of blackness at the rear of the close.

Even without going into the close at all you can feel the dark menace, for in a quiet street at night, your quiet footsteps abruptly throw back an echo each time you pass a close. You look in quickly, and there's that dark limbo at the other end. Or you force yourself not to look round, but you can feel the blackness through the side of your face, and you break into a run, but that merely quickens the rhythm of your unease, for as your feet echo past each close, you realize that something is running along keeping in step with you *at the back of the building*, hurdling the back court walls effortlessly with its long legs . . . and how many long legs?

So when you see a boy running on the pavement and uttering a sharp hoot as he passes each close in a Glasgow street, he isn't doing this merely to enjoy the echo and annoy the burghers. He is shouting his defiance at something in the back court that keeps pace with his every step.

And he is listening to it shouting back.

There was a doleful ballad of the First World War called *Suvla Bay*, and we grew up in Gallowgate singing our own words to that too, and they said:

> 'Why do I weep?
> For Flannelfeet
> Is up a close
> In Bellfield Street.'

I wanted to know who Flannelfeet was, but nobody could tell me very clearly, and I never found out, and later I didn't want to find out. What I do know is that the closes in Bellfield Street were the worst.

Shopped

Sam the grocer had a daughter the same age as myself, and I can't remember her name, but I know she had a red coat with white fur round the collar and she might well have been called Betty. It was always bright and cheerful in the shop, and one afternoon I got in to play with Betty and keep her out of Sam's hair.

Soon we found the best place was behind the counter on **our hands and knees, dodging Sam's feet while he served**

18

and popping up to startle the customers. He must have been a long-suffering grocer as grocers go. But he had a girl assistant in the shop too, and she began to prey on my mind. She was a big, healthy girl with big healthy legs, and every time I caught sight of them from my position on the floor I got confused again. I was sure she was wearing silk stockings, the fine flesh-coloured kind, and I knew about them because I had four sisters quite a lot older than myself. But surely even fine stockings would look more like stockings? These looked just like skin. You couldn't see a thread or a wrinkle. She wasn't wearing stockings at all, in fact. And yet the next time her calves passed in front of my face I felt sure I had been right the first time. After about ten minutes of this my eyes were shrinking to pinpoints and I couldn't bear the uncertainty, so I finally reached out, while she was cutting a pound of cheese, and touched her calf to make sure.

The cheese flew across the counter and she screamed. It seemed a terrible fuss to make over an act of simple curiosity, and I tried to explain that I had just been settling my mind, but I was ordered to get into the back shop and stay there.

Betty was a nice little thing. She spoke school even when she was just playing, saying 'down' for 'doon', and 'I' for 'ah'. This put me instantly in her power. We ourselves grew up trilingual. We spoke the King's English without any difficulty at school, a decent grammatical informal Scots in the house, and gutter-Glasgow in the streets, and we never mixed the three or used the wrong one except as a joke. There was nothing wrong with people who spoke school English all the time, but they were a little cut off from real life, or suffering from harmless pretentiousness, or maybe just foreigners who didn't know. All the same, when Betty said things like 'down' for 'doon', or 'girl' – an alien, English usage this – instead of 'lassie' – when she did this, she somehow acquired authority with her strangeness, and with that and the fact that it was her father's shop and not mine, I was as putty.

'I like sticking my finger in the flour,' she told me

19

warningly. There was an open sack of flour just inside the door of the back shop.

'Do you no' get intae a row?'

'Nobody would know.' And she stuck a finger into the white flour and pulled it out white and slapped her hands together to shake the stuff off. It looked like a good idea, so I stuck my finger into the flour too.

'Daddy!' she shouted, 'He put his hand in the flour!'

Sam came back, muttering and said to me, 'Any mair o' that, and right out the door.' I shook my head and looked innocent with the flour dropping off my hand on to my jersey. As soon as Sam had gone back to the front shop, Betty said, 'I won't tell if you do it again.'

'Ye will.'

'No, honestly, I won't tell.'

It was irresistible – all that lovely white flour crying out for a hand to be stuck in it. I stuck my hand in again, and Betty shouted again. This time Sam was quite angry. I was put out of the shop and barred for life. It was the first time I had been deliberately deceived. I couldn't understand it.

Blood and the Demon

Glasgow stands on sixty hills where Rome can claim only seven; and it stands on the three principles that have made it famous over the world – drink, violence and crime. It isn't very long since an American evangelist incited the headhunters of Borneo to pray for the soul of this brawling sinful city. It oppresses me to think of all those well-meaning headhunters praying at me and me not able to do anything back at them. But the drink and crime legend has got to the pitch nowadays at which Glaswegians slily encourage it as Aberdonians give currency to Aberdeen jokes.

There were gangs in Glasgow in those Gallowgate days of the twenties all right. They blossomed redly after the world war. It wasn't until years later that I learned anything intelligible about them, because talk of such things was never encouraged at home, maybe on the principle that if you pretend they're not there they'll go away. As Rangers and Celtic were the giants of football – I didn't even know there were other football teams until we had left Gallowgate – the Billy Boys and the Sally Boys were the giants of gangdom, and we sometimes played Billies and Sallies the way we played cowboys and Indians, although cowboys and Indians was better. We knew all about guns and bows and arrows, but we had never heard of razors.

The gangs of the twenties grew out of depression and unemployment as gangs have done in other places at other times in history. Glasgow, in spite of its sooty grey look, or maybe because of it, has always needed colour and the gangs gave colour to some people if it was only the colour of blood. These were never comparable to the Prohibition gangs of Chicago. The American gangs were illegal business enterprises that used violence and death as trading methods in the rational pursuit of profit. The Glasgow gangs never made any money for anybody. They existed for fun. Gang bosses never graduated to Cadillacs or even Austin Sevens, far less villas on the coast and political pull. They just wanted a fight. They started poor and they finished poor and they stayed poor in between.

One of their best excuses for fighting was religion. The Billy Boys took their name from that remote Protestant gentleman King William of Orange and the Sally Boys took theirs from Salamanca Street, where the founders lived. But I never yet saw a Billy Boy or a Sally Boy to identify, though my father once had to nip up a close smartly to escape being mixed up in a brawl and maybe arrested since he was small-built and not likely to give the police trouble.

It's odd that not only Glasgow's Catholics but Glasgow's militant Protestants take their aggressive inspiration from Ireland, for Ulster is the home of the Orangemen and a place given to good rousing religious bigotry just as Eire is the fount of the Fenians. Not that I would deprive

21

Glasgow of any of the credit for Billy and Sally. Long afterwards, when I had read Sean O'Casey and heard about the 1916 Rising and once even met face to face the late Jim Larkin, senior – the titanic Irish patriot who came to Liverpool and told the authorities candidly that the purpose of his visit was to overthrow the British Government – these years later, I acquired a kind of astonished liking for the Fenians, astonished because such a thing denied the very principles of my childhood. And even before that I had taken a kind of scunner at the Orangemen, and not on religious grounds at all. It was the music of an Orangemen's band that drove me away.

It must have been the day of an Orange Walk – 'The Twelfth of July, the Papes'll die' – the formidable anniversary rally of the Orangemen when they gather from all airts to spend a day dedicating themselves to the downfall of Rome and the restocking of their fervour. It's a poor Lodge that doesn't have a band.

This one marched up Cubie Street on the way to some railway station to join the rally, and I caught the words 'Orange Walk' from passers-by with a strain of apprehension in them that infected me too. If they were Orangemen, then naturally I was on their side, but the way people said it suggested that they might decide to hit somebody, and how would they know I wasn't a Catholic? But they didn't hit anybody. They just marched up Cubie Street, wearing fancy blue sashes over their good suits and playing the strangest things – flutes. Now there's nothing wrong with a good flute, but a chorus of flutes and nothing but flutes has a surprising quality, like a first acquaintance with those twenty-four-note Oriental scales, and the oddity of it combined with the tangible unease in the people listening, put me off; and to tell the truth, I thought that in spite of the blue embroidered sashes they looked a bit scruffy, and pretty silly too.

The reason for the flutes, I imagine, is only partly historical and partly because a flute is cheaper than a trumpet, and Glaswegians of any denomination were not too rich. But who would ever expect a thing like a flute to be a recognized religious symbol? One of the oldest

Glasgow jokes is about a new Irish immigrant who went looking for work to a Glasgow Corporation building foreman, who he had been warned was Irish.

'Hallo,' he said, making the sign of the cross, 'have ye ony jobs, I don't suppose?'

'Aye,' said the foreman, imitating a flute player, 'start on Monday, I don't think.'

So on the twelfth of July, although at any other time we played with the Catholics of the neighbourhood and never noticed it, we would be exclusively Protestant, and always ready for the challenge from any other wandering gang—

'A Billy or a Dan or an auld tin can?' The wrong answer might mean a stand-up fight and personally, I always said an auld tin can because there was no known procedure for that. I suppose it meant a religious nothing, so it was prophetic. Still today, the day of the Orange Walk produces its little spots of trouble in Glasgow, for there's nothing like religious zeal to put a man in the mood for a fight, and, not to shilly-shally about it, after the Walk some of the boys are not above taking a dram.

And then there are the songs to go with that flute music. Because people in Glasgow are always singing or dancing or both, as you can find in any side street in the slums any dry day of the year. Whether I was an auld tin can or not I could sing the fighting Orange songs with the best. There was one that went to the tune of 'Marching Through Georgia'.

'Hullo! Hullo! We are the Billy Boys.
Hullo! Hullo! We are the Billy Boys.
Up tae the knees in Fenian blood, surrender or ye'll die
For we are the Brigton Billy Boys.'

I liked that. Another adopted the melody of 'The Girl I Left Behind Me'

'King Billy slew the Fenian crew
At the battle o' Byne Watter
A pail o' tripe came over the dyke
An' hut the Pope on the napper.'

23

Good, vivid imagery. You could actually see the pail, and when we were far enough out of earshot of home, it was something worse than tripe that was in it. The Catholics must have had their songs too, but apart from plainly Irish songs, there was little evidence of them. As well as the bloodthirsty songs, there were other Orange ditties like a sad-sounding ballad that drunk men often intoned with catches in their throats, and it still sounds hysterical to me.

> 'If you want to see King Billy
> Take a tramway to the cross
> And you'll see a noble soldier
> Riding on a big white horse.'

It went on and on, but it was hard to pick out any of the following verses as I never heard anybody singing it due sober. But the choicest of the factional songs I didn't hear until we had moved away from Gallowgate, and it was given to me as the signature tune of a Catholic gang that neither I nor anybody else had ever heard of. It had the tune of the 'Irish Jaunting Car'.

> 'Oh we are the Shettleston Antique Boys
> We are Fenians every one
> And when we meet the Billy Boys
> They will make us Fenians run.'

It was my brother Jackie who sang it to me, and I objected that they wouldn't sing a song like that.

'They have to,' he pointed out, 'because it's true.' Jackie could convince me of anything, being the natural boss of our age group in the family. The family started with Harry my eldest brother, then the four girls one after another, then Jackie, Jimmie, myself and David the youngest.

But that was the sum of the gang warfare and religious riots of my experience – a tootle on the flute and a handful of lyrics about long-ago battles that were never explained. I didn't even know that what I sang as the Byne was actually the Boyne.

There was the General Strike of 1926. And Gallowgate didn't miss it. To this day the family still recalls the day of the big riot when the shop windows were broken and not a hundred yards from our close there was a rollicking looting party at McBride and Black's the grocers, and scruffy brats were scuttling down Soho Street hitting whole cheeses before them with sticks as if they had been girds. Jackie and Jimmie and I accepted without question the dogma that people in Soho Street were a pretty low-class crowd by our standards, but we thought the cheese trick was great, if it ever happened.

All I can say myself is that I was living in a house with a grandstand view of one of the busiest main streets in working-class Glasgow and I never saw or suspected a thing. I recall with wonderful clarity that I was in the front room one day – not a very usual thing when there were no visitors because the front room had the good furniture and the alabaster model of the Taj Mahal my father had brought from India – and later I had the impression of recollecting rows of big brass spikes, as high as tramcars, standing up obliquely all the way along Gallowgate. I'm not suggesting that there ever were any such things. I do know I was taken away from the window in a hurry, and I decided afterwards that the oblique brass spikes were an optical illusion caused by my being yanked abruptly back into the room before I had a good look at anything. My mother was interested in my description of the spikes at the time, but she possibly didn't want to tell me what had actually been going on, thinking it might frighten me, and by the time I was old enough to be told without catching the vapours she herself had forgotten.

And that wraps up my analytical history of the causes and effects of the General Strike of 1926 in Glasgow.

Then there's drunkenness. At that time I knew what drunkenness was all right. It was never hard to find a drunk man in Glasgow if you know where to look – straight in front of you. Jimmie, who is three years older than I am, and was always a man of the world, explained to me that drunk men were really mad men, exactly the same thing, and he had the conscience to dissuade me from joining the crowds of kids who gathered round mirauc'lous drunks in the hope of pennies. For a real Glasgow drunk, if he doesn't want a fight, wants to give his money away. That's why they love Glaswegians in Blackpool and the Isle of Man. The English industrialist may tip sixpence and the American millionaire may put a comptometer on the bill to check mistakes in addition, but the Glaswegian on a spree wants rid of the filthy stuff. When the genuine Glasgow keelie steps off the train or the boat in Glasgow after his holidays, he thinks he has cheated somebody if he has enough in his pocket to pay his tram fare home.

And the drunks *did* give pennies away. They swayed on the corners and dug into their pockets for more pennies. Jimmie said that their wives needed those pennies to buy food for their children, and I didn't want to have their children starved, but I did feel that if the pennies were being handed out and the kids would starve anyway, I might as well have a penny as anybody else. That was before I discovered where Jimmie had picked up all this inside stuff about liquor. The Band of Hope, of course.

You can't have Glasgow without that because it illustrates one of the truths about the Glaswegian: he takes a mad breenge at everything he goes for. Glasgow drinking is savage and Glasgow temperance is practically lethal and it's hard to say which one is the cause of the other.

Jackie and Jimmie took me to the Band of Hope, in the Wesleyan hall in Wesleyan Street, and I got my first year's membership card and my first stamp on it. Without the membership card and a good show of attendance stamps you were kept out of the annual dumpling night at Christmas. Well do I remember the stunned, incredibly innocent faces of the rejected on dumpling night – most of them gatecrashers from other branches or the Chapel or England, even.

We sat at the back and joined in the hymn, an old Band of Hope favourite – 'Dare to Be a Daniel, Dare to stand alone', and a very useful watchword for five-year-olds in

26

Glasgow. It meant that no matter how much your school pals joshed you, you had to look noble and skip your turn at the whisky and soda.

>'Dare to have a purple film
>And dare to make it known',

Jimmie sang.

'What's a purple film?' I asked him, fascinated.

'It's in the hymn. I'll show you it next week.'

Next week I caught on. They had a magic lantern and a dim purple light shone out at the back of it all the time it was performing. But I still couldn't see what Daniel wanted a purple film for.

After the hymns and prayers the Band of Hope put on the main event. Many of these star turns stick out in my recollection, because even after we moved away from Gallowgate Jimmie and I kept going to another thing called the Guild of Honour, which was exactly the same as the Band of Hope except that it sounded higher-class and less proley.

The routine entertainment was a visiting speaker with a cute kind of title for his lecture, like 'More Precious than Gold' (water) or 'The Secret Enemy' (alcohol). Some brought anatomical charts to unroll and pictures of human tripes and cirrhosed liver sections, and so on, the kind of thing that interests toddlers to under-tens. Some of them didn't altogether grip their audiences, and the Band of Hope was a noisy kind of evening, but not so noisy as when the arrangements broke down and a speaker didn't appear. We had all the peevish impatience of a Roman arena crowd when the Christians have been withheld. All the same, I took everything in with passionate fixity. They didn't have to work hard on me – I was their boy from the first hand-coloured liver section I met. The first rumblings of disaffection didn't stir in my mind until the man with the water speech, which was years after my initiation.

He was a good enough performer, a bit on the thin nasal side vocally but fast and slick and well able to shut

27

hecklers up without any help from the chairman's gong. But he was just obsessed with water. He wasn't satisfied to take the traditional swipe at alcohol – *any* liquid except pure water was a fraud according to this fish. Tea was an insidious drug; coffee a rampant poison; cocoa an innocent enough thing in itself but dangerous and futile because, in making cocoa, you actually *boiled the purity out of the water.* You could see that given half a chance he would turn against water itself and leave us nothing to drink except saliva. I got so fed up with water that I finished up de-converted.

Apart from dumpling night, the star bill was easily the magic lantern. You could tell a magic lantern night instantly, from the mounting excitement in the hall and the burgeoning fear among the officials on the platform. They could put on as many hymns as they liked and stretch the prayers out till their throats cracked, but sooner or later they were going to be forced to bring on the big moment – Lights Out. And if we were a Roman arena mob in the electric light, what would we be in the dark? But why ask themselves the question? They knew the answer.

As Jimmie's command of original mythology grew, and how it was to grow! he revealed to me privately the reason why Big Jake always sneaked into the meeting with his young brother on lantern nights. Jake, a likeable shambling youth of nineteen or so and long past Band of Hope age, always sat right at the back.

'He's operating an illicit still while the lights are oot!' Jimmie told me.

Finally the lecturer had been introduced and the moment of truth couldn't be delayed longer.

'And remember, boys and girls,' the chairman cried, trying not to snarl, 'Mr Johnson is a stranger – he is our guest, and we must treat him as a guest, mustn't we?' And the girls, in their solid segregated block to the right of the aisle, chorused, 'Yes!' Confused shouts came from the male block on the left aisle and the chairman's eyes narrowed.

'And if any boy interrupts . . . or *throws anything* . . . he will be put out at once – and not only for tonight. He will miss Mr Johnson's lecture and *he will not be allowed back in. Ever again*!' The words struck an answering spark in our hearts as we groped through pockets for jauries and crumpled paper and pencil-stubs. But we kept an eye on the lecturer too. Would he have a clicker, or bang his pointer on the floor, or just snap his fingers? It was too much to hope that he would just snap his fingers. But some of us had clickers of our own.

You could never tell what system he would use if he had any experience in this grim trade. He knew the value of surprise.

'And remember, boys,' the chairman roared, 'there will be a monitor standing at the light-switch and I will not tell you when the lights are going to be switched on!' There were mutters of 'durty shame!' and 'Get them oot!' and finally they went oot.

Mr Johnson's assistant stood at the rear end of the aisle, among us, operating the lantern and changing the slides. Before he even had the first one flashed, some fool would start blazing away with his clicker and give the game away. Mr Johnson, smiling loftily to himself, would abandon his clicker and do his signals to the assistant by banging the pointer on the floor. It looked easy to impersonate this sound, but we never tumbled to it that the assistant knew Johnson's patter too, and blandly ignored all the thump-thumps on the floor from our boot-heels. They didn't really sound right anyway, but when one very rare effort did fool him, we were insane with joy. Once the darkness had grown familiar and safe a shower of pellets and bits of pocket-lumber started flying across the light beam. They were thrown so that they would register on the screen as well as landing on the defenceless rows of sanctimonious girls on the far side of the aisle. And now and then a desperate character would manage to escape from his seat and stick his hand right in the beam, a surefire show-stopper for the pew-sitters in the immortal words of Variety. It didn't happen often because there was a monitor at the end of nearly every row, ready to beat back rioters with his bare hands.

Suddenly there was a sharp movement from the platform and the house lights went up.

'*That boy*!' the chairman yelled. 'That yin there!' he added, his well-controlled English shattering under the tension.

'Me?' A beetle-browed lout near the front gazed up, hurt at the accusation. 'Ah never done anythin'!' Instantly everybody near him shouted, 'That's right, it wisnae him, sir!' and the chairman, losing the initiative, lifted his little gong with its wooden plinth and thundered with it on the table. 'If there's any more noise youse'll *all* get put out and there'll be *no lantern night*!' He sounded as if he meant it.

The barrage thinned out and the screams were muffled to mere yelps and Mr Johnson resumed his unflustered routine like a real pro. And it was a great show, when you could get a second to look at it.

'The Wrong Door.' How's that for a title? In full glowing unnatural colour too. You must remember that we were well into the movie era, although Al Jolson and the first all-talking, all-music film hadn't quite reached Glasgow. Still, we had Chaplin and Douglas Fairbanks and Theda Bara (my fidelity to whom has never wavered), and Fatty Arbuckle and all the others, every Saturday at the penny matineés at Scoats Pitcher Hoose in the Gallowgate. We were sophisticated children of the mechanical age, and the lantern nights were something of a return to the primitive – stooky pictures, I mean to say. Like many religious bodies, the Band of Hope was usually some years out of sync with the times. As well as being stooky (still), the characters in 'The Wrong Door' wore the proletarian uniform of a generation earlier. They were principally a family – a big family, all merry and bright and knowing their Place in the World, living in a trim little kitchen with bright flowered wallpaper and a rash of little red shield-shaped inspirational texts pinned up on it. Mother and Father and the wheen of weans were discovered in the first shot sitting round the family board, which had a lot of plates but nothing to eat that I remember except a dish containing about half a hundredweight of boiled potatoes – good homely fare and to hell with that balanced diet nonsense. Mother was ladling out spuds to the chuckies, Father was patting the infant on its big fat head and everybody was happy, so insistently happy you knew something frightful was being saved up for them and you were glad.

In the second shot father was leaving the gates of the factory where he worked – always an ominous step in the world of stooky pictures. Two or three of his workmates, easily identified as low-life, foul-mouthed Lombroso specimens and thoroughly interesting chaps, were trying to induce him to go home by their route, but Father was answering with a painful stare of horror and pity and refusal, with unlikely quotes supplied by Mr Johnson, who fancied himself at the Man-with-a-Thousand-Voices business.

The third episode was soggy with the sudden illness of the wean, round whose miserable cot the whole tribe was kneeling, and towards shot five or six, Father, his honest brow corrugated like a washing-board, was actually accepting the base invitation of his degenerate chums to get his feet in the sawdust on the way home – Just One Drink, of course. And Oh, boys and girls! how many poor men have uttered those Words and never realized what they were letting themselves in for which! Quick shot of a batwing door, period 1830, Golden Gulch – I told you the Band of Hope stuck to its own century – another quick cut to the bar, Father facing a brimming beaker, quick cut to Father downing it in one, slow sequence of Father insisting he must go – D. W. Griffith stuff all the way, or maybe Eisenstein; anyway, Mr Johnson's assistant was flipping slides through the machine like a Mississippi card-sharp and Mr Johnson's pointer was rattling a rhumba on the platform.

And what of Father's little ones? Those innocent little spud-gobblers with pasty smiles who were waiting for his return? Yes, there they were, the whole flaming shower, lined up by a stroke of telepathic genius right outside the pub door; Big Teenie joggling the wean in one hand and shoogling the pram in the other, and the remaining dozen

31

or so strung out along the frontage with their wee noses dripping and somebody shovelling torn-up paper on them from the flies. It was more than flesh and blood could stand. Back to Father – alas! the brain was fuddled and the beastliness that lurks in all of us was coming out in his frantic bid to buy another round for his chinas. It was the old, old story. He had belted the grape and the grape had belted him right back. And Mother? My God, here was Mother hanging upside down from a bosun's chair – no, it wasn't a bosun's chair, oh, hurray! Heh, heh! Stamp your feet and coup the bench – Mr Johnson's smart-alec assistant had finally got one in the wrong way up. Shut up at the back, here it came again, Ah, it wasn't a bosun's chair at all, it was the kitchen table, and Mother was sitting at it stricken with grief and shame.

In the interval since Dad left the factory gates, the paper had peeled off the walls, sizeable pieces of the ceiling had fallen, somebody had raked out the fire and thrown the coal away and the kitchen door had half a mind to come off its hinges. It was strong beer they sold in those days. Mother had shed about ten pounds of flesh too, and the mice had scoffed the last tiny tattie.

From that point on there was a definite decline in the dramatic value of the entertainment. Father, reduced in about four hours to a shambling alcoholic shell, reeled from the pub straight into another door – The Mission! (In those days they sent missionaries out to us to win us over to the Great White Father and the Queen-lady Empress far-off in heap big kraal by'm call um London.) Next minute a smirking individual was handing Father a tract which hit him like a prairie oyster, and putting his nerveless fingers round a pen poised above a pledge form.

The table-cloth re-materialized, the plaster flew back up to the ceiling and the paper went back to the wall, the Belfast boat came in with another forty tons of wholesome, nauseating potatoes, and Father resumed his place at the head of the table with his moon-faced smiling bairns. And if you wonder what they had to smile about you've missed the whole point – maybe it was *you* that was throwing that orange peel at the lantern! Yes, you in the third row with no behind in your breeks.

High Living

A terrible thing the drink, and no defence for us against it except the Band of Hope chant . . . 'honour my father and my mother and refrain from strong drink as a beverage . . . ' But it wasn't the drink that led us into crime. We couldn't afford any kind of steady drinking on a halfpenny a week pocket money. We just turned naturally to law-breaking out of the badness of our hearts. Even I, essentially a sensitive, pure-minded keelie, was a hog for bad company. Something, I don't know, some original flaw in my character hurled me into the arms of any fast set who were up to something no good if it looked easy enough.

So maybe it's just as well we flitted. That old Hanley wanderlust was stirring in the family, and shortly after my fifth birthday I found myself in the middle of the delirious excitement of a flitting.

Everybody else seemed to be busy hauling chairs and ornaments about, but in the middle of this Mary found time to wash my face. A few minutes later Johanne noticed me under somebody's feet and for want of anything better to do with me she washed my face too – 'You want to look nice for the new house,' she said. That was all right with me. When nobody bothered with me for ten minutes or so I went back to the jawbox and ran the tap over my head. I wanted to make a proper job of the thing while I was at it. The flitting was abandoned while half the team pulled me out from under the tap and dried me off, but nobody was much upset. One more little thing couldn't make any difference at a Hanley flitting. Soon afterwards I was hurried, wrapped like a mummy to keep the pneumonia out, downstairs, across Gallowgate and upstairs again. We had moved from the second floor flat on the south side to the second floor flat directly facing on the north side. We had begun to carve our way up through the amorphous social strata of the city, for there's no doubt that from the new windows, the old building was patently on the wrong side of the tracks. Instead of a long thin lobby, the new house had a square hall; and a bath, in a dim dark room off the hall shaped like a three-decker coffin. We had a big, opulent front parlour too, with a vast oval table supported in a tentative manner by a three-legged curly mahogany thing. It was a splendid table with a heavy chenille mat draped over it, and it took us years to get rid of it – in the end, a friend and I carried it between us to a school jumble sale, dumped it in a corner and denied all connexion with it.

There was more room in the new parlour too for my musical experiments. No Hanley was ever entirely un-musical. We could all at least sing, and usually did, sometimes in opposition, though Flora was the only one who showed the distressing mannerism of joining in somebody else's song note-perfectly but in a different key, almost the most disquieting sound ever made. Harry even had a saxophone at the time, and there was a harmonium in the parlour I could practise on. It had to be pedalled all the time and I was too short to reach the pedals from a chair, but I could cling with the left hand to the underside of the keyboard to support my body, pedal like mad and play with my right hand. I don't know which I liked more – doing that or taking up the same position at the sewing machine and pedalling it. There were so many of us in the house that we had tea in two relays, and my finger was wandering idly over the mighty keys one evening as I waited for the kids' shift to start when Mary heard me and cried in amaze:

'Look at that! He's playing on the black notes as well!' And me only five.

We had a party in that house too, the first I ever remember in our own house. There was a lot of home baking and dishes of almonds and sweets on the oval table, and some neighbouring children came in and we roasted chestnuts at the fire. It was a warm, friendly feeling, and I still remember the feeling and the bright red of the big fire and everybody laughing, although I can't think what else we did. Why do kids nowadays want all their pleasure manufactured for them? We busied ourselves with the simple things then, roasting chestnuts, fretwork, petty theft, and we were just as neurotic as they are without half the expense.

The backward pull of the old gang on the wrong side didn't weaken, all the same. Our new house was a posh affair, with a tiled close too – the ultimate seal of solidity in Glasgow society; but the new back court was a wee toty thing, shaped like a bannock and bounded by the highest wall in the world. Besides, most of the people we knew still lived on the even-numbers side of Gallowgate. I made friends with a wee boy who lived up our close, an awfully nice wee boy, but there's something limiting about a boy who wears new hand-knitted Fair Isle jerseys all the time and whose idea of a wild time is trying to sail a lead boat in a two-foot puddle round the back. I pointed out to him that my big brother (Jackie, this time) had spoiled boats-in-puddles for me by running a *railway* through a puddle. It was true. My father brought him a stupendous American-style clockwork train set home from one of his trips, with a cowcatcher engine, and Jackie re-enacted a scene from the current horse opera showing at Scoat's Pitcher Hoose by taking the whole thing down to the back court and running the Dodge City Flier through the flooded Yellow River. It never went really well after that.

Abandoning the sinking ship in the puddle, I scouted across Gallowgate one afternoon and met Leo Gourlay. He lived in Cubie Street, and he was on his way with some of the big yins to steal rides at the grain store. That sounded more like it.

The grain store had that mesmerizing grain-store smell of dog-biscuits and peasemeal and clean jute, and the floury smell was even stronger in the cul-de-sac alongside the store where the lorries loaded up for deliveries. The big yins were doubtful about my fitness for the job, and so was I when I thought it over, but one of them said it was all right, just do what he did. We lurked till the lorry was ready to go, then nipped out and caught hold of the back end. We didn't jump aboard, just held on behind and ran, and as I write this now it still sounds like a damfool trick. I got myself a little hook to grip on to, and the lorry swung out and away down Cubie Street like the hammers. It was great. Your feet hit the ground every twenty yards or so. I loved it and then I hated it, and my instructor shouted to me 'Don't lit go!' But I had had enough. I abandoned the lorry.

Nevertheless, I kept on moving behind it as if I were still hanging on. Only my feet weren't touching the ground at all now. I landed squarely on my face and ploughed a yard-long furrow down the middle of Cubie Street, and I knew I was dead. I wasn't, but when I felt my face and brought away a handful of gory grey dust, I could picture myself rubbed absolutely flat. Jimmie appeared from somewhere, horrified, and took me home, and my mother heard me yelling before we even reached Gallowgate.

'Ah fell in Cubie Street!' I said. Jimmie looked disgusted.

'He was haudin on the back ae a lorry.'

'Don't you ever run after lorries, son,' my mother said as she uncovered my features with warm water. 'If he'd been haudin on a lorry he'd have been killed,' she dismissed Jimmie's story. She was right, of course.

Disaster nearly always visited my crimes. But running after lorries had none of the beautiful neatness of a confidence trick Jackie discovered. There were two wee sweetie shops, one in Cubie Street and one in Soho Street, each selling the same brand of lemonade at a penny a bottle. I don't know why I said lemonade – ginger, of course, is the name for any bottled soft drink. Owing to some book-keeping quirk, the Cubie Street shop gave the bottle out on trust, while the Soho Street shop charged a penny on it; a perfect set-up for a racket. You couldn't make a lot of money on it, but if you could raise an initial capital of one penny, you could drink an awful lot of ginger. Jackie employed me, in the old tradition, as runner – one runner couldn't go too often because they're suspicious people in Soho Street. I stood with him in

36

Cubie Street and got a swig from the bottle, and then took the empty round to collect a penny on it from the other shop. I was so delighted with the system that I ran recklessly round the corner and fell, but never thought of letting loose the bottle. I was led back up to the house gushing blood in three places just as Harry arrived home from a trip abroad, and his first domestic duty was to paint me with iodine and wrap me up while Jackie stood by stricken, not only with sympathy and remorse but with the fall of his ginger empire and his lifetime supply of free drinks gone for ever.

Desperado though I was, my morals were offended by the sight of two boys pelting past McBride and Black's the grocer's shop and scooping up potatoes as they ran, from a basket of spuds displayed outside the shop to lure the customers. I ran into the shop like a true Wesleyan Hall boy and told the man, but he refused to give chase. 'We'll no' miss a tottie or two,' he said callously. When I went back out, aggrieved, I found the thieves had dislodged several other potatoes, so I picked one up and trailed after them. What kind of thing to steal was a potato? What could you do with it? It wasn't the tottie-gun season and you can't chew a murphy raw.

They were mending the road in Cubie Street, and the robbers were crouched beside the tar-boiler. Underneath it, the road was sprinkled with ashes and hot embers raked out from the boiler fire, and among the embers were the stolen potatoes, and here was I with a potato of my own. I threw it under beside theirs and gave up my principles. The only thing that went wrong with that escapade was that my potato roasted better than theirs did, and one of them claimed it as his own in exchange for a very inferior piece of cuisine he had already started eating. But there's something about a tottie roasted under a tar-boiler; all that lovely carbon, and the blisters it leaves on the fingers; something no home-cooked potato can compete with. Some day I'll get enough money to buy an old tar-boiler of my own and hire somebody to steal me a few potatoes from McBride and Black's. I still feel cheated of that potato.

There was nothing casual or wanton about Jackie's approach to crime. He didn't really have a decently developed criminal streak at all, merely a simple curiosity and a simple faith in his chances of getting away with it. One quiet afternoon he got himself hidden in our bedroom, overlooking Gallowgate, and sent me down to stand on the pavement underneath. In a few minutes a tin can came flying down from the building across the street and I nipped into the road and picked it up. It had a string attached to it. My job was to tie to the can another string that Jackie was letting down from the window, and then he pulled the whole thing up. I ran back up to the bedroom.

'Whit is it?' I knew it must be something great.

'Ssh! It's a telephone.' I believed him. In the house across the street George Gillan had the other end of the string, with another cocoa tin fastened to it. I got putting Jackie's tin to my ear.

'Ah canny hear anythin',' I complained.

'The string's goat tae be tight. Ssh!' I jammed the tin against my ear and walked sideways back into the room but only got a lot of mush on the line, and Jackie finally took it off me and started a conversation with the other end. Slim McCann reporting, did you get them bank robbers? and so on. I felt proud and awe-stricken.

Later there was a knock at the door, and my mother was appalled to find a policeman investigating an odd phenomenon that apparently led to our house. There was a piece of string, or rope, lying right across the overhead tram wires, and apparently coming from our window. Jackie, trapped in the bedroom, and with a bright red circle round his ear from the pressure of the can, overheard and made frantic efforts to contact Captain Q across the street, but there was a hitch in transmission and he was caught red-faced. The law, cackling to itself, said it was afraid the apparatus would have to be removed from the tram-lines.

That's it, you see. People give the world a new contribution to gracious living, and bureaucracy crushes it under foot. It's a dampt shame, so it is.

The Bridge

The trams ran along Gallowgate in both directions to places that were so vague and remote they barely provoked my curiosity then, and beside the green trams ran the red GOC buses that were just about to vanish entirely. To the West, they headed for the toon, a big place away past Bellgrove Street, and to the East they went through Camlachie to a place called Parkhead and even farther.

South of Gallowgate meant down Cubie Street and Soho Street, and I never went down Soho Street. Even Cubie Street petered out in a dark mess of streets a few blocks down, streets I never explored then and which are still a blurred area in my mind's map of Glasgow.

It was always to the north that our wanderings took us, the north separated from Gallowgate by the railway but simple and unmysterious. You went up Bellfield Street to the top, where it ended in a wooden fence, and at one end of the fence was the long footbridge running straight over the railway yards to Dennistoun. The first time I crossed the bridge was one morning when Jimmie took me to school with him when I was about three years old. This was a great thing in schools like Thomson Street School – taking your wee brother or sister to school with you. It happened when mothers were ill, or away at a funeral, and there was nobody at home to tend the infant, and there was nothing the teacher could do about it once the child arrived. But I will say teachers never seemed to dislike the novelty as far as I could see, and pupils, especially little girls, often took their toddler brothers to school not from necessity but in pride of possession.

That was my first crossing of the bridge. It was a beautiful bridge; wide enough to let crowds walk abreast, but so long that it seemed slender and even dangerous. A mile long, I told Jimmie and he groaned contemptuously – he didn't really want to take me to school with him. He was a boy.

'It would take you *days* to walk a mile,' he told me. 'You don't know what a mile is.'

It was true. A mile was a thing like a million, the biggest thing of its kind, and it was so for years. We knew that you could get distances of hundreds of miles, but they were only for talking about. No movement of our own, on foot, could possibly exceed so noble a figure as a mile. All the same, it was a long bridge. It had a cement floor, slightly cambered, and walls made of iron plates too high to see over, and the plates were joined across the top by iron arches every few yards, as if the bridge-builder had been planning to make a roof too but had left it unfinished. Being on the bridge was like being on a bus, or in an aeroplane, or in a tunnel. Inside its high iron walls it had no connexion with the railway below, only with the sky above.

In the fence that ran across Bellfield Street at the bottom end of the bridge there was a door that led down steps to the coal ree. It was always closed, but sometimes you could open it, and if you did, you shouted down into the ree:

> 'Grease Berd
> Penny a yerd
> Tuppence a wee bit longer!'

The first time Jimmie did this, to demonstrate, I was frightened and tearful. If the ree looked empty, there was no sense in shouting at a Greasy Berd who wasn't there. But if he was there, he might be too near the steps to give you time to get away before he ran up and caught you. I know that he never did run up the steps, and I even know that I never saw him at all. But at the same time I knew I had seen him, his face hidden and faceless behind his greasy beard, which was big and shapeless and greyish-green in colour, for that is the colour that the word greasy suggested to me. When I was alone, I never opened the

40

door and shouted down at him.

A little later I was crossing the bridge every day to go to school. I had enrolled at the age of four because my fifth birthday fitted awkwardly into the school term dates, and I never lost my delight in the long walk through that sky-covered tunnel. We carried a piece to eat at playtime, often a roll and jam. When we had a roll, we would take it out quietly in the class before playtime and sit on it to squash it out flat and make it bigger. But sometimes I ate mine straight away on the way to school. I had just turned into Bellfield Street, chewing it, one morning, when we found a tar-boiler bubbling and reeking at the corner. I threw the roll on the ground.

'It's a' taur,' I said to Jimmie.

'The taur never touched it.'

'But the smell touched it.'

'If you keep it for efter the smell will go away.'

I picked it up.

'You canny eat it noo,' he said. 'The Devil's licked it.'

It was the first time I had heard of the Devil licking food that touched the street, and I couldn't accept it. How could his tongue get through all that stone? I picked up the roll and carried it beyond the smell of the tar-boiler. By the time we were up the steps of the bridge it tasted like a roll again, but as I bit it a woman coming down the bridge laughed at me and said:

'My, that's a terrible sore haun you've got!' No, I shook my head, there was nothing wrong with my hand, but this made her laugh more and Jimmie told me she was talking about the roll. I couldn't understand why a play-piece should be called a sore hand, but it always is. Maybe she thought the roll was a bandage, I thought. Her laughter was quite kindly and friendly, as if she knew me, and when I got home I asked my mother who the woman was. This is why I remember the business of the roll – it got wrapped up in a bigger puzzle.

My mother didn't know who the woman was because she hadn't seen her. I tried to explain what her face looked like, but it was impossible to explain although I knew what I meant.

41

'What do I look like?' I asked after a while.

'Like yourself!'

But that wasn't enough. I knew what the boys in my class looked like – their names went with their faces and that was how I recognized them. But what was my face like? I found it impossible to see a recognizable name-shape in my face, and I started to worry. I wouldn't recognize myself if I saw myself in the street.

I got back to the woman on the bridge and tried to explain that she had the kind of face you *know*, and my mother was tickled, but baffled. I meant that the woman had a general feeling about the shape of her face that was intimate and familiar – just the *ordinary* face, that made me sure she was an acquaintance of the family. But how do you explain a thing like that?

It was not simply a childish whim. Throughout all the years afterwards I kept seeing the same kind of face with that same quality on scores of people. Nobody could ever understand what I meant by it. It's a 'plain' face, and it evoked a mixture of reactions in me. Familiarity, still – the face of somebody easy to know; sometimes friendly, sometimes hostile, but always knowable. If I had known how to explain it then, I would have said it was a proletarian face. It is often broad in the nostrils and round in the chin, and with a lot of big teeth that show themselves easily, and it's a face that is often red and sometimes rough as if it had been whipped by a hard wind.

Many of the friends of my youth had this Face, and it often went with a haircut that was common then and never seen today – the whole head cropped close, 'right into the wood', and a tuft left at the front to keep the childish face from looking totally bald. The boys of well-off families never had this haircut, and they didn't have the Face either. A reassuring thing about the Face was that you could flit to any part of Glasgow you chose, and you would still find it, making a familiar human background in a new place; but at the same time I could never expect to find any mystery or glamour in it. It was not the face that a fairy princess or a mysterious beautiful lady would wear; a face to know and even like, but never one to fall dreamily in love with, for love on those terms needs mystery.

If there is such a thing as a Glasgow face, this may be it. At least it is one of Glasgow's faces. I saw it twice again last year in the Norwegian town of Bergen, and I don't know how it got there and learned to speak a Scandinavian language, for by that time I had identified it to my own satisfaction, and it had no connexion with the north. It was one of the faces that came to Glasgow from Ireland, and it still abounds in Glasgow and always puts me in mind of poverty-stricken Irish acres and a chancy potato crop back in the eighteen-forties.

It's easy to say that Glasgow is the most democratic city in the world, and it quite possibly is, but that doesn't mean it doesn't have its own shades of snobbery and blood-pride or money-pride. Growing up in Gallowgate I imagine I was no more snobbish than any of the other kids, and less than some, but I felt these subtleties in some way, and the red, cheerful Glasgow-Irish face was involved in them, one I made my mind up about when I was quite young. I was always trying to get life classified so that it would be easier to grasp, and my classifications were quick and rigid, until I had to bend them in the light of later experience. My feeling of affection and superiority to the wearers of the Face lasted a long time until I found that a minute difference in the length of a nose or the curve of a chin might put the mystery and glamour back into any racial face, and that the brother of a rather dull peasant might resemble him almost like a twin and yet be as handsome as hell.

And of course, I had my mind made up about the Face before I ever learned anything about myself and my own Irishness, and suspected in alarm that the Face looked familiar because it was my own. Looking in the mirror, I wouldn't say so. But a mirror never does what you expect it to do – it doesn't give you a stranger's eye to classify a stranger's face.

Somebody's Wean is Lost

As well as the school, the long footbridge led to the rest of Dennistoun and to Alexandra Park and the lucky middens. There are lucky middens everywhere in Glasgow, as a matter of faith. What we called middens, upper-class people described as dustbins. The older name must indicate an enduring rustic tradition, and middens mean a lot in the culture of the young of Glasgow – the insult that comes most easily to the tongue is even midden, or sometimes durty wee midden.

Every street has its own middens, but the Lucky Middens, like the Hesperides, are always the middens in some other street, some fabulous street where millionaires live, who throw almost-new umbrellas and cars and boxes of chocolates and worn money into the midden every night, and all you need to acquire this loot is the secret of where the Lucky Middens are. When we set out on explorations the Lucky Middens lured us on like Montezuma's gold.

One afternoon in summer I joined a gang on its way to Campbelfield Street, because somebody thought the Lucky Middens were there. It didn't seem likely, because Campbelfield Street was too near home, leading off Gallowgate and still on the south side of the railway. It was a genuine cul-de-sac, with no long bridge to connect it to Dennistoun, and to my eyes it seemed unnaturally filled with people and children and dogs, moving about in the street itself as if it were a stage. The life of the street seemed to go on visibly and outside the houses, as there were no trams or buses thundering east and west to interrupt it. There was no question of searching the middens – it was the wrong kind of street, where the back courts could be reached only through the closes under the eyes of the natives. The mythical middens were always gained by a deserted lane at the back of the building. But the candy-rock man was there.

The candy-rock man needed a street like that, with no through traffic to spoil his act. He must have been selling something – candy-rock, I suppose – but to us he was a pure entertainment and a free treat because we had no money in any case. I went back to Campbelfield Street often in the hope of catching him again, but never saw him except for that first time.

The children of the street crowded round him and he waved them away, pretending to be angry. They backed into a circle, but warily and ready to rush him again. Then he shouted:

'Who likes Candy Rock?'

And hopping with excitement, we shouted back:

'Me!'

He took a piece of toffee wrapped in paper from his box and made to throw it, and we ran a few steps and then back, for he liked to fool us. Then he looked quite angry, and threw it far over our heads and there was a terrible, panic-stricken race for it.

'Ah telt yiz tae keep back!' he bellowed. 'Who likes Candy Rock?'

'Me! Oh, *me*, mister!'

He turned his back on us, and some of us made to run to the other end of the street, but some hung back. Then, while the first half were running past him to catch the next lump of candy-rock, he put his feet wide apart and threw the piece through his legs and past the crowd who were still hanging back but getting ready to follow.

I never saw the candy-rock close up because I was too small to get ahead in the race for it, and we waited for a long time for the next bit, but he didn't throw any more, and the children of the street started running to their mothers for halfpennies to buy candy-rock. We had no mothers to run to, and we gave up and went back to Bellfield Street and over the bridge.

As far as my mother was concerned, we were on our

way to Alexandra Park, a legitimate place to visit. Sometimes the whole family or as many as were together at one time, went to the park, in fact. There was a paddle-boating pond, a paddling pool and a model yachting lake, and Harry had brought Jackie a real model yacht back from one of his trips to sea. It was christened 'Thistle', and the label on it described it as Clyde Built, which made it the best boat in the world, and Jackie would have Jimmie and me pelting mile after mile round the lake to catch it and point it back to him while my mother and probably my sister Mary, would sit on a bench with David, the baby, and admire him and call to us not to fall in.

Well, when we went off on our own we did go to the Park but the route was different. We started raking the middens somewhere near Armadale Street, in Dennistoun, behind a red sandstone tenement that had a lane along the back courts. We didn't find any lucks, but we started combing the back courts and climbing walls until Paddy Dunnigan had his famous accident.

Paddy Dunnigan wasn't much older than I was. He would do anything. He had once stolen a 'Keep Off the Grass' sign in the park and thrown it in the fountain, and if you asked him to, he ate worms. When we came to a low brick wall separating a stretch of waste ground from a back court, Paddy said he could jump it, and he ran up for the jump and went over in a kind of vaulting leap, and disappeared. The rest of us rushed up to the wall and found that although it was only two feet high on our side, the back court at the other side was four or five feet lower. It looked like a cliff. Paddy was lying on his face in the back court, with his bow legs twitching. Some cried out that he was deid. The thought was terrible and frightening and thrilling. But while we hung over the wall he jumped up and started dancing about on one foot, grinning at his own cleverness.

A bigger boy, well-dressed and wearing a school cap, came out of the back of the close and shouted, 'You get out of this back, you wee scruff! Away and play in your own back.'

46

'Aw haw!' we shouted. 'Whitehill pup wi' yer tail tied up! Whitehill pup wi' yer tail tied up! Away hame tae yer maw!' Whitehill was the big school in Dennistoun, a toff's school.

It was nearly impossible to sneak into the paddle-boat pond on Alexandra Park. The parkies always marked us as soon as we went into the park and kept appearing behind us. The pond had iron railings round it, and inside the railings, a dense growth of shrubs and willows, and sometimes, if we actually got over the railings, there would be a parkie inside, patrolling the shore, to throw us out again. It was different on Sundays when we went to the pond with the family, all scrubbed to death and in our good go-to-meeting suits, and were taken on the paddle boats respectably. We just looked different, and unsocial, by ourselves. We couldn't get up to anything, and Paddy suggested that we should wander ourselves. I never knew whether people were serious or not when they talked like this, and I had a stab of fear. I took it for granted that being wandered meant being wandered for life, and never finding the way home again.

Beyond the Park, Riddrie stretched over the skyline absolutely alien and unknown, and somewhere away beyond that lay the Sugarolly Mountains, which I suddenly found I didn't want to see after all, even if you *could* eat them. Being one of the infant hangers-on, I listened to the argument about getting wandered and just prayed everybody would decide against, but the gang actually split into two factions, and I stuck with the respectable half who were for staying in the park and having old-fashioned fun.

The wandering section went off towards the canal, and as far as I know, got tired after a while and went home. I went with the others into the paddling pool. My crowd were the better-dressed, better brought-up members, and the leader was quite a big boy called Teddy Young, a nice, respectable name. I believed his family actually had a billiard table in their house. He was carrying a billiard cue at any rate, as a walking-stick and badge of authority, and he let me watch it while the rest of them went in to paddle. He laid it down on the little sandpit beside the pool, and when I looked down at it, it was gone. I thought he had lifted it up again, but he came out of the pond in a temper and started to shout at me for losing it. His anger developed a nasty edge to it, and the rest joined in with him, but I was more bewildered than afraid, and when he threatened to go home without me I knew he was only trying to frighten me to punish me for letting the billiard-cue be stolen. I walked round the pool to have another look for it, and when I got back, they were all gone.

I was the one that had ended up wandered. The idea of finding my own way home, to the other end of Dennistoun and over the bridge, was one that never entered my head for a second. I ran frantically looking for the gang and shouting their names and felt sick with loneliness. In the end a parkie got me and gave me to a policeman.

My mother had always told me not to be afraid of policemen, and Jimmie had told me that policemen were not real – they were just men, wearing policemen's suits. But this was the first time I had actually liked the polis. He was quite young, I think, and enormously tall. I wanted him to take me straight home, but he took my hand and we got on to a tramcar, without paying any fare, and when we got off, he took me into the police station. Men in police suits but without helmets spoke to me, and a big fat one gave me a piece on jam. What was worrying me was that I knew – a boy at school had once told me – that if a policeman took you home, it was free. But if he took you to the police station first, your mother had to pay a shilling to get you. What if my mother didn't have a shilling? She always told me that she had no money, when I was asking for a halfpenny. And although I had seen money in her purse when she said she had none, this might be the time when it was true.

After a while another policeman put on his helmet and walked home with me. It wasn't late, but the rest of the crowd had come home and reported that I had run away by myself, and there was the commotion in the house that

48

always happened on the very rare occasions when a policeman came to the door.

'I didn'y run away – they ran away an' left me!' I insisted. I wanted justice done. Adults tutted and smiled wryly to one another across my head and said you could never tell what kids would get up to. My mother was still nervous from the shock of opening the door to a policeman, but when I asked her if she would have to pay him a shilling to get me back, she laughed and kissed me and sent me to wash my hands and face for tea.

I Am The Ghost of Gogar

My sixth birthday got lost somewhere between number 628, Gallowgate, and Sandyhills. It was a thing I brooded mutinously over for a long time. There was no tradition of birthday presents in our family – we were so many that the presents would have been cropping all year round until we were sick of saving up our no money for them. But we never failed to have a dumpling, with thrupenny bits in it too. As it happened, Jackie, Jimmie, David and I all had birthdays falling in October, and sometimes the four dumplings would be telescoped into one big one, but joint or separate, there was always a dumpling, and when we found ourselves living in Sandyhills I kept looking for my birthday because I couldn't remember any dumpling, and that meant there had been no dumpling, and that meant I was still five. Wearying of the subject, my mother told me we should have an extra big dumpling for the next birthday – the biggest dumpling ever, made not in a pot but in the clothes-boiler that stood in the kitchen of our new house. Even that doesn't quite make up for losing a birthday without trace, but I think I'm getting resigned to the loss now, I haven't worried about it for a year or more.

The clothes-boiler was only one of the peculiar, exciting things about our new house. We couldn't have been in the second flat very long, even allowing for that lost birthday, because we had only one Christmas there, a terrible Christmas I never liked to remember when my father had just gone to sea and there was no money for presents and the Santa Claus legend had vanished like smoke and an awful dark loneliness was hanging over the house. But in the spring, we got on to one of the green trams passing the close and went away from Gallowgate. I was only slightly sullen because I had wanted to travel on the lorry that was carrying the flitting, but I was too stimulated by the move to nag much about that, and I was already perceptive enough to know there are some times you can nag and get results, and other times nag and get a quick clout.

It was a total change. A new house that was literally new and not merely new to us. My mother, always too inoffensive for her own good, had, all the same, brow-beaten some Corporation official into recognizing what she saw as justice and handing over the magic key. The house was the end of a terrace, with a garden back, front and side. The front garden was small and consisted entirely of a steep little hill running from the front path to the pavement, and it was made of reddish clay that ran in coloured streams down the front steps each time it rained. There were no windows on the gable end, and we could play in the garden at the side without being seen from the house, a cherished form of secrecy. Three elders that were planted later, close together, made an impenetrable screen that hid the side strip entirely and left it dark, sunless and secret.

Jimmie, who *had* travelled on the flitting lorry and explored before I arrived, took me out of the front door and round to view the side and back garden, with all the pride of a tenth-generation squire. I was worried by another door that gave into our garden from the back of the building, and incredulous when he insisted that that door was ours too. He even claimed that hot water came out of the tap, but when I tried it, Flora rushed at me and turned it off and warned me that it was *her* hot water. Everybody, except Jackie and Jimmie and me, developed a passion for baths, but Flora most of all, and when we were fighting with her, which was reasonably often, we would wait till she had gone upstairs to the bathroom and then quickly turn on the hot taps downstairs to empty the hot tank before she could run her bath.

We were still in the pioneering days of Glasgow's massive rehousing operation. Sandyhills was a small, tidy district, but it still had unbuilt ground that was corrugated from the recent passage of a farmer's plough. I discovered that the move, in a way, was a return home for the Hanleys. Sandyhills lay between the old villages of Shettleston and Tollcross. My mother had been raised in Shettleston and had worked in Tollcross as a girl, and on learning this I first became preoccupied with the effects of time. I tried to picture the place when plough-horses walked over the ground our own house stood on, and when the stagecoaches clattered through Shettleston on their way to Edinburgh. It wasn't easy, for even the empty farm land around us was being cleared and built up all the time.

The place was so raw and virgin as a community that the back garden was littered with builders' debris – not just odd slates and broken chimney pots, but one whole concrete doorstep and such-like chunks of masonry. A kindly neighbour admitted to us that as we were the last to move into the block, the people in the other houses had heaved the rubbish from their gardens into the empty one. Jimmie and I instantly heaved some of the smaller pieces of concrete back into the yard next door, but they returned on the following day, and we finally had to drag them, in the dark, into even newer gardens of other unoccupied houses. This clearance work was our own idea entirely. My mother was shocked to learn that we had wished the stuff on other innocent people, but she didn't go to the length of telling us to bring it back.

By Gallowgate standards our new house was a vast and palatial affair and we were intensely proud of it. Until

51

David stopped being an infant and became a toddler and a pest who always had to be watched or taken for walks or tagged on to our games, as I had been tagged on to Jimmie's in my time. I slept with Jimmie and Jackie and we shared a secret society in our bedroom tucked upstairs. Jackie was the king not only because he was the oldest, but because he had such a persuasive talent. As the oldest, it was his privilege or duty to sleep on the outside of the bed, but he hated wakening up with the blankets pulled off him, and he induced me to take the outside position just once, and then twice, and then for a month. After the month was up, he would take it for a month, which was only fair, as I readily saw.

At the end of the month he arranged an extension, but this time he would sleep on the outside forty times for every time I did, which was even fairer. By the time David had grown up a bit, and the four of us moved into the bigger bedroom to share two double beds, he owed me about 120 years of outside turns, but since he and Jimmie were in one bed, and David and I in the other at the far side of the room, there was no easy way of repaying them.

My school-teacher in our new school, Miss Sheppard, was a gentle, good-hearted woman, very unlike the last teacher I had had at Thomson Street, who incensed the family by caning me on the hand with the classroom pointer. Miss Sheppard did the teaching business well, as far as I can judge, but she found time for reading a lot of stories to us, and even encouraged us to put on a play of our own in the dead period of Friday afternoons. Every night in bed I had to tell the latest story I had been hearing in school; prissy little fairy tales about snails who turned back into princes and defeated wicked witches, but Jackie always insisted on hearing them and giving them a fair hearing. Sometimes, if we didn't feel like sleeping, we would take a blanket each and drape it over our heads and prance over the bed knocking one another down and groaning.

'I am the ghost of Gogar! No one shall dare defy me!' The Ghost of Gogar was Jackie's own making, but occasionally we would terrify ourselves with the standard horror stories of Gallowgate, which we knew by rote but which never lost their power.

Once upon a time there was a wee boy and his maw sent him for a fish supper. And here when he was nearly comin' hame wi' it he met a black man up a close and the black man said: 'Gie's a chip, son, ah'm stervin'.' And here, the wee boy said: 'Naw, they're ma maw's chips for ma daddy's supper,' and so here, the black man said: 'Ah'll pey you for a chip.' So the wee boy said: 'How much?' So the black man said: 'Ah've got nae money, but ah'll gi'e ye wan o' ma black fingers if you gi'e us a chip.'

So here, the wee boy said: 'All right, here's a chip,' and the man said: 'All right, here's ma black finger,' and here, he pulled aff wan o' his fingers and gi'ed it tae the wee boy. So the wee boy took the fish supper hame and put the black finger under his pillah and here, he forgoat a' aboot it and then he went tae bed, but efter everybody was sleepin', the wee boy wakened up and here, he heard a wee noise ootside the windae in the back court, and he listened, and it was a wee voice sayin': 'Gi'e me back ma black finger! Gi'e me back ma black finger!' But the wee boy was too feart tae go tae the windae, so he just lay there and says tae hisself, 'The man'll never know whit hoose ah'm in.' But the voice aye kept moanin': 'Gi'e me back ma black finger! Ah want ma black finger!' Nearer an' nearer, through the cloose an' up the sterrs, 'Gi'e me back ma black finger! Gi'e me back ma black finger!' Up the sterrs and through the door and through the loaby an' intae the front room, gettin' nearer an' nearer the bed, moanin' 'Gi'e me back ma black finger . . . *Ah've goat ye!*'

And whoever was telling the tale would make a grab at whoever was hearing the tale, and we would yelp with conventional terror that wasn't only conventional terror. And if it was late, Flora or Johanne would call through from the other bedroom telling us kids to shut up and get to sleep.

One of the most obvious things about Glasgow today, a great thing in its way but a worrying thing too, is the way the Corporation housing programme has expanded. It's great because people shouldn't be living in dank old slums, crumbling and congested and insanitary, and the new houses have light and space and baths and the physical decencies of life that folk should have whether they have money or not. But the new housing schemes have spread so far and fast that something has been lost in the flitting, and I think it's the spiritual vitality of the old slum streets – the songs and the games and the social manners and the homely feeling of living in a place that has got used to people living in it, and is adjusted to people.

It's easy to say this from outside Gallowgate or Gorbals, when nobody in his senses would deliberately choose deliberately to live in Gallowgate or Gorbals if he didn't have to, and like all reminiscers, I would never expose my own children to the uncouth accents and rowdy adventures of my own childhood. But something has gone out of life in these great airy suburbs. A string has been broken and left the children rootless and starved of tradition, and tradition means a lot to children. They don't have the handed-down legends of the slum streets, and they don't have the different legends of children in country villages. The people in the enormous new suburbs know this very well in their hearts. There's an unease and an unrest in the biggest of the new districts, and television isn't a complete substitute for the feeling that has gone.

This unease isn't just a matter of not having the old neighbourly feelings. The suburbanites have plenty of neighbours. Sometimes they have too much of their neighbours, as most of the postwar houses in Glasgow are less soundproof than the persistent old stone tenements. Up a close in Gallowgate, in fact, a family could very well keep itself to itself if it didn't want to mix with the neighbours, and a lot of families did and do today. Maybe it's because the far-flung suburbs mean a complete separation of domestic life from work and all the other social activities.

In Sandyhills in the 'thirties, things hadn't developed

that way. We arrived with our childhood traditions intact, and the place was so small, and so close to the old villages that merged into it on either side, that there was no break in the continuity of what you could call cultural life. Life was merely more hygienic and less dusty and had more open spaces for playing in.

The old games still persisted, as they do still in old Glasgow. Peeries and billy-nuts and moshie and rounders came round in their time, without conscious choice on our parts but in obedience to some invisible rotation of seasons.

The girls played ropes, pavey-waveys or French ropes or Belgiums, as they still do to the ancient chants in Glasgow side streets.

I remember how embarrassed we were at school for an English boy who had come to live in the district, when he referred to a peerie as a top. But it gave the thing an exotic touch to hear him call it a peerie in a Cockney accent. It was a halfpenny for a flat-topped peerie, a halfpenny for a whip with a leather thong, and a halfpenny for a box of coloured chalks. We never ever whipped a peerie without chalking a design on the top to make it look like something decent when it was spinning. We believed that a good design made it spin faster and stay up longer too.

The object of peeries is to acquire merit for your own peerie by knocking down other peeries with it, and a peerie with a big score of successes is naturally a prize peerie. This is one of the dirtiest games in the whole field of sport.

In the first place, the shop whip, a twelve-inch dowel with a fifteen-inch leather thong tied to it, is soon discarded. The leather keeps untying and string has to be fitted instead; or the sorry bit of dyed stick snaps. During one peerie season in Sandyhills, people started using garden canes for whips, and a new terror trend was set as longer and longer canes became popular, and longer strings to go with them. The short whips were driven out entirely. It was too dangerous to square up to an opponent if you carried a short whip and had to stoop close to your peerie while he could stand well back and slash the air, and probably you, with a thing like a coach whip.

An unscrupulous player, on the pretence of whipping his peerie nearer to yours for the necessary crash, might easily reach farther and nudge your peerie over with the end of his cane; or accidentally lay a swipe across your legs to put you off a stroke; or get his own peerie going well and then entangle his whiplash with yours, so that by the time they were disentangled, your peerie had fallen dead while his was still spinning and triumphant.

Finally there was a move that year to discard whips altogether and use the boot. A boy up the street, who played football for his school, had developed the art of kicking his peerie a glancing blow that kept it whirling; but I always managed to kick mine square on and send it flying, dead, out of sight.

Bools or jauries are a more subtle and skilful affair. At that time we used almost nothing but the old wally jauries, fairly crude earthenware marbles just under an inch in diameter, for ordinary games. They were sold in bulk. The smaller glass bools, the glessies, beautiful little things with graceful spiral lines twisting inside their hearts, were all right too, but more expensive and harder to hit. The king bool was a plunker made of iron, but in an engineering city, somebody could always produce a giant steel ball of nearly two inches diameter, designed for a ball-race, and such a one was worth dozens of jauries in a straight exchange.

Quite grown-up boys, fifteen or sixteen years old or more, joined the moshie schools in the coup behind the Honeymoon Building in Shettleston Road, where you could always find three decent holes set in the correct triangle by some previous moshie school. While the jaurie fever was on, even food became trivial. We played at liney in the playground, nearest the line takes the lot; or chalked a circle and aimed to knock bools out of it. And on the way home at dinner-time or four o'clock we stooped along the gutters playing the straight game all the way home and back again.

It was noisy and emotional. There are three basic throws, and the right one can mean win or lose. Sheevies, an underhand bowling movement; knucklie, in which you grip the jaurie between the thumbnail and the index finger and flick it forward; and pots, in which you lift the jaurie in the air and lob it at your opponent's. When two jauries landed close together, if it was your turn, you tried to shout 'Sheevies' before your opponent could shout 'High pots!' or even 'Knucklies!' We got home hoarse and breathless in the jaurie season.

The girls chalked complicated beds on the street for ba' beds or peever, and I started a movement at one time to crash into this. It was amusing for a while, but it could never come to anything, of course. It was untraditional.

One of the most accomplished jaurie-players in my class was a big red faced boy called Hugh Smith, but he was a person who was accomplished at every sport. Even his close friends called him jammy for his unfair ration of luck, and it was widely held that if he jumped oot a windae, he would fa' up. He amassed a monstrous horde of hard-won jauries, and wore a special glove, with the finger-tips cut off, when he was playing.

When we first moved to Sandyhills, I disliked him intensely. At Thomson Street school, I had accepted the fact that I was the best fighter in the class. I didn't come to the point of fighting anybody to prove it. You're the best fighter in the class if people think you are. When I went into Eastbank school, the first thing that smote me was the number of bigger people than me, and Hugh was the biggest, so he was the leader of the gang. Even in Thomson Street, I was short in size as five-year-olds go, but I got away with it, and now I couldn't. When I did find somebody in the class that I felt I could tackle, he turned out to be a friend of Hugh's, and Hugh warned me off.

Soon I found that there was a class division in the class, that emerged into class war from time to time. The two sides were Hugh Smith's gang and Eddie Kirkwood's gang. Some boys swung from one to the other at different times, but the main cleavage was quite easy to define. Hugh led the well-dressed, well-fed, respectable crowd, and Eddie led the crowd that came from poorer houses. I don't think there was any strong personal enmity between them, but each represented his own type and accepted the responsibility of leadership.

When I had adjusted myself to the class and established my personality, I found I didn't particularly hate anybody after all, and I attached myself to Hugh's crowd from motives of respectability. I was welcome, because the war usually took the form of dunting. It was a form of knightly jousting in which one knight on horseback tried to bump another knight off his horse, or even knock both of them off balance. Hugh and Eddie were natural born horses, and at my weight I was a natural knight. The war never decided anything or produced any conclusions. Later I found that Eddie liked me and I transferred to his gang. He was shorter than Hugh, but broad and as solid as a building, and he was practically unbeatable as a horse. Eddie had that Glasgow Face and a great personality with it, and a beautiful ugly smile. He was a very lovable character, but he moved to another school and I never saw him again. Hugh went all the way through school with me and seemed to stay jammy and well-omened all the way.

Not on a Lamp-post, Surely

There was an epidemic of bikes one year – it was probably at the same time as Hitler's Jugend business. Everybody wanted to get away somehow, away to Loch Lomond or Largs or the Three Lochs, and everybody wanted a bike. The kids didn't want to get away, they just wanted a bike. Flora was always in the van of every modern movement, but she had never learned to ride a bike, and I can still see her learning, intent and laughing and terrified and wobbling. Later I read a piece by H. G. Wells in which he pointed to unexpected bits of progress, and instanced the fact that in his youth, cyclists went to teachers and took a course of lessons on bicycling whereas in modern times, people were evidently able to ride almost as naturally as walking, taking for granted what their grandfathers had painfully to learn. He wasn't entirely right about that.

What I really wanted was a pony. I dreamed about ponies all the time, and planned to stable mine in the garden and let it eat the back lawn for food, and I ran alongside ponies when I saw them pulling little carts in the street and resented their being wasted in shafts when I might be riding them. I suspected that saddles were hard and chafing, and I reckoned that I would have a good soft cushion tied on my pony's back to make it easier.

The hunger grew so fierce that I began to tell people that I had a pony in fact, until one of them blurted it out to Miss Sheppard in the class, and I had to confess my imposture. But I wanted a bike too, because I knew I would never have a pony, no matter how much I persuaded myself that one day a farmer would stop me in the street and say: 'Look, sonny, I was taking this pony to sell it, but I want it to have a good home. You take it.' Soon I began to imagine men stopping me in the street with exactly the same story, but with a bike instead.

Jimmie Paterson, a boy at the foot of the street who became friendly with Jimmie, had a bike, a full-sized bike, but there was a bedraggled fairy-cycle in the family too. The pedals, cranks, crank-wheel and chain had come off and got lost, but it still behaved like a bike if it was going downhill, and I was given it for a whole afternoon. I stood on the crossbar at the bottom and pushed it along a flat street for a while, like a scooter, and knew I could never balance it, but eventually I wheeled it up our own street, which was short and had a good slope, and tried it timidly from the lamp-post at the top. In about an hour I was able to travel twenty or thirty yards before I took fright and fell off sideways. There was no brake.

Soon it was clear that I could stay upright as long as I could keep it going, and the sensation of new-found power surged through me. I rode it right to the bottom of the street, shouting to people to keep clear. I could turn sharply into the street at the foot and slow down on the level there. But two girls were playing a great long skipping-rope right across the foot of the street, with only a yard clear behind each of them, and a third girl was standing in that three feet of space at the side I was aiming for. I yelled at her to give me room, but she glared back and told me she wasn't moving for anybody. I yelled that I had no brakes.

'That's your funeral!' she shouted.

'Ah'll hit ye!' I pleaded.

'Oh, naw ye'll no!'

I hit her, of course. It was glorious. But after the bike season was over, we all played mixed games, boys and girls together, including the one I had so much enjoyed knocking down with my crippled fairy cycle. The cold weather and the dark finished off many of the manly games we played by ourselves, and brought a tentative interest in girls.

They were the old street games; but when we dispersed and hid ourselves for Leave-Oh or Kick-the-Nacket we could lose ourselves in the back gardens instead of up closes. There was the added excitement of a hot-blooded girl named Louise who would cuddle you if you landed in the same back garden together to hide. It never happened to me, but I always thought it might. Even out in the street in communal games like Charlie Charlie, it was noticeable that after a while, people started favouring particular people and becoming known as pairs.

Charlie Charlie is a game with odd implications. One player is It, and stands in the middle of the road as Charlie, while the rest line up along one pavement. They chant together:

'Charlie Charlie, may I cross the water?'

'Not today but yes tomorrow,' Charlie answers. Then the crowd ask how deep is the water, how wide is the water, and Charlie answers evasively until the last question – 'How cold is the water?'

'Put your hand in and see,' says Charlie. They all dip their hands in an imaginary river and cry:

'Oh, I've lost my golden ring!' And at that they make a dash for the opposite shore, while Charlie tries to catch one who will be Charlie next time.

Most of these old street games derive from the more macabre incidents in actual history, and a few years ago in an article on Charlie Charlie I proposed the theory that Charlie was not connected with the obvious Bonnie Prince Charlie, but was a version of Charon, and his deep cold river in which the victims lose their golden rings was the Styx. Leslie Daiken, the Irish–Londoner who wrote the most authoritative book on the subject, was provoked into writing to me and applauding the theory, and it stands unchallenged to date. I was mystified then, and still am, by Glasgow's version of 'Ring o' Roses', which goes:

> 'A ring a' ring o' roses,
> A cuppa cuppa shell
> The dug's away tae Hamilton
> Tae buy a new bell.
> If you don't tak' it
> I'll take it tae masel',
> A ring a' ring o' roses
> A cuppa cuppa shell.'

The desertion of the old tenements and the move to the suburbs may eventually kill the very Glasgow chant to the same tune:

> 'Murder murder polis
> Three sterrs up
> The wummin the middle door
> Hit me wi' a cup
> Ma face is a' bleedin',
> Ma heid's a' cut
> Murder murder polis
> Three sterrs up.'

61

We mixed well-bred prissy games with bloodthirsty chants and platonic comradeship with old, old suggestive stories, quite indiscriminately. It was left to Jimmie to invent a completely new sport.

The garden next to ours was enormous and lay in a hollow, and its clayey soil was the toughest in the street. Jimmie discovered that a piece of this gritty stuff rolled casually in the hand and flung on the street looked exactly like a dog's dropping, and started to lay specimens artistically at the foot of every lamp-post in the street. Then he thought of putting one on a clean doorstep, and everybody joined in, in a wave of hysteria. We moved pounds of clay and decorated every single doorstep in four streets.

My mother was coming home from somewhere when she caught me at it, and was stricken with shame and anger. I slunk back into the garden and removed the offence, and was taken home to bed early. She didn't learn for years that there were a hundred more doorsteps involved.

The most bewildering aspect of this outbreak of shocking dog behaviour, however, was the result of Jimmie's final inspiration. On the following morning, early risers found not only doorsteps and lamp-posts defiled, but along four streets, the same decorations on the crossbars of the lamp-posts, eight feet from the ground.

The Secret Life of the Baron

We were surrounded with eccentricities and mysteries.
Children didn't go in and out of one another's houses.
When we called to see if somebody was coming out to
play, we knocked at the door and waited outside for him.
What was actually behind the doors was secret and
strange, and anything could be happening. Jackie and
Jimmie always had clear-cut information about the secret
lives of our neighbours, and my mother worried in case
anybody outside the house should hear what they were
saying. Some of the time I accepted their stories as true,
and there was often fact in them, but I was growing to the
stage where I could help to construct the stories myself.

We did have a simple eccentric handy, Mr More, who
was always going in and out of business ventures. He was
an educated well-spoken man, always nice to meet on the
street, and his wife and son and two nearly-grown
daughters were good-looking and refined without being
affected. Everybody felt they gave a nice tone to the
neighbourhood, and everybody liked them, but poor Mr
More took a terrible drink from time to time. One of his
businesses was a travelling pie shop consisting of a little
open van, and occasionally Jimmie came in to report that
three hundred and fifty pies were laid in a wavy line from
Sandyhills to Parkhead Cross. What did happen was that
one night I was coming up the street when Mr More's van
shot past me weaving wildly from side to side and shot a
mutton pie neatly into my face. But the idea of the wavy
line of pies gave me one of my own silliest ideas.

There were motor-vans selling ice-cream at the time,
but more common were the pretty little ice-cream carts,
shaped like sedan chairs and painted and decorated like
canal boats and drawn by handsome ponies. If lawns were

being mown when the cart came round we always rushed to feed the pony with handfuls of fresh-cut grass. The ice-cream people didn't like this very much, but we liked feeding horses, and one Sunday afternoon after the Mr More story had taken root in my mind I persuaded Jimmie to join me in laying a wavy line of grass cuttings down the street and up on to the pavements here and there. A few minutes later the regular ice-cream cart arrived, driven by an elderly man with a lame foot. He couldn't bound out of the cart to take the grass away and he couldn't get the horse to stop. It meandered along the wavy line from side to side and finally stopped when it couldn't pull the cart between a lamp-post and the garden railings.

The Martins were legitimate characters. They were a whole crowd of sons, all grown up, and they lived a life of cheerful rackety squalor. The varnished wooden surround of their living-room fireplace, a standard fitment in Corporation houses of the time, was pitted and etched with their practice at knife-and hatchet-throwing.

In warm weather one or more of the brothers would sit on the front doorstep singing and whittling pieces of wood, like characters in a Western film; the Martins and McCoys, in fact. From time to time hellish shouts and crashes could be heard from the front window to indicate that two or more of the boys were having a serious tussle, and Jimmie swore that when he was in the house once he saw a whole cheese on the bare table with a dagger stuck in it so that the boys could carve off their supper as they came in.

Pete Green, a boy in my class at school, lived in an even more hectic house. He had so many brothers that there weren't enough beds to go round them all, and the last one home at night had to go without, for even the shakedown in the loft would be occupied. The boys kept fairly loose hours, but even an early homecoming was no firm guarantee of a good bed for the night. A later arrival might think it was worth while fighting over it, and sometimes a sleeper would be heaved out of bed and out of the room and the door barricaded against him, before he wakened up and realized what was happening.

One night the oldest brother came home last and found one of the other brothers curled up asleep on the stairs, bedless. Al, the oldest one tried all the doors and found them barred, and the ladder pulled up into the loft, but he dragged the kitchen table upstairs and climbed into the loft anyway. The brother in the loft camp-bed refused to give it up, and soon they were punching each other back and forth under the sloping roof. The loft was only part-floored round the camp bed, and the struggle was decided when Al fell through between two joists, through the plaster ceiling and into bed on top of his father, who got up swearing to kill him if he ever saw him again.

But the best of the characters was the Baron, because Jimmie and I invented him almost from scratch.

He was a miner of some kind, and worked on varying shifts so that he was home at unexpected hours. He was thick and short and had a broad aggressive face, and he smoked a jaw-warmer, a clay pipe with the stem broken off and the bowl held upside down as he puffed it. We first seized on him when we saw him cycling home one afternoon on a bike painted bright orange – not gleaming orange enamel, but thick, lumpy orange paint. Jackie had started working by this time, and by the time we told him later, we had extended the possibilities of the story.

'The whole bike was orange,' Jimmie said.

'Even the chain and the tyres,' I said.

'Stolen property,' Jackie said, his eyes narrowed dramatically. 'He painted it to disguise it.'

'He carries a tin of orange paint in his pocket,' I suggested.

'No – *inside his clay pipe*,' cried Jimmie.

'Yes.'

We all paused, stunned by his fiendish cunning. That's when Jimmie christened him the Baron, meaning Baron Munchausen, for we decided that he was absolutely bland and insolent in the face of accusations and would have a glib, unbelievable explanation ready for everything.

'It's a different bike every day,' Jimmie pointed out. 'All painted orange.'

'He jumps on a bike and paints it while he's pedalling away,' Jackie explained.

We all waited tremulously for the next evidence of the Baron's crimes. A few days later Jimmie came in puzzled and disappointed and said the Baron had just come home driving a horse-and-cart.

'What colour?' I asked him. I could see his face lighting up from within.

'Orange! An orange horse. Even its teeth are orange. He's gone into the rustling business.' One thing that struck us was the fact that the Baron had always wheeled his stolen orange bikes into the passage between his house and the next, and the passage was too narrow for a cart. But on thinking it over, Jimmie decided it had been a one-wheeled cart, with the wheel right in the middle. That night in the bedroom I asked Jimmie which direction the wheel had been fixed in. He caught on at once.

'Side-weys!' he whispered in the dark. 'So that he can run it up a close when the polis are trying to head him off.'

Jessie, Ah, Jessie

We felt we were actually living in the country and not the city, and we were right enough, because there was grass everywhere. One of the good things about Glasgow is that it's easy to leave. In any direction from the centre of the city, you can strike green fields and rusticity in half an hour, and we were right at the edge of it. A real burn ran through Sandyhills on its way from north Lanarkshire to the Clyde, clean and country-style. At least one child was drowned in it while I lived there, but we played in it all the time. We would never drown. It ran under wide streets so that its bridges were more like tunnels, usually choked

66

with tree branches and flotsam. In rainy weather we often crouched along one of the tunnels on stepping stones to shelter from the rain. In sunny weather we crept along the tunnels for fun.

We even had a Big House, an Estate, in fact, owned by a Cassells family. It was an enormous house, in fact, with twenty or thirty windows on the visible side, standing in wooded policies bounded by an eight-foot sandstone wall, and there was a whole tennis court in the garden. The life that went on inside the stone walls was a total and endless mystery having no connexion with the life we lived just outside. One Sunday afternoon a two-seater monoplane appeared over the district and did some simple aerobatics and people said it belonged to, 'young Cassells', but nobody really knew. A crowd of us pelted up to the estate to see if it would land among the trees, but it didn't. Once I got inside the garden by the main gate when I was helping Jimmie on his newspaper round, and a manservant took the afternoon paper. It was the first manservant I had ever seen outside of a film, and the experience should have been thrilling, but the mystery remained. Sometimes we would climb up and sit on the wall behind the house and stare at the windows, in which no movement was ever seen. One small window was nominated as the cell in which somebody had been locked up to die, or walled in, or committed suicide centuries previously. I often walked up and looked at the place to make sure it was really there, to make sure I hadn't invented it.

When there was some sign of real life, it was on a day when three of us had sneaked into the policies by wading across the burn, which ran along the foot of the estate. We had barely landed when a gardener type of man rushed out of the trees roaring at us. The sheer shock of finding an emotional human being in the place unnerved us, and when we had splashed back to the safe shore, I found I couldn't get a foothold on the steep slithery bank. He was still shouting from his side, and at last I made a mad effort and fell back into the burn. He stopped shouting then and went away.

Why the panic? He would never have followed us across the water, after all. That doesn't matter. We were in a foreign country and nobody likes being walled up in a cell even with a tennis court outside.

The very back courts in Shettleston had a rural flavour, for grass grew in them and was even carefully nurtured for bleaching greens. I often played in one of them with Johnny and Joe, one of several pairs of inseparables in my class at Eastbank. We played at pole tig and dreeped from the wash-houses, but it was something different that kept them playing there when we might have been anywhere else. They refused to tell me what it was, but they kept hinting about it, and often with the undertone of dispute. I asked them what the secret was, but the one thing they agreed on was that nobody else could ever know about it. Then Johnny told me when Joe wasn't there. It was a girl.

Afterwards Joe told me too, when Johnny wasn't there. Her name was Jessie and she lived up the next close to Joe, and she sometimes played in the back court with another girl, Jane – not that Jane came into the thing at all. She was the kind of girl everybody likes, but nobody chases. We were all ten years old.

Several times we gave up waiting for Jessie to appear, and went to steal turnips from the gardens in Sandyhills or ask a man to take us into an evening football match at Wellpark. By the time Jessie did appear, we all knew that the secret was out. All that remained was whether she preferred Johnny or Joe. They were ready to fight each other over her, and yet their love for Jessie was another bond between them too. Only they knew how nice she was, nice-looking too, lovely hair and all.

We played pole tig, the five of us, Johnny, Joe, Jessie and Jane and me. You can't be tigged while you touch a pole, only when running between poles. Johnny and Joe warned me that Jessie could run faster than a boy.

She could, and I didn't care if she tigged me. It was thrilling to watch her running. She wore a yellow dress and yellow ankle socks and her short brown hair tossed as she ran, as she ran on long brown legs with her hair tossing

68

up and down on her neck. Her face was brown with the sun, and she smiled often, in pleasure when she tigged somebody or in despair when she didn't. Her teeth were small and white and even and they lit up her face when she laughed. There had never been anything so beautiful as her face when she laughed.

We sat on a wash-house roof and talked afterwards. Jessie and Jane both read the *Girl's Own Weekly*.

'You should read the *Wizard*,' Johnny said. 'Captain Q is rare.'

'I like school stories,' Jessie said. She was shy and bold at the same time, not sure of me because I was a stranger. She liked school stories. I dismissed Captain Q.

'You should read the *Magnet*,' I told her. 'Harry Wharton and Billy Bunter at Greyfriars.'

'English schools, yah-yah,' Joe said.

'Billy Bunter?' Jessie was excited. 'His sister's Bessie Bunter. She's in the *Girl's Own*'

'Who writes the stories?'

'Hilda Richards.'

'That must be Frank Richards' sister,' I said, eureka, I have found gold.

We talked about the boys of Greyfriars and the girls of Bessie Bunter's school. We knew the same families in a way. Johnny and Joe, who never read the *Magnet*, were contemptuous of the whole thing, and apprehensive. Jane sat there talking with us and knew that we were all trying to impress Jessie and I think we all knew this and were sorry for her, but that didn't stop us. I didn't care about Johnny and Joe. They were both too stupid to know how lovely Jessie was. Nobody but myself could appreciate her. She looked at Jane most of the time and hardly ever at me except when something excited her, but there was something in the way she didn't look at me that meant something, I was sure of it.

After a while the girls went up the close to sit at a landing window and talk. It was a routine move. As soon as they were gone, Johnny and Joe looked for pieces of paper to write letters to Jessie.

'I'll write one as well,' I said. Johnny looked at me narrowly.

'It's nae good – she disnae know you, just me and Joe.'

'Let him write wan if he wants,' Joe said. I would have written one in any case. I know what Johnny and Joe wrote. *'Dear Jessie, I love you, do you love me?'* I wrote, *Dear Jessie, I love you. Let me be your hero and protector and tell me if you love me. Yours forever, Clifford L. C. Hanley.*

It was a document calling for the full name and initials.

Jane came downstairs in a few minutes and we handed over the three letters for her to deliver. Then we sat feeling glum and happy and tried not to argue about Jessie. It was quite a long time before Jane came back with three answers. I took mine and glanced at it and pushed it in my trouser pocket. It read: *I love you. Yours forever, Jessie.* Johnny and Joe read theirs too, but they were not downcast. This ritual had been going on for a long time, and never anything but an evasive answer yet. Joe's only worry was that Johnny might have finally won, and Johnny felt the same way about Joe.

'Some day ah'll make her love me,' Johnny muttered.

'Maybe we could dae somethin' brave,' Joe said. 'Rescue somebody.'

'An' get wounded – wi' a bandage an' a sling. Ah like slings. Ah twisted ma erm last year an' ah had a sling, it was great, a wummin gave me a penny.'

I held my joy quiet, not only to spare their feelings but because I couldn't let it speak. When Jessie came back downstairs we didn't say anything to each other. Later she told me why she had favoured me. Johnny and Joe had written such ordinary letters.

'They didn't say anything, just the one thing, just—'

'Uhuh,' I said.

'I liked what you said.' She was shy.

'Did you? Honestly?'

'Mhm.'

That same month there was a change of classes and Jessie came into our class. I had always been the bright scholar, and now I answered questions and finished first with long division like a monkey doing cartwheels, to please my love. She was pleased and even awestruck.

We never met each other alone, only when the five of us played together and sometimes crawled over the bleaching green looking for a four-leaf clover. She could still run faster than a boy and she always looked lovely. Although we boys knew we knew everything and had a store of dirty jokes, I don't think I ever even kissed Jessie. There was a time when I might have, when Jane had a Hallowe'en party and we were all there, but right at the beginning of the party I bumped into a chair and knocked off a wart that I used to have on my left knee. It wouldn't stop bleeding, and Jane's father was dabbing it and bandaging it and putting ointment on it almost till the end of the party. That was of no importance, I didn't want anything from Jessie, only to know that we loved each other. We loved with scarcely a word spoken, and in time we drifted away from each other again without a word, and I was angry and sorry.

Here's The Lions

One of the oldest Glasgow fighting stories starts in the Emperor's palace in Rome, where the Emperor was livid to find that a crummy little shape on the Roman map of the world, North Britain, didn't have a wee Roman flag on it. He sent a legion to annexe it, and when the legion vanished without trace, sent ten legions after it, and then a hundred legions. After years of silence, one ship of the Roman fleet was seen approaching Rome, charred and tattered, and with a terrible commotion visible on the deck even from a mile away. The commotion was caused by two undersized, unshaven creatures, with ten legionnaires trying to hold each of them down. The ship carried the only survivors of the 110 legions, and the only prisoners. The Emperor was speechless with disbelief.

'Your Imperial Majesty,' said the surviving centurion, 'It seems impossible, but every other man you sent has had it. We can fight any army, but yon was ridiculous. We reached a place called Glasgow, and they don't fight by the rules there. They land you one with a bicycle chain or a broken bottle or give you that knee in the crutch and then disappear up things called closes, your Imperial Majesty. We only managed to capture these two prisoners because they had been at the wine and they were paralytic drunk. Honest, it was a massacree.'

'What?' hooted the Emperor, 'creatures like these two, two wee bauchles?' At this, one of the prisoners spat expertly in the Emperor's eye, and foaming at the mouth, he ordered them to be thrown to the lions instantly. The whole population turned out for the circus. After an hour's struggle, the arena guards managed to shove the two prisoners through the gate to the arena and drag back their unconscious comrades to safety. The two prisoners walked round for a look at the place.

'Heh Wullie,' one of them said. 'Nice statues they've goat therr. Who're they apposed tae be?'

'That yin wi' the baldy heid is Julius Caesar, a right stupit-lukkin nyuck, int 'e? That other wan is Tiberius, a rotten sod, that wan.'

'You're right educatit, so ye ur, Wullie. Who's that wan – that good-lookin' burd wi' the big dug?'

'Eh, that's, eh, ah know it, ah jist canny think. It's on the tip ae ma tongue. It's . . . uch, ah'll tell ye in a minute, here's the lions comin'.'

Well, it's all very well talking about fights, but it's a different thing fighting them except when you know you'll win and you won't get hurt. I never liked getting hurt. There was one afternoon I deliberately picked a fight with a boy in the class who wore an expensive blazer and had curly hair and a transparent complexion and talked like a jessie, and maybe he was a jessie, but his arms were about two feet longer than mine, and every time I made a run at him I ran my face straight into one of his fists, and when I started running back from him his arm could still stretch faster than my feet could move and all I wanted to do was be somebody else, in another country for preference. It wasn't the humiliation that worried me so much as the discomfort of being punched on the face, and once he had discovered the thing could be done, he was all for doing it all night. But I knew later how he felt because I had it the other way round and this time I didn't want the fight in the first place.

To be frank, I had given up the fight game for life. But there was a crowd of older boys with a pack-sheet tent pitched on the coup one evening, and they sponsored the match after this other boy of my own height and weight had landed an unprovoked stone on the back of my head. They wanted sport, and I felt that I was armed with justice, so we squared up. I'm not even sure of the other boy's name, but I think it was Hannah.

We sparred for a few minutes, and the big boys got impatient and shouted for action, and at last I forced myself to aim straight at his face, and hit him hard in one eye. I was ashamed at once and sorry for him because I knew what it was like to be punched. But although he was half-hearted about it and didn't fly into a killing rage, he went on fighting, and I hit him in the face again. The big boys cheered me and patted me on the shoulder, and I felt flushed with victory, but I hated them too and they disgusted me, for they were risking nothing themselves and nobody was punching their faces, and I hated myself a bit for playing up to them. I was hoping Hannah would run away, and I wouldn't chase him very fast, but he suddenly kicked me.

Dirty foul! One of the spectators was so hot on fair play that he was making to kick Hannah from behind to prove it, but missed him, and I was smarting slightly from the kick on the shin and justifying myself while I hit him again. And then it got hellish. He was either blinded or posing as blind, and it doesn't matter which, because he just stood with his hands in front of his face and I punched through his hands and hit him again and again until a man working in a garden across the street came over and stopped the fight and gave the big boys a telling off and said I was a bully.

'He hut me furst!' I said.

'Get away home out of here,' the man said, and I went.

It was always bad to see older boys urging young boys on to a fight, because they were always liable to throw in a clout or two themselves, if they didn't like one of the fighters, and they were just as liable to turn nasty with their favourite if he didn't produce enough action. Even among ourselves I didn't often see a fight that was deliberately sought and willingly fought. There was a standard practice at this time for satisfying honour. Fights usually started in the playground, and the contestants couldn't fight there. They would promise or threaten to meet up the Muck at four o'clock, and by four o'clock the thing would be forgotten.

The Muck is a piece of made ground with a cinder track on it used for training by Shettleston Harriers. It may have another name, but nobody knows it.

In the playground one afternoon I was tripped on my face by Willie Cairns. He was one of a big family of Cairnses who lived in a little low old row of cottages in Shettleston Road, since demolished and gone, and the Cairnses, about five of them all at school, were known for two things. They were all sneaky wee pukes and their mother was a terror.

After I was tripped, Willie was laughing in his Cairns way. I said:

'Ah'll get you.'

'Ah'll ge-e-et ye!' he mimicked. It was a catchphrase. 'An' if ah don't get ye, the coos'll get ye!'

The bell rang. 'You wait,' I warned him. 'I'll see you up the Muck at four.'

'Gi'e him a towsin', Willie,' one of his supporters said. 'Don't worry,' Willie said. We glared at each other as the lines went in and made a threatening gesture with our right fists. For this gesture, the left shoulder is pushed up and forward and the right forearm is tucked well into the body pointing towards the chin, and the fist is clenched, but with the thumb poked through between the first and second fingers. We regarded this form of fist as correct for a killer punch. In practice, if you landed a punch with the thumb like this, a stab of pain shot up your arm to the shoulder and paralysed the thumb.

I knew my Willie. There would be no fight up the muck at four. In the crowd leaving school at four o'clock, it was easy to get quietly lost before anybody could find you. But I had friends, and Willie had friends, and friends love somebody else's fight. Willie would have got clean away at four o'clock, and good luck to him, but for his friends who wanted his honour defended, and my friends had me trapped before I was out of the classroom. We took our positions before an audience of fifty or sixty, or rather, inside an audience of fifty or sixty, for everybody wanted to crowd round for a ringside view.

I had no fear of Willie. On the other hand, even a Cairns fist can be sore against the nose and was undesirable. We set to in the first position, arms tucked into the body and right shoulders forward, and then we did the usual thing. I said:

'Well?'

And Willie Cairns said:

'Aye – Well!'

'Well, whit'll ye dae?'

'You'll see!'

'Well, whit?'

'Ah'll dae a loat.'

Somebody in the crowd shouted:

'Aye – in yer troosers!' Shouts from every direction. 'Hit im wan!' 'Gi'e it tae 'im!' 'Whit kinna fight is this?' 'Baste 'im!' 'Gi'e 'im the auld wan-two!' Some of the spectators would demonstrate the kind of uppercut they fancied, and accidentally nudge another watcher, and arguments spurted up here and there. Willie Cairns and I were breathing heavily at each other, then I made the first attack, by leaning forward and bumping him on the shoulder with my shoulder and upper arm. He missed balance and staggered back a step, then stepped up and gave me a dunt with his shoulder.

'Well?' I said. 'You want a fight – let us see ye fight.'

'Ah never wanted a fight – you asked for it!'

'Ah don't want a fight.' These were the only honest remarks made all day.

'Well, yur gonny get wan!' a spectator shouted. Everybody was blood-mad to fight; except me and Willie Cairns. Somebody shoved Willie from behind to get him started, but he kept his balance and swung round angrily to curse the shover. It was a diversion that might end the main fight, but the crowd stayed in a solid ring and he finally had to give up arguing and turn back to face me. It never occurred to me to punch him while he was off guard. I don't say I was too honourable. He might have punched me back.

Somebody shoved me, and I was off balance. I cannoned into Willie and he fell back shocked. 'Hit 'im!' 'Uppercut!' 'Solar plexus!' I didn't know where the solar plexus was. Willie straighted up and aimed a swinging punch at a point two feet in front of my chin. 'Get in therr!' I aimed an uppercut about eighteen inches from Willie.

As I swung it, somebody shoved him again from behind, and his face crashed on to my fist. 'Uppercut!' the crowd shouted. 'Oh boy, did ye see that?' Spectators demonstrated the uppercut that I had landed. I danced about now, red and heavy-breathing and looking as if I meant business. I had put an uppercut right on the button. I was a real fighter. Willie swung like a woodsman again, but this time he was peevish and didn't care even if he hit me. He hit my shoulder and I lashed out, terrified of myself, at his face, and struck bone. I never liked Willie, but I was grateful to him then. He didn't get angry, he surrendered the fight. He put his hands to his face as if he expected the jaw to be smashed, and reeled about drunkenly and decided not, after all, to fall down. It was a poor fight, as usual up the Muck. But my friends loyally made the best of it, and there were even some sycophants

76

from Willie's camp who wanted to shake my hand and pat me on the shoulder. Soon I let them persuade me that I was a real killer. I lapped it up. I went home with fans on both sides of me and behind me shouting:

'You basted 'im! It was a massacree! Wan, two, bang!'

They stopped shouting. One or two of them left the procession and hurried ahead, or turned aside. We had reached Shettleston Road, and a big red woman was ten yards away facing us. She had Willie Cairns by the hand, and he was weeping floods and moaning. His eyes, which I had never laid a finger on, were raw red where he had rubbed them himself, and he had apparently sprained a knee and broken both arms on his way home, from the way he was walking. The big woman was Mrs Cairns.

'Aye, it's me! You come 'ere tae ah get ye, yah wee devil! Proud ae yersel', eh? Ah'll soart ye!'

'He started it!' I retorted. I was just as angry as she was, and I wasn't afraid either.

'Aye, an' ah'll feenish it!'

I ran like hell. She shouted after me:

'Ah know where ye live, ya bullyin' wee nyaff! Ah'll get ye!'

That was something I could worry about later, as long as I got out of reach of Mrs Cairns in the meantime. She wasn't like Willie. Mrs Cairns *could* fight.

That Music Stuff

'The Old Rugged Cross' had a particular place in my musical taste, from which nothing has ever moved it. It was a street song. It sounded religious, all right, but I had never heard it in church or Sunday School, or on the wireless, and I never imagined for a second that anybody had put it on a gramophone record. It was one of the songs that people sang for pennies in the back courts of Gallowgate or in the streets of Sandyhills on Sunday mornings in the nineteen-thirties. Not really a hymn and not a song, but a pious thing written for beggars to make money. Although I wasn't good, I was religious, at times passionately religious, and a church choir singing with the organ full out could bring quick tears to my eyes. But I still hated that song, and I didn't like the religious buskers because they looked vicious rather than holy. The other buskers I liked, from the spoon-rattlers to the accordionists.

One thin old man was a regular turn on Saturday afternoons, with an English concertina and a tune called 'Butterflies in the Rain'. He played it fast and he never played anything else. The spoon-rattlers were going out of fashion, but I fancied this kind of music. It was difficult, because I often tried to get the tremendous rolling rattle using both hands and rattling the spoons on my knee like the professionals, but they just fell out of my hands. And that was the great day of the dulcimer. This is a form of harp on a sound-board, like a zither, but played with two thin iron cleeks. For a long sustained note the cleek is bounced rapidly on the string, so a dulcimer solo has a trilling effect and usually almost no connexion with the original timing of the tune.

The same thing applies to Glasgow's traditional singing style. There is always a lot of singing in Glasgow, everybody does it. It was the thing that most struck two French girls from the melodious south who spent a holiday with my family some years ago. They had never heard anything like the incessant urge of Glaswegians to burst into song. Burns songs, pop songs, folk songs, operatic songs, patriotic songs, all kinds of songs. But mostly, in terms of sheer bulk, passionately sentimental songs.

Every wedding in Glasgow proves that every family in Glasgow has at least one singing uncle, usually called Uncle Willie, I have sometimes noticed. He either carries his well-worn music in his pocket on the chance that he may be persuaded to favour the company, or is prepared to go on unaccompanied. The Uncle Willies tend to choose songs with a bit of tone, like 'Red, Red Rose', or the 'Rowan Tree'. Both of these are certain death to amateur singers, but they die happy and proud. They take pride in a good-going tremolo, produce very rolling r's, very broad a's, and o's and u's so narrow you could slice a cheese with them, and whatever the tempo, when they hit a good note fair and square, they hang on to it till they've milked it of every drop of passion.

All traditional Glasgow singers do this, drunk or sober – give their best notes all the time they need. It may express their rugged independence of restrictive practices like Time.

Singing is not permitted by law in Glasgow pubs, because Glasgow understands the dangerous power of music, which inflames as readily as it soothes; especially as pub singers would always be liable to come up with 'The Wild Colonial Boy', or 'Ra Sash my Farra Wore', either of them guaranteed to spark off a crusade. But buskers sing outside the pubs, and customers sing after they leave the pubs. They still cling to their ancient favourites, for instance:

'Ra pale mune wos raaaaaaaaaaaaaaaa-ising,
Above rgrnmounte-e-e-e-e-e-e-e-e-ens . . .'

Or the song that is the Glasgow drunkard's national anthem, although Glasgow (and Will Fyfe) gave the rest of the world 'I Belong to Glasgow' for the world's drinking parties. Glasgow's own choice is 'The Bonnie Wells o' Wearie', pronounced 'Rab Onie Wells a Wee-a-rie'. Glaswegians never sing this song sober because it is believed to bring on rain.

The thirties were the great days of the buskers because honest men with honest trades could find nothing better to do. The depression was awful in Glasgow. Men used street corners as their club meeting-places in dry weather, and just stood there all day. They wore mufflers in place of collar-and-tie, and usually no overcoats even when it was cold, and when they had nothing to say, they shuffled from foot to foot, weaving their heads, in a neat co-ordinated movement that was almost like dancing, or

79

shadow-boxing, and clapped their hands and rubbed them together with the elbows pointed straight out sideways. When an acquaintance passed they said: 'Aye!' which meant, 'It's a cauld day', or 'Good old Geordie', or 'It's a helluva life'. And they gave the Glasgow nod, a funny movement difficult to describe and difficult for a stranger to imitate. It is a shake of the head, just one movement, that brings the chin up to the left and causes a slight twitch of a one-sided smile, and as well as greeting, it means affection and encouragement. It is practised in every social stratum.

And the men on the corners did a bit of punting with their spare coppers, or a bit of busking sometimes. It got beyond the stage of the spoons and the accordions. Whole revue companies worked the back courts and the side streets. There was one group that we trailed all round Sandyhills one summer evening; five clean, respectable young men dressed alike in khaki shirts and flannel trousers. They carried among them a saxophone and a fiddle, a megaphone for singing through, a board for tap dancing, and wheeled a kit of drums and an upright piano. They might even have been professionals suffering from the depression that had hit the theatres too. They unpacked in seconds, played a couple of band numbers, one of them sang, one tap-danced on the board and another did acrobatic turns. They were good.

Another group of three turned up. One played an accordion, another a saxophone, and the third took off his coat to reveal long thin legs and a very short kilt and put on a false Charlie Chaplin moustache and did comic songs, dances and jokes.

It must have been a terrible time, but not to us. We knew we were poor and we hated it, but nearly everybody else was poor too. There was always something happening and there was always music somewhere. Flora sent away for a banjolele at a shilling a week, but none of us except Harry could wring a tune out of it. I got a sixpenny mouth-organ and after some time I stopped giving recitations at the Guild of Honour soirees and played harmonica selections instead, just as good as the recitations. If we hadn't been respectable, I would have busked in the streets without a second's hesitation. You could always get by in Glasgow if you were musical.

Okay, Well, Draw!

When Jimmie started his newspaper round he was still at school, and quietly hating it, or at least quietly hating one of his teachers who didn't appreciate him. Jimmie never had any more difficulty than Jackie had in making a place and a name for himself in any society he liked, but there were always some people who could take a dislike to him and his attitude to life. It might have been hereditary. The same teacher, a woman with an obsession for neatness and order in life, took a dislike to me too. In Jimmie's case, I always felt that she was just blind to his brilliant grasp of inessentials.

He was spending a lot of creative energy on observing the teachers in the secondary school and teaching me to do impersonations of them so that I would know them when I moved up, and in inventing fantasy lives for them. He combed the French and algebra books for material for jokes, and maybe he had more natural talent for this than for French or algebra at the time. When he spoke about life in the Higher Grade, I thought it sounded glorious and free and full of intellectual mysteries and sophisticated entertainment. He taught his class to chant 'ee-hee-hee!' to the first three notes of Dvorak's 'Humoresque' every time the French teacher left the classroom, and the noise didn't merely irritate other teachers, it bewildered them. What did it mean? Where was the point of it? There was none, except a calculated subversion of logic. Words and sounds interested Jimmie so much that he made up his own to play with. Jackie started it, but Harry had done it before him. When Harry bought us a schipperke terrier pup and named it Roy, he gave it the alternative title of Schnyippie because the word Schipperke amused him. Jackie extended this to Schnyippie Schnyen and Jimmie called the dog Lippy Len, or sometimes just Sssss. It ended up answering to anything at all.

But this surrealist nonsense didn't impress teachers, and Jimmie began to develop a despised and bitter reaction to them, and to that one woman in particular who found a vulnerable place in him and jabbed sarcasm through it without mercy. At length he abandoned school in his own mind and simply endured it while he looked forward to something else, and in the meantime he started delivering papers before and after school every day. The job gave him a new set of people to study and entertain.

Jackie had started work in a little family engineering factory along the back road in Shettleston. I went to see him once or twice, sometimes with a jug of soup at lunchtime, and when I felt noble and unselfish I helped Jimmie with his newspaper deliveries. Mostly in summer, because I was almost incapable of being roused from bed in winter at six in the morning, no matter how faithfully I had promised the night before.

The best things about the newspaper business were being free to hang about the newspaper shop, and going up in the afternoons to hang about Shettleston railway station waiting to collect the evening papers from the train.

My recollection of this period is involved with guns and crime, although these couldn't have been more than momentary incidents. Guns had always fascinated us. Jackie once acquired a single-shot blank cartridge pistol, and when he learned something about working with metal, he sawed off the barrel and bored it through to the chamber, so that it could fire real bullets made by sticking an air-gun pellet into the nose of a blank cartridge. He demonstrated it about a dozen times firing at empty cans in the coup, and then intelligently dismantled the whole thing in case it caused any trouble. Then he bought an ordinary Diana air rifle, the kind any boy could buy in a shop without formalities, and fired at cans and egg-shells.

He was playing with it in the back garden one Saturday afternoon when I came up the street and passed within his range of vision. The boy next door, who was with him, said that an air-gun could never fire *that* distance, Jackie thought the gun was unloaded, and put it to his shoulder and fired. I hadn't even seen him when I felt a burning pain in my chin and leapt into the air yelling. He hid the gun and rushed out to me in terror and remorse, and I knew without argument that the shot was an accident and must not be mentioned, but a neighbour had seen me dancing in the street, and she brought it up when she was in the house that afternoon.

'He never mentioned it,' my mother said, puzzled.

'Somebody threw a stane at me,' I muttered, hating the neighbour woman.

'It's broken the skin,' my mother said, turning my face up to the light. 'He could have put your eye oot.' I wriggled away but the neighbour peered at me and said:

'That's a funny mark – it's as roon as a bullet hole. Was it no' that gun your Jackie's got?'

'Jackie would never dae a thing like that,' my mother said, offended in her innocence. 'The wean would have telt me if Jackie had fired at him.' The neighbour humphed, but I stared at her ready to stick to my story if it killed me and she didn't say any more.

Then Jimmie bought an air-pistol. It was five shillings, the kind with a telescopic barrel that cocks by pressing one half of the barrel back into the other half and shoots out the hidden half when it fires. This odd action gave it a tremendous kick upwards, and it had to be aimed about forty-five degrees below the target, so that strangers to the gun could get nowhere with it. It was the envy of every other newspaper boy in Shettleston.

When I helped with the newspaper round I got shots with the gun, usually over the coup where I couldn't hit anybody and get into trouble. We lived a lot on the coup.

Shortly after the air-pistol appeared, a lorry dumped a

load of curious slabs of baled straw, flattened into big cakes with some kind of cement, and Jimmie started to build a den where nobody would find him while he was out shooting. There was no cover on the coup because it was dead flat from one end to the other, but there were heaps of rubbish here and there, and Jimmie's cunning plan was to build a den that looked exactly like a heap of rubbish. The two of us hauled these straw cakes to a likely spot and piled them up and leaned them together until we had a heap that was hollow inside, with a slab that could be pulled over the opening from the inside.

It was more perfect than we could have expected. Lorries with loads of rubbish drove straight past it. Gardeners walking across the coup to their allotments came within feet of it without even looking at it. It was so secret that we had to let other people in on it in order to enjoy their admiration. We didn't do anything in it except crouch in a circle, Jimmie with gun drawn, waiting for an attack. Then, very gently, the idea ran amok. Jimmie Paterson liked the den so much that he wanted his own room in it, and he dragged more stuff over to build a lean-to extension. When it was finished, he got empty wooden boxes and fitted them in as cupboards, with tuppenny tins of meat paste and small loaves and bars of chocolate on the shelves for the big siege. Everybody else wanted a private apartment too. The heap of rubbish started to grow in all directions. There was no science in the method – the idea was to keep it looking like a heap of rubbish. The weather was dry and it stayed intact overnight, and overnight again, and for a week, and all the time it grew. At the end there were ten separate rooms inside it, some of them no broader than a telephone box, and with holes poked in the partition heaps for whispering through.

We still didn't *do* anything in it. We just sat in our separate apartments, whispering through holes in the walls to one another or peering through slits at people passing unconsciously by, and we felt perfectly glorious. When old Ballantyne, one of the allotment diggers, walked past, we crowded to the lookout slits and watched him stumping across the coup. He was a short-tempered man and wore breeches and leggings, like a farmer, and to stare at him and know that he didn't even know he was being watched, was a pent-up delight.

The den had been standing for nearly a week when he did notice it. Jimmy and I were in the main chamber alone when he looked at the heap in passing, and he looked suddenly irritated. Jimmie called his expression baleful malevolence. He took two steps off the path and aimed three or four kicks at the den with his tacketty boots and then walked on, well pleased. The whole affair, so gently tended by us delinquents, collapsed and buried us.

The slabs were too light to damage us and we just crawled out of the wreckage, but we felt baleful and malevolent too. When the rest of the gang turned up to crouch in their apartments they had the heart knocked out of them at the sight.

Jimmie took the gun with him to the railway station when we went to meet the newspaper train. There were twenty or thirty newsboys in the crowd, and the station staff hated us. At first we waited on the platform or in the waiting-room, but from time to time a porter cleared us out into the yard and then would wheel the bundles out on a barrow just to keep us out of the station itself. Jimmie worked for Big Geordie Forbes, the best boss in the business, with the biggest delivery rounds and the highest wages, and big parcels of evening papers that had to be wheeled in a barrow from the station to the shop. Some of the other shops had only a dozen or two of each evening paper, tied up in string. When the parcels arrived the newsboys threw themselves in a heap on top of them to find their own, and heaved any others up in the air or over their shoulders or on to the railway lines. They could never do that with ours – the parcels were too big. But that was why the porters liked to get the papers clear of the station before we were allowed to fall on them.

We whiled the time away waiting for the train in trying to pat an elderly retired Shetland pony that grazed in a yard adjoining the station, and some of the boys tried to mount it, but it was too slick for that, and most of us objected to actual ill-treatment of the wee thing, although the crowd was fairly rowdy and illiterate and just the kind of crowd that railway porters and policemen don't like. When Jimmie started bringing his air-pistol to the station, the pony was forgotten for a few days. He was cagey about giving a shot to most of the boys because some of them would have blazed away at the station windows without a moment's thought, but we put cans and pieces of wood on top of fence posts and shot at them.

Not understanding the amount of kick in the pistol, the rest of the boys fired all their shots into the air. The biggest of them, a simple lout called Big Feeney, made up his mind that the gun was a fake. Jimmie and I and Neil, a school-friend of mine, had all hit the tin can and nobody else had even nicked it, and Big Feeney shouted that it was a trick.

'The gun disnae fire at a',' he sneered. 'When you bang the gun, your brother flings a stane an' hits the can!'

'All right, look,' I said, and fired instantly at the can, and missed. 'See? Whit did ah say? It's jist a trick,' Feeney gloated. It was Neil's shot of the gun, and Feeney pushed his luck too far.

'Goan, hit ma haun,' he shouted, and held his open palm straight out from his body. Neil fired from the hip, Big Feeney's eyes popped and he started flicking his hand to shake the pain off. Then he started to grin mournfully and showed everybody the mark, and the train came in with the papers. Jimmie left the gun at home after this.

The next night there were two policemen waiting at the station when the newsboys arrived. At the sight of them I wanted to run, but it was too late. When Jimmie and I reached the crowd there were mutterings about finger-prints. The policemen were talking in a reasonable, friendly way with Big Feeney. I swore to myself never to touch another firearm as long as I lived, and waited while one of them looked slowly round in our direction.

Then it turned out that they didn't know anything about the gun. Somebody had been trying to break into the chocolate machines on the station platform, and the search had been narrowed down to the newsboy crowd.

A sense of innocence is a wonderful thing.

I hadn't even been in the station during the estimated days of the crime. In fact, the suspect was practically fixed, and he was nowhere to be found. He was one of the regular gang, a high-spirited foul-mouthed character known as Sticky. The two policemen had got that far and were trying to unearth his full name, but nobody knew it. He had never been anything else but Sticky, and he lived in Shettleston, and that was all anybody knew about him. Nobody could even remember which shop he worked for.

In spite of that, the police didn't take long to track him down. But it wasn't his crime that excited us all, or his punishment, and I never discovered what that was. It was his name, the name of the character who had never been anything but Sticky. It was Aloysius Fitzgerald. I never felt the same about him after that.

A Friend Is A Friend

Years and years later, when Sticky was grown up and married, Jimmie and I met him in Shettleston again. He was limping and he had a terrible story to tell.

He had been called up – this was still during the last war, and after a few months in the Army he had deserted.

'Natcherally,' he added. 'Ah couldny stick it. That's how a' broke ma leg.'

'What – you broke it in the Army?' I asked him. No, no, that was the story. He had stayed with his mother for a while in case the Military Police were looking for him at his own house, then went to live with his wife when he thought the heat had died down. One night while he was in bed, he heard a battering at the door and a voice on the landing shouting 'Come on, Fitzgerald – we know you're there!'

'Ma wife shouted "It's the polis!", an' ah dived straight oota bed – in ma shurt – and jumped right oot the windae withoot waitin' for ma boots, landed right on ma feet an' broke this leg. Next thing ma pal was roon the back tryin' tae lift me an' nearly greetin'. It was him that had shouted at the door, the stupit f— b—. He was tryin' tae be funny.

'He had tae cairry me up the sterrs an' get a doactor tae fix the leg, an' he was just aboot greetin' a' this time.

'So therr was ah lyin' wi' a broken leg, an' ah said tae the stupit f— b—, "Ya stupit f— b—," ah says, "As soon as this gets better ah'll gi'e you a doin', ah'm tellin' ye, ah'll gi'e ye a kickin' if it's the last thing ah do."'

While Sticky was mending his remorseful pal kept him and his wife going in money and cigarettes.

'He turned out all right after all,' I suggested.

'Sure, there's nothin' wrang wi' him,' Sticky agreed. 'But what a stupit f— maniac. Ah said ah would gi'e him a kickin', an' the minute ah goat the plaster aff ma leg ah gi'ed him it. Ah half-kilt him.'

Roosty Pockets

A terrible lot of people get married in Glasgow, and when we were young, we tracked down weddings greedily for the scrammle. Then my own family started to do it, and I was on the other end of the scrammle. The first big wedding in the family I was old enough to appreciate was Mary's, and I remember it because the house was packed with presents weeks before and because I was old enough to be entitled to ask Neil to the reception. A thing about big families is that family affairs in the ordinary way are already so crowded that there isn't much room for outsiders, and especially children; and young children in a big family never get an inflated sense of their own importance because they have to take their chances against the competition of their older brothers and sisters. While we all lived at home we had to have two sittings for evening meals, adults first and kids afterwards, simply because it would have been too crowded to do it any other way.

Neil was to come to the house before the time and travel with us to the hall, and I was at the door to see him coming down the street, all clean and brushed and with a parcel in his hand. Mary, still in the house, was surprised and touched that his mother had gone to the unnecessary trouble of sending her a wedding present, but a terrible moment occurred as he was coming up the front steps.

'He's bringing a sugar-and-cream – the parcel's the shape!' Mary wailed, looking out of the window, and then told me to stall Neil at the door for a few minutes. She had just been counting the crystal sugar-and-cream sets among the wedding presents, and they were laid out on the living-room table, sixteen of them. I kept Neil standing at the door until my mother opened the living-room door behind me and asked me why I hadn't brought him in. Mary was just jamming shut the door of the sideboard and turning the key to keep the piled-up crystal from cascading on to the floor, and when Neil handed over his sugar-and-cream she was perfectly honest in her thanks, but she hid that one too.

Everybody I knew was crowded round the front gate by the time the taxis arrived. As we got into the cabs the crowds chanted, 'Hard up! Roosty pockets! Hard up!' and we affected to ignore them. The shouts got louder when the taxi door shut behind us, and when we started to move away my own friends were screaming. Some of them were really frightened.

'Hard up! Hard *up!* Hard *up!*' Neil and I had been given the throwing money, and we waited until it looked as if we were going away without throwing it before we wound down the taxi windows and heaved handfuls of coppers into the street.

It was one of the sweetest, lordliest sensations in my life to be throwing the money instead of shouting 'Hard-

Up' and scrambling for it on the pavement, and the moment would have been complete if I could have thrown it and then joined in the scramble too.

The only ominous note at Mary's wedding was symbolized by the presence of Neil. He was always nice and clean and well-brought-up, but his father was a Socialist town councillor, and already my mother was worried at the influences that were working on me.

In the only election I remembered from Gallowgate days, all the kids had roamed the streets singing:

> 'Vote vote vote for Campbell Stephen
> Vote vote vote for a' his men
> And we'll buy a penny gun
> And we'll make the Germans run
> And we'll never see the Germans any more.'

And it looks pretty silly now since Campbell Stephen was a pacifist all his life. Still, we sang it, but we didn't know who Campbell Stephen was and I didn't care. We had always been good, God-fearing Conservatives and respectable people, and there was pain in the prospect of one of us being wooed into some ugly heresy. These things started with street-corner politics and could end with the abandonment of God Himself.

Not that there was any danger of that. I was firm in my faith in the truth.

Never Look at Your Face

One day the minister, on one of his regular visits, was talking to my mother when I came home from school. He was a big rugged bass-voiced man, and I thought he was great, but he had the minister's trick of speaking about you to yourself, and he turned round when I came in and said:

'I was just saying to your mother, Clifford, that I had been telling my wife you would go far because you have the greatest asset of all – a smiling face.'

It wasn't true anyway, a boy at school was always dripping at me for looking gloomy. My face fell into a glum shape when I wasn't doing anything with it. But people shouldn't say such things in any case; they make the possession of a face a conscious burden. I had enough trouble already trying to discover who I was and what kind of human being I was. At school I was one of these recognizably irritating little boys who pass exams and pick up prizes without making any effort, so that teachers either like them for being so responsive or hate them for being so arrogant. I assumed without question that I was a genius, and it was both a blow and a relief later to realize I wasn't. At least I was too clever to let people know my opinion. I knew that a decent modesty pays better. I was skilled in annoying teachers to amuse the class, the easiest way to cheap popularity, and cheap popularity is nice to have. But I was shy too, apart from my passion to make an exhibition of myself.

Knowing my own strength, I took care to avoid the discovery of my weaknesses. When everybody else was discovering that girls were a good thing, I avoided them and made up good reasons for myself.

During this time I assumed that practically everybody

else in the world simply did what they felt inclined to do, without thinking it over and over, and without wondering what kind of fool they might make of themselves. There were always two or three girls each year who became the favourites of the class and were pursued by several boys at once, and I rigorously refused to concede these girls any attractions at all. It was a shock when I was forced to speak to one of them one day and she answered with every sign of friendliness. I had got myself so disgusted with her popularity that I was convinced I hated her and that she must hate me. That's the cure for adolescent broodiness, by the way – being chased by beautiful girls. I organized this very badly.

At the same time, we all had a whale of a time. We realized we were the elite of our generation, in a secondary school. Eastbank was the only secondary school in a wide radius, and its old name, still carved out on the stonework, was actually Eastbank Academy. There was a school badge and a Latin motto and we were conscious of our high-class destiny and our social superiority, from time to time. We denied this, of course.

I blamed my diffidence on various things. My teeth were uneven at the front, absolute death to any lad's career. I never had much money to spend, and *that's* no fun. While everybody around me was beginning to sprout to man's size, I was still short for my age, and it is well known that no girl in the world likes short men.

But every so often I would break out despite myself. When I first got into the school debating society I got so drunk with an atmosphere where argument was actually encouraged that I conducted the discussion session practically solo, and when Neil chivvied me afterwards about overdoing it, I didn't give a damn. I was reeling with new-found power.

On the night the debating society held its mock election, the political cleavages in the school abruptly gaped deep and unbridgeable. My mother, who was always hoping that I would triumph over temptation, had become derisively resigned by this time, and merely laughed when

I raked through the house to find a red scarf to wear at the election. I didn't wear it in any case. I had to lend it to Neil's sister, who was leading the ILP ticket.

I have always been glad I grew up in a violently political city like Glasgow. Anything is better than a place that doesn't care one way or the other about politics, and Glasgow has never been a place for taking an impartial view. By this time I had learned that people who said they didn't believe in politics meant that Conservatism was the normal state of affairs and anything else was politics and therefore absurd. I was a passionately convinced Socialist, with all the aggression of an ex-Calvinist, for my mother's worst forebodings had come true and I had abandoned God as well as Toryism. I was all for abandoning everything. Gothic architecture, the institution of money, sexual morality, nationalism, the English language and clothes.

We lost the election. But I could feel the tide was turning. There had been a time when Neil, and then Neil and I together, had had to take on the whole class in our political fights. We were beginning to find allies in all directions. But at the same time, our Tory schoolmates were acquiring new arguments too. We had Communists. After a holiday in Germany, two or three people came back with Blood-and-Honour daggers and swastika badges and advocated Nazism with all the complacent superiority of people who know from *actual experience*. There was a boy who tried in vain to expound the doctrines of the British Israel World Federation, and when his arguments petered out, used to clinch the thing by saying:

'My father has maps in the house that prove it.'

It was difficult to teach us any subject that might touch even lightly on politics, because we were always ready to protest to our teachers against anything that smelled of propaganda. When the same woman teacher who had persecuted Jimmie started reading aloud to us, for relaxation, a chapter from a book by Beverley Nichols about how a lone English official had silenced a howling mob of Egyptians, I leapt to my feet and demanded to be excused from any attempt at Imperialist indoctrination. I was never forgiven, but I hugged my principles and my courage to my bosom for weeks and looked the world straight in the face – with a straight face, too.

The Scottish Nationalists were strongly represented. In fact, we were in truth subjected to Scottish Nationalist propaganda by a teacher. He was Donald MacCormick, brother of John MacCormick, the Scottish Nationalist leader. We called him Monty, and he taught English and history, with brief digressions from time to time to correct any false impressions we might have picked up from our England-biased history text-book. And, of course, presented with so blatant a propagandist, we didn't protest at all, but encouraged him and asked innocent questions to lead him on and enjoyed sharp, witty political speeches when we might easily have been studying the history in the curriculum. He had the advantage of being a born teacher and a good man who was loved generously by most of his students, but he didn't convert a one of us, even although all his criticisms of our English history-book were absolutely fair to the best of my knowledge.

He always wore brown, very dapper and nicely built with broad shoulders although they were curved in from an asthmatic condition. When he thought nobody was looking he sometimes executed little steps of a foxtrot or a rhumba and whistled through his teeth. He died young, a terrible thing to me because I loved him.

Hugh Smith, still as big, burly and straightforward as he had been in the role of a knight's horse, was stoutly Tory. He had grown out of the phase when he proved that Conservatism must be best because nearly all the Peers in the House of Lords were for it, and he admitted that his father voted Labour, but he would concede nothing more. The real basis of his political faith, I think now, was that he was so reasonably balanced and uncomplex that he felt the world was a good place to be in and there was no reason for wanting to change it. He was honest and healthy and people liked him. He ran well and played football like a well co-ordinated bull and although he broke a couple of bones at different times playing games he kept on playing them. He pursued the favoured girls of the school with that unselfconscious gusto I envied so much and was the automatic choice for school captain when the time came.

Hugh had been on the organized ten-day trip to Germany that had stimulated some people to a brief passion for the Nazi idea, but it had no effect on him. One of his regular companions and girl-chasers who had been on the same trip was a tall, slim, handsome, naif character called Alfie Hendry, who sported the Nazi badge to assert his independence when Neil and I cornered him and preached the pure doctrine of socialism to him. He played the piano and made thousands of model aeroplanes, and he was infuriating because he was impervious to argument. Alfie didn't want to be persuaded or converted. He just wanted to be a hit with the girls, and with one in particular, and to make toy aeroplanes or fly real aeroplanes. He had been aeroplane-daft since he was six. I liked him, partly because he too suspected that I was a genius.

The third member who made up the girl-chasing pack was Big Bob Hughs. They were all of a height, and Bob had been famous among us in his younger days for his ability to draw cowboys. Later he started singing, and knew the words of every popular song the minute it appeared. So did I, and this formed some kind of bond between us.

The school solidarity, regardless of politics, burst out in Coronation year when the Town Council decided to celebrate by chartering Clyde steamers and taking whole school populations for a sail on the lochs of the Clyde to Ardgoil. Our school shared a steamer with another school whose name I have long forgotten, but it was from the other end of the city and was a Catholic school to boot. We had a good day for the trip, and I remember part of the time umping into a forbidden area of the steamer for a bet, and part of the time doing my suave man-of-the-world act leaning over the rail and talking to three girls in the class about the best part of the Argyllshire coast for building a dream cottage. So it was possible to speak to girls socially after all. The one who was most fervent for the quiet life among the mountains ended up living in the middle of Paris, last I heard of her.

When we reached Ardgoil there was an issue of buns and milk and we spilled on-shore with a warning to get back for sailing time. Teachers who had spent the voyage patrolling the alleyways now patrolled the countryside, looking wan and apprehensive. In the big field near the pier was a square wooden platform on trestles, about the size of a boxing ring, used for Highland dancers during the local Highland games. During the middle of the afternoon an Eastbanker wearing spectacles rushed into a crowd of us and reported that he had been thrown off the platform by a crowd from the other school.

A few people strolled towards the platform looking for excitement, but nothing was happening. Two of them jumped up on to it and still nothing happened. But by this time the fiery cross had gone round the glen. A spearhead from the other school appeared at the other end of the platform and headed for the Eastbank representatives, and within five or ten minutes hundreds of us were trying to scramble on to a square that might have held fifty. I found at once that you don't have to be big or strong or vicious in a free-for-all, you just have to keep your eyes open and move fast; and keep away from the edge of the platform where somebody from below could yank the ankles away from you.

The teachers of both schools stopped looking wan and leapt across ditches and fallen trees to stop the fight, but there was nothing they could do. When they called on a boy by name to desist, he looked helpless and fell back into the crowd. Two teachers who lost their patience and climbed up were carefully mistaken for mere schoolboys and heaved off. For a minute it looked as if we might get the teachers worked into the fight, but somebody slicker than the others started calling that it was boat time, and we were swept by a mass terror of being abandoned among the hills.

When the platform was finally cleared, the boy wearing spectacles who had started the whole thing was left standing in the middle of it, looking fulfilled.

On the trip home, we moved about the steamer in fours or fives, but the teachers moved in twos and nobody was thrown overboard. The girl who had wanted the cottage in the mountains sneered when she learned that I had been in the juvenile squabble on the platform. I sneered back. We got on fine.

You Learn Things, Travelling

For several years in the 'thirties, Harry was among the great crowd of Glaswegians who were thrown idle without hope of work ever coming back to the Clyde. Idleness was a staple industry. He redecorated his house and made furniture and ran a Boy Scout troop and a St Andrew Ambulance section just to keep himself from atrophy. Engineering apprentices were being meticulously trained for the dole – as soon as they completed their apprentice-ships they were paid off. When the slump hit Jackie he decided to join the Navy.

Mattie, my eldest sister, was married to a regular Naval petty officer, and Bill was a figure of heroic romance to us all. He had specialized in dismantling faulty torpedo-heads and at one time had played a glass piccolo in a Navy band, and he was a person of authority and poise and very likeable, and if he was the Navy, it seemed bound to be a good thing. I was torn between admiration and my conviction that navies and armies were bad things, but I could quite see why Jackie wanted to go. It's an easy step from Glasgow to the sea, and it was always particularly easy for the Hanleys. Jimmie finally despaired of his prospects as an engineer and followed Jackie to join up.

The urge to move was an epidemic. Neil's family had as guest for a while a political refugee from Austria, an enormous young man in lederhosen who had hitch-hiked across Europe to Britain, and he reeked of the freedom of the wanderer. Hitch-hiking was almost unknown in Britain, but we decided it was the only way to travel, and in the face of bewildered opposition from both our mothers, we borrowed rucksacks and headed for London in the last fortnight of a summer holiday from school. Neil was thirteen and I was twelve. We had thirteen shillings between us, and our parents felt reasonably sure that this would cut the trip short and bring us home disenchanted, but we reached London with the thirteen shillings untouched – one motorist who picked us up insisted on standing us a day's keep and gave us four shillings. We actually lived on a shilling a day between us.

The 400 miles took two days of hard thumbing and we went on to Kent to put up with Mattie, who had bought a house in Gillingham to be near the Naval barracks. The story, told with loud modesty, blotted out everybody else's holiday adventures when we got back to school. Alfie wanted to join us the following year and other people made plans to form their own teams, but we ended up by ourselves again. In the third year we wanted to strike farther, and I got a job as a boy on a little cattle ship from the Clyde to Montreal.

It took ten days each way, and it wasn't as much fun as I had to claim afterwards. I was sick without respite for the first three days out before I was even able to talk intelligently. After that I ate with terrible greed. I had never met food in such quantities, and my memories of leaner days drove me to eat rather than throw anything away. My main duty was to fetch the meals from the galley and dump any surplus over the side in case the cook served it up again, and the dumping was real pain to me. In five days I grew a paunch. I was sixteen, short and slight, and my pot was the silliest thing I ever saw. It went away in a week or two.

About half of the seamen – there were ten of us in a

little L-shaped fo'c'sle with two-tier bunks on three walls and a table in the middle – were Islandmen, one of them a giant with a face the size and shape of a kitchen window and the heart of a child. The first time ice was sighted, he remembered I had never seen an iceberg, and lifted me, on my mattress and pillow and still wrapped in my blankets, and took me out to the deck, and then wakened me up to show me the berg. When I opened my eyes and saw ice and sea instead of the fo'c'sle I thought we had gone down and started doing the breast-stroke in desperation.

There were four sailors from Glasgow. One was a thin, gangling boy of about my own age who was celebrated for having got drunk in Montreal on the previous trip and caused a riot in a brothel. The second, Willie something, was a few years older, short and tough and given to passionate cursing. He fascinated me with his descriptions of the Montreal bordellos. This was real life, I thought. Before we had passed Ireland on the trip out he had started promising himself a big time in a new place in Montreal, and on the whole trip back he raved about two girls he knew in Govan.

'Wait tae ye see St Dominic's, Peggy,' he told me. 'A film star fur a dollar. A film star!'

'Rin Tin Tin?' I asked him.

'Oh, ye can laugh. But ah'm comin', Lulu! Ye don't believe me, Peggy' (Peggy is the duty name of the deck boy), 'but you'll see. Naw, mebbe ye'll no' – you're too young. You can haud the jaikets.'

'Leave the peggy alone, Willie,' one of the Islandmen told him. 'Wan horny tink like you iss eneuff on wan shup.'

I could have listened to Willie all day, and I had to, most days. He reminded me of Sticky – no real harm in him. His ravings about his plans for Montreal didn't shock me at all, I was sophisticated and broad-minded. I was also mad to see a brothel, a real den of sin, so that I could take the story back home. Any reservations I had about it were not on moral grounds. It just didn't sound exciting to my tastes from Willie's descriptions.

The third Glaswegian in the fo'c'sle was Jimmie Wilson, a tall, quiet young man with deep brown eyes who evidently knew his trade but didn't speak much and never used bad language. I did. I fell into Willie's style as a mimic. The fourth was Alec, sharp-faced and argumentative. He considered himself the intellectual of the seamen's fo'c'sle, and after a few days of chumminess towards the new Peggy turned nasty when I didn't agree with him. He used to lie on his bunk thinking out traps for me.

'Peggy!'

'Uh?' I learned to be suspicious.

'Where is heaven?'

'I don't know, I've never been there.'

'Don't get smart. Where is it – whit direction?'

'Give in.'

'Come on.' His temper was slipping. 'You're supposed tae be educatit, answer the dampt question!'

'There's no dampt answer. Heaven's no' a place.'

He hated this, and me.

'It's up there, isn't it?' he demanded.

'All right, it's up there,' I agreed.

'Oh, is it?'

'I don't know – it's your idea.'

'Don't be so bloody cheeky – an' don't start backin' oot. You said it was up there!'

'All right,' I said.

'Oh, is it? Well, whit aboot the Australians?' It was so obvious it was wearisome. 'You need a bit mair education before you'll be a man!' he crowed. And another time:

'Peggy!'

'I don't know.'

'Whiddye mean, you don't know, ah havnae asked ye anythin'.'

He was about twenty-eight, and a head taller than I was.

'Whatever you're gonny ask, I don't know.'

'Watch your lip, you're no'an AB yet.'

'That's right.'

'Can you box the compass?'

'Sure.'

'Let's hear it.'

With an air of long-suffering indulgence I boxed the compass, and he prepared to fault me, but somebody else in the fo'c'sle patted me on the shoulder and said, 'Good man, Peggy, you'll be a sailor yet.'

'All right,' Alec said. 'All right, since you know everythin' aboot navigation – whit shape is the horizon?'

'A straight line.'

'Ah! Ahah! Eh! Well, where are the ends?'

'What ends?'

'The ends o' the straight line! A straight line's got ends, hasn't it?'

'Uhuh,' I said. 'But in mathematics there is no such thing as a straight line. It's just a line of such slight curvature that we call it straight for convenience.'

'Convenience! Away back tae school, whatever kind a ragged school you've been at, an' learn somethin' before you start shown' aff.'

On long voyages, the sailors sometimes occupied themselves in chewing over such insoluble problems for weeks on end. On a previous trip the fo'c'sle had debated for over a week the question of how Solomon had seduced the Queen of Sheba. Nobody considered looking for a Bible to check the story. That would have killed the debate. Nobody had ever failed to fall for Alec's two prize puzzles of heaven and the horizon either. I could understand why he hated me. I was an evasive sea-lawyer.

My first evening in Montreal was spent standing watch over an open hold full of whisky. When I related the story I was standing watch with a loaded revolver, and I related it so often that I can now see myself clearly with a great heavy Smith and Wesson in my hand, but I should think I am certainly deceiving myself about that. On the second night in port I went to watch a football match between our ship's company and another, on a piece of waste ground in the suburbs. Little knots of spectators turned up, and several middle-aged women spoke to me when they learned I was from Glasgow.

101

'How is Argyle Street, son?' one of them asked kindly.

'Fine – still the same, big crowds on a Saturday night an' buskers playin' the flute.'

'Oh, my God!' She started weeping, but took a hold of herself. 'It's that nice tae hear a good Scotch voice. Could you no' take me hame on your boat, son?'

'I wish I could,' I said in desperate pity.

'Ah know, ah know, son, ah wish you could tae. Don't you ever leave yer hame, son, it's the best place in the world. Ah wish tae God ah had never left dear auld Glesca.' She patted me on the arm as if I were the one who needed sympathy and walked away dabbing at her eyes. After the game we climbed on the back of a lorry and had a frightsome ride back into the city. There was some argument about what should happen to me, but finally Willie said I should stick with his crowd. We went for a drink. The waiter refused to serve me beer and brought a Pepsi-Cola instead, which was all right. At a suitable time Willie suggested a move. He had a late attack of moral scruples.

'Mebbe you better get back tae the ship, Peggy,' he said dubiously. 'Your mither widnae like you bein' in company like this.'

'He would get loast,' somebody else said.

'Ah would gi'e him the money for a taxi,' Willie protested. 'But ah've only got three dollars left. Stick wi' us, we'll look efter ye, Peggy. See a bit a life, boy!'

Willie knocked on a door in a quiet street and a little peep-flap opened, just like speakeasies in the movies. The door opened and we went into a little lounge with a parquet floor and seats round the walls. There was a juke box in one corner and Bing Crosby was singing 'El Rancho Grande'. Five girls were sitting round the room, one in a one-piece bathing suit and the others in underclothes. They looked agreeable and dull. I sat in a chair at the door with the boys' money in my pockets. The scene was sharp and distinct and quite unbelievable, it had nothing to do with excitement or vice. Two of the boys danced with two of the girls, and then Willie came to me

102

and asked for one of his three dollars.

The madam was a very short, very fat woman with a fat worried face. When Willie gave her the dollar she pulled up her skirt and tucked the bill into the top of her stocking, where there were lumps of bills tucked already. I was too stunned to laugh when she gave him a green ticket from a roll in her pocket like a roll of cinema tickets, and he went out of the room with an apathetic black-haired girl, waving the ticket in the air but quite subdued and for once not talking about sex. Bing Crosby sang 'There Ain't No Sweet Man That's Worth the Salt of My Tears'. I listened to the juke box and kept my eyes open for details to make the story sound more convincing when I got back to school.

We got back to the Clyde at the end of July, and a few days later Hugh Smith got a trip to Canada too, as a passenger, on one of the Rhodes Scholar jaunts. He never saw a house of sin, but he met more girls.

Have You Ever Been A Public?

'Ladies and gentlemen,' I said quietly. 'Ladies and gentlemen.' One of the workers looked up at me and grinned. 'Try just a wee bit louder.'

'Ladies and gentlemen!' I looked down at him. 'It sounds daft – there's naebody here.'

Councillor Davie Gibson looked up. 'You're doin' fine, Cliff,' he assured me. 'Just get them warmed up – they'll come all right when you start.'

'Comrades and friends!' I yelled, and took fright at the sound, ringing across empty space in Tollcross Park. 'Comrades and friends,' I whispered, and then forced myself to it. '*If you listened to the six o'clock news you would hear that British troops have bombarded* . . .' It still

103

sounded silly, but the workers nodded happily and I went on.

It was a summer evening during the war and the ILP was bringing the message of pacifism to the people, but the people weren't there.

I had never had any doubt that I would be against war. Everybody was a pacifist in the 'thirties, but I was always resolved to keep my peaceful principles pure no matter how inexpedient they might seem. I had joined the Independent Labour Party, the only remaining champions of international sanity and the brotherhood of man, and we were a bit insane ourselves, of course. I would have been one of the regular public speakers earlier, but I was always discouraged by the extent of my ignorance. Now I was taking my first training venture as chairman of an open-air meeting. We had a speaker's stool, some bills advertising the *New Leader 2d* weekly, and a supply of pamphlets, and Councillor Davie Gibson as principal speaker. If it had been Jimmie Maxton, the crowds would have given up sunbathing in the park and rolled round, as Davie cheerfully admitted. Still, he had his own record as a box-office buy and there we were; Davie and me and four supporters. The stool was pitched on one of the open bits of the park, near a main path, and surrounded by nobody.

It was a flaying experience. I discovered that when I was put to it, I could spout fluently enough and keep on thinking of something else to say, and it would have been easy with a couple of dozen listeners. The chairman's job was like a carnival barker's. He had to start up and keep up a noise until curiosity drew the crowds. It isn't easy to address nobody with confidence and passion.

At first I kept breaking off and smiling down, stiff with embarrassment, at our lonely supporters, but after a while it was less embarrassing not to stop, and I landed on the old barker technique by force of necessity. The stool commanded a view of the path for a length of 300 yards or more, from where it started at the park gate to where it vanished behind a clump of trees. People could walk along it and ignore us altogether.

So I kept my eye on the gate at the far end. As soon as an innocent stroller appeared through it, I bellowed straight at him. He had 300 yards to walk under my eye and defenceless. A sitting duck.

'Are you aware,' I howled, gripping the edge of the rostrum and wagging my finger straight at him from the distance, 'Are you aware of how many millions of pounds are being poured into the prosecution of war at this moment? And not only by Britain – Oh no! Are you aware—'

'Good stuff, Cliff!' somebody grunted. I got cocky.

'Are you aware – yes, you!' The victim was still too far away to make out the actual words. 'You with the mouthful of marbles! Walking through the park as if you didn't have three wives suing for alimony! Are you aware, but no, not *you*! You don't care, do you? Dead to your own interests!'

'Watch it, he'll hear you in a minute.'

'Okay. Are you aware of the incalculable cost of pursuing a modern war whose only result is final poverty for the whole world? Not only in blood, sweat and tears do you pay, but in the prosperity of generations unborn. For what will be the end result, the final curtain, to this war? The bleeding nations will have to find a way of living together in . . . the . . . end . . .' He was almost opposite the stool, and now he was the embarrassed party, at a loss to know whether to recognize the speaker, turn his head, stop or charge straight on as if deaf. He finally charged straight on, to the shelter of the clump of trees, and without pausing in mid-sentence I picked up a couple who emerged from the opposite direction and fired a continuous burst dead on target until they escaped, walking fast, through the park gate.

But it was a bad night – the sun was too warm and the grass was too green and nobody wanted to be bothered. I was ashamed to have to call on the speaker without having collected any audience for him. Davie, an old hand, didn't let that inhibit him. He delivered the message with fervent sincerity that renewed his own faith. Two or three, maybe seven or eight people paused at a safe distance so that they could hear without being dragged into the meeting, but at the end, when I called their attention to the fascinating literature available, they drifted rapidly away.

'Sorry, Davie,' I said. 'I didn't get much of a mob collected – we've wasted your time.'

'It always does some good,' he warned me. 'We've got to show the flag, anyway. I'm just going for a word with that sailor – he hasn't come forward, but he's been standing there since I started and he's still there. Maybe he's a wee bit shy.'

'What sailor?' I asked him. I looked round. 'I'm awful sorry, Davie,' I said. 'That isn't a sailor – I mean, it's a sailor all right, but he's my brother. He's waiting to take me for a drink.'

The Gutters Will Run With Tea

Red Clydeside is a terrible place, seething with beetle-browed proletarians in bunnets and mufflers with their fists clenched, spherical black bombs in one pocket and chinking roubles in the other and a good supply of clothes-rope in the cellar ready for the day when the aristos and the middle classes will swing from the lamp-posts in Argyle Street. But you can see it clearly in these terms only from a distance, like the distance from here to Mars, for instance. Observed in close-up, the Glasgow Reds are innocuous people in good suits with a distaste for fireworks and a passion for justice and cups of tea. Even with wartime rationing, the ILP in Glasgow went through whole plantations of tea.

It was made up of too many individualists to arrive at anything like a rigid party line, except on the unifying hatred of war. In the party, we used to joke indulgently about the Anarchists. 'They tried to start a brass band,' we used to say, 'but everybody played a different tune.'

So did we. The reason why the party stayed together was that there were so many nice people in it. It was a better club than the House of Lords, and a lot more intellectual when it felt disposed, which admittedly wasn't all the time.

There was plenty of elbow-room for conscience in the party, and if everybody in a small branch had agreed even on some fundamental issue, they would have felt that the organization was going decadent.

A strong rivalry flourished between the Shettleston and Tollcross branches, which in any cold, efficient organization would have been amalgamated, they were so close and so small. Shettleston had its own premises, with lavish facilities for making cups of tea, and had a vigorous programme of Saturday night socials. In Tollcross, where we rented a kind of dungeon under a tenement for our weekly meetings, we viewed these affairs as lowbrow deviationism, or something. We devoted our energies to the eternal questions such as who was prepared to be minute secretary and what we could do about arrears in the payment of dues.

But every organization of any political colour spends more of its time wrangling over book-keeping details than it does on working out policies and principles. The ILP meant a lot in Glasgow because it kept its hands clean and stood by its principles even when they had become unpopular, and there is nothing laughable about the brotherhood of man.

And even if one of our meetings in Tollcross Park failed to turn the nation from war, others did draw crowds, and Glaswegians who were convinced that Germany must be conquered were still, usually, prepared to see that the anti-war stand of the ILP was honest and reasonable. There were exceptions, but Glasgow is not Burns-daft for nothing. The idea of the equality of man evokes a deep and instant response in this city. When even a maudlin

Glasgow drunk declaims that 'A man's a man for a' that', he means it.

Our excitement in the ILP was the headiest excitement of all, the conviction that we were right, that we were in a minority, and that we would proclaim the truth to the last ditch, or Saturday night social, whichever was later. In the Tollcross branch, we were nearly all young and read everything, and we got tired of discussing the trivia of administration and got ourselves a series of lectures so that we could examine the nature of mankind and the meaning of society and other such useful things. We never agreed; it was wonderful.

An argument I recall most vividly was the possibility that in extreme conditions, men might discard every single ethic and inhibition that made social life possible – for instance, men lost in the Arctic might turn cannibal for survival. Or would they?

We spent most of an evening projecting ourselves into the characters of starving men in the Arctic, and what impresses me now is that although we differed violently, we all believed that there was a firm, true answer to be found. And we were prepared to struggle all night to find it. Sometimes I used to walk home with another member, who lived two miles beyond my home, to continue the argument. We walked slowly in case he reached home before the thing was properly thrashed out.

We were living up to an ancient Glasgow tradition. Two centuries previously, we would have been thrashing out an impossibly obscure issue in theology, for Glasgow produced theologians in thousands, and when theology faded out there was Marxism to take its place, and even anti-Marxism, because to confute Marx, it is necessary to know him. There are always pairs of Glaswegians walking slowly home at night and pounding flat some esoteric point in religion or politics or art or jazz, and the jazz theologians are about the worst.

The other influence that held the old ILP together was Jimmie Maxton, still then the Member for Bridgeton, where at general elections they didn't count his votes, they weighed them. Some people might have deserted the party now that it had lost its power and its numbers, but few people could have brought themselves to desert Maxton.

The difficulty in speaking of Jimmie Maxton is that so many people have picked over his character already. He was a man who had no acquaintances, only friends. Among the scores of thousands of people who met him in his lifetime, hardly any will say they knew him slightly.

My first sight of him was when I hitch-hiked to London with Neil, and we spent a night on sofas in his flat on Clapham Common. On the following day we were to meet him and be shown the House of Commons, but another Member had to rescue us and take us to the Stranger's Gallery. The other Member was the fabled Campbell Stephen I had sung so unconsciously back in Gallowgate. Maxton never quite got to us because as soon as he appeared in the lobby he was buttonholed by a disgruntled citizen who couldn't find his own Member, and Maxton was incapable of brushing him off. Another supplicant was hovering and then another, and soon there was a queue, or crowd, pouring out its troubles to him while other Members thankfully got about their business. In his thin ravaged face with lank grey-streaked hair falling over one eye, his eyes burned with a gentle warmth rather than a passionate fire, although he could burst into flames on a platform with such effect that he grew tired and slightly suspicious of his talent for exciting audiences. The real test of his mere talent as an orator is that the jokes he told that convulsed his listeners turned out to be very mild chuckles at best when anybody retold them.

Listening to him orate was a lesson in master craftsmanship. The voice was not beautiful, as some people claimed, but throaty and metallic, and he pronounced 'r' sounds with a guttural burr not uncommon in Scotland. It was the personal warmth in it that gave it its magic. He would rise on a platform like a badly-made scarecrow and begin quietly, with little expressive movements of his thin hands, and then, without any effect of calculation, swell the volume and hold out ideas at arm's length till they became visible. The effect was irresistible because out of this eccentric figure with its odd haircut came words of shattering simplicity. If other orators pull out stops like cathedral organs, Jimmie Maxton was a seventy-piece orchestra.

If he had been only that, he would have been nothing. His real eccentricity was that he loved mankind both in the mass and face to face. It's true that he was capable of political blindness and even political petulance. When he led the ILP out of the Labour Party he led it out to the wilderness and it died there when it no longer had his enchantment to feed on. But he was never a politician in the clever sense. He just wanted to fight for the underdogs of the world, and he fought with everything he had, which was plenty. If he had never been in politics at all he would still have been Jimmie Maxton, I think. He made everybody he met feel that it was a great thing to be a human being. Nobody can do more than that.

Hard-bitten News-Hawk

By the time the war was properly started I was working as a reporter in a little news agency up three flights of stairs in a side street and doing my suave man-of-the-world act to my friends while I scrambled to keep my feet in my job. The writing bit was no problem, but on the job I never knew from day to day whether I was going to be glib and masterful or timid and suicidal. Sometimes I walked up and down outside for half an hour or more before I could find the moral force to knock on a door to interview some total stranger. When I was rebuffed by somebody I wanted to interview I walked away quickly with an imitation smile and hid myself because I knew everybody would know at a glance what had happened to me. For a reporter digging out copy for the *News of the World* this is a lousy way to start life, but it got a little better. I could see the same thing happening to other people.

What is wrong is that in this condition at this age you regard other people as fixed stars and yourself as a planet, compelled to orbit round them. You don't imagine they are important or even right, but they know who they are. That was how it seemed to me. All these unknown people had their place in the universe arranged, even if it wasn't much of a place, and short of becoming one of them, which was impossible without knowing the secret, there was nothing to do but swing round them in space and hope for the best. It was only after getting to know people that it came to me gradually that most of them were swinging about in space too, but it was a long time before I could convince myself that people I didn't know were just as unfixed. I wrote several short stories every week, mostly about girls, and I realized afterwards that the girls in these stories weren't people so much as Things, or fixed points of reference, which didn't react to events but simply were. One of the most exciting things about girls in real life, in fact, was that they did react to events, and that I was an event to them just as they were events to me. The adolescent attitude to people and sex is a bit inhuman, in fact. Other people tend to be taken as the furniture of life, and even if the furniture moves about, it's still there mainly for comfort or for tripping over.

This was one of the great mysteries the gang used to discuss at the public library or in the hut. The gang was an assortment of people from the old school. Some of the boys played football on the school playing-field one evening a week, and some of the girls played hockey on the same night. Some of the boys played hockey too, I had always preferred it myself because I would rather be clouted with a hockey stick on even terms than charged on the basis of fourteen stone against eight stone. Most of us had helped to lay out the playing-fields by our own sweat while we were at school, and collected funds by odd tricks like cards in which people had to pierce holes with a pin each time they handed over a penny. The funds and the sweat made good playing fields but they didn't run to any fancy accommodation, and there was a second-hand railway carriage for dressing-rooms. We sat in it by candlelight after playing and argued and talked and got to know the girls. They were nearly all nice-looking girls. I liked them all. I liked looking at them playing, neat and agile and small-waisted, and talking in the carriage afterwards and sometimes playing cards, for pennies, was a kind of exercise in relaxed mixed company I felt I had missed up to then. It didn't stay relaxed for ever, of course. Later on, odd important things happened to it, but in the meantime it was fine and unstrained.

The library was over in Tollcross next to the park, and we used it as a club and a casual meeting place too. Some of us were reading our way doggedly through it, and it's a big library. I was in a kind of passion to know everything and pack my life with variety and somehow for one winter I was playing hockey and taking four WEA classes at the University at nights and getting into politics and doing my damnedest to grow up overnight. These things weren't separate activities, they were all a bit of the same thing.

It wasn't enough to be interested in girls, we had to know everything about them. I had started on the Penguin editions of Freud just before I left school and we all swapped books and hunted down authors like beagles, Ethel Mannin and Havelock Ellis and Tom Payne and Oscar Wilde and all the world-breakers. I mixed this with Dale Carnegie and Jane Austen and Ibsen and read textbooks for my class in Drama Production, sometimes going through six books simultaneously, but we never thought of ourselves as crazy-mixed-up kids. It was the world that was mixed up and everything would sort itself out when our generation took charge.

We were sorry for our parents because they hadn't had the educational chances they had given us. It wasn't their fault they didn't know the principles of psychology and had grown up choked with inhibitions and complexes. I used to think what a wonderful world our own children were going to inhabit, because my generation was on to all

112

the secrets of the full rich life and wouldn't have to make the old mistakes. Even with the stupidity of war going on, you could tell that truth was surging to the top and ignorance and superstition were on the way out. Almost by chance I hit one spring evening on Bertrand Russell's *Marriage and Morals* in the philosophy section of the library, and within a month or so it was elevated to the status of a new bible for us all. It wasn't only lucid and convincing, all this wonderful destruction of primitive sex taboos looked like being a lot of fun if we could only get enough girls to read it too. The difficulty was that we hadn't reached that plane of discussion with the girls on the hockey field, and the most successful collector of other specific girls, was Big Eck, who was shaky on his Russellism. He even said it was tripe. But he could play football and he had a broad oafish leer and girls liked him. The whole thing was unjust.

Shettleston Road was one of the regular Sunday-night pads, but nothing ever came of it in my direction. There were hundreds of girls on it, walking a mile or more back and forward in twos, and the idea was that they were looking for boys in twos, but they never admitted it, and the job of tracking two down and insulting them or flattering them from two yards behind until they wore down and started acting human, was too wearisome to be suffered. It's nearly impossible to pay a compliment to a Glasgow girl straight off without a long ritual of chatter. Her instant reflex is to tell you to chase yourself, and when a girl says this I'm so well-mannered that I obey without question. You have to be really desperate to walk the pad in hopes of finding a girl, and if there is a good-looking girl on the pad, she always, absolutely always, has a grisly friend functioning both as foil and jackal. In half-hearted efforts to click two girls, we always muttered to each other:

'I don't like the wan you're gettin'.'

But that sex morality stuff is perfectly useless as a mere theory, and it was becoming urgent to get some fieldwork in because youth and life were slipping by and I was nearly eighteen. Finally girls began to happen spontaneously, too fast.

You Should Have Listened, Lily

Big Eck was studying civil engineering, which explains why he was still at home when he had his twenty-first birthday, and he threw a party in the Plaza Ballroom, a private table for about twenty of us and buffet and lemonade thrown in. Most of us turned up unpaired, with a selection of the playing-field girls to keep things even, but there were three or four new girls brought as partners by the boys who had been scouting on their own, and it's always easier to get to know a girl when she already knows somebody you know, when she's come with one of your best friends for instance. One of the crowd had produced a nice number absolutely new, from Paisley, where legend said that the girls outnumbered the men by eleven to two – I never got the length of checking the figures. Lily would have got off all right even in Paisley, anyway. Obviously, Joe had brought her and Joe would have to take her home, but I pulled him aside during the evening to make sure that he had no permanent intentions towards her, and he shook his head and said she was too strong-minded.

'You dance like gossamer,' I told Lily, and she said:
'I must have stood on a spider's web.' That answer practically made her an intellectual. I sang to her while we danced, always a perilous venture, and she joined in while we quickstepped round and round the fountain. 'How about jumping in,' I said, 'and I'll prove myself by rescuing you.' She said it was only three inches deep, and I said: 'That's all right, I can't swim either.' It wasn't the jokes so much as the atmosphere. I felt I was getting across loud and clear. 'Let me show you the enchanted

114

waterways of Venice,' I whispered huskily into her ear. 'I think we're going to Dunoon for the holidays,' she whispered back passionately. She went straight to my head. I was fond of Joe, but I was sorry he didn't develop stomach cramp that night. I hadn't even got to the point of getting her telephone number when we left.

Saturday of that week I spent as always on the stand-by shift at the office, a whole evening with nothing to do but call the police, fire and ambulance services every hour in case something big had broken. In the intervals I ate sandwiches and wrote curtain speeches for the plays I was going to write some day. Sometimes people who hadn't been able to get into the pictures or who had been dissied by girl-friends, came up to sit at the fire and talk, and this week it was Andy Skinner, a rather viscose youth who liked to sit at my feet and hoard my wisdom and practise to be a big newspaperman like me. I found myself telling him about Lily, and after digesting the words I had whispered in her ear – I improved them in the telling, he shook his head and wished that he had my born talent for wooing.

'Not born,' I corrected him. 'The simple result of training and application. Anybody,' I said like a fool, 'can dazzle women if he gives it a little thought.'

'Go on,' he said. 'Phone her while I'm here – I would love to hear it. I don't know what it is,' he added glumly, 'I never say anything *interesting* to girls.'

'It doesn't need to be interesting, just smooth,' I said, not airily. 'She'll be out somewhere – it's Saturday night.'

'You could try. You wouldn't feel embarrassed with me listening, would you?'

'Me? Embarrassed? Huh!' I gave my short laugh. He had the telephone book open, working down the columns of Frasers, who, I thought, thank God are such a vast clan we'll never find the number. But we did, at least we found a number that looked likely and Andy sat with his big idiot eyes glittering at me and his tail wagging. I gave him a sympathetic, spurious smile. My big success with Lily was shrinking in recollection to nothing. Finally I took the telephone and a chair over to the fire so that I could put my feet up on the mantel and feel masterful, and got the number in Paisley.

Lily was surprisingly and unwelcomely at home that Saturday night. It took an ominous amount of preliminary talk to recall my existence to her and somehow, without the fountain bubbling in the middle of the dance floor, the effect wasn't the same. She did remember me, though, and she wasn't actually hostile, yet.

'Somehow you've haunted me ever since,' I said.

'Probably because I'm freezing to death,' she said. 'This telephone's in a draughty lobby.'

'The draughts are warmer in Venice,' I pointed out smoothly, while Andy nodded and winked his stupid eye at me from the other side of the fireplace. All he was worrying about was whether he would remember verbatim or whether he should take the whole thing in shorthand. 'I thought we might catch a gondola there soon. Have you an evening next week you could spend in the Adriatic? Sunshine and magic and song.'

'Look,' Lily said. 'I really am freezing.'

'Well?' I said.

'Well what?'

'Next week? Or better still, the gay exotic night life of Sauchiehall Street? Wednesday?'

'No, I'm busy next week.'

'Good.' I nodded meaningly across at Andy. 'And how about later?'

'No, I don't think so.'

'Well,' I said, smirking. 'That takes care of that.'

'Can I go back to the fire now?' Lily asked.

'Your wish is my command,' I said, in an imitation husky voice.

'Okay. Thanks for phoning.'

'It's nothing, nothing at all.'

'Well, goodnight.'

'Fine,' I said, and she hung up. Andy was still hanging on the words, and I went right on.

'No,' I said. 'It just took a little detective work – Paisley is a small place. I called the local police and asked them where I could find the most delicious creature in the town, and I got your number at once.'

'No, no, not at all.'

'Yes, I would love to dance again too. Sure, through the streets.'

'But it's a long walk home from Paisley, and I'm going to need my feet again – I play the accordion with them.'

'But would your family not object? They don't even know me.'

'Never fear, I can sleep on anything. You realize this will compromise me, of course.'

'Hee, hee.' Andy was getting his money's worth. He was frothing with excitement and admiration.

'Will I pick you up?' I said to the dead telephone. 'Yes, six o'clock is fine, even if it kills me.'

'Please! Remember I'm an innocent young man.'

'Sure, six o'clock on Wednesday. Goodnight, Lily . . . Yes, I'll be thinking of you too. Incessantly.'

I thought I had overdone it, but when I put the telephone down Andy just stared at me shaking his head in awe.

'Just wait,' I said. 'Wednesday will be the day I get sent to Cladhnacuddin on a story and miss the last train back.'

'Could I go in your place? Just send me a telegram,' Andy pleaded.

'But you don't look like me,' I said.

'What does Lily look like?'

'Kinda nice,' I underplayed it. I was speaking part-American at that time. I hated Lily in my heart. The only consolation was the brilliant performance I had given for Andy, a thing satisfying in itself, but unsatisfying because nobody knew about it to admire it. I nursed this until the next Saturday night, and he came up to the office again and asked breathlessly how Wednesday night had gone off.

'Kinda nice,' I said. But he was going to press for details, and I changed my mind. 'I have a confession to make about Wednesday night,' I told him. Then I told him it all. He was aggrieved for a second.

'When exactly did she hang up?' he wanted to know.

'Practically instantly,' I said blithely.

'My God!' he said. 'What a performance!'

'Mean.'

'But how can you talk to an *empty phone* like that?'

'It's easier than talking to Lily,' I insisted.

'She'd be livid,' Andy said, 'if she knew what she had missed.'

'Well, that'll larn her,' I said. 'Let other dames be warned.' I began quite to like Lily again.

Green and Pleasant

It was during the war that Glasgow's corner boys adopted the bicycle chain as a weapon in their search for novelty. The blackout was unpleasantly convenient for casual violence and odd, novel little crimes like yanking women's fur coats off their backs and vanishing in the darkness. It wouldn't do to exaggerate this, of course. Although I was now professionally interested in crime and spent endless evenings all over the city I never had the luck to come across any criminality by chance. What the war meant mainly was that the city was seething with unexpected people, like an international settlement, Tangier plus fish suppers. It was an actual strain trying to keep track of all the new people and things that kept turning up, and I couldn't bear to give up any of them.

There was a new Polish community, hundreds of them, mostly in the emigre Polish Army and a few of them privates or sergeants. The others, even the civilians, all seemed to be officers. I used to wonder what happened at parades. There were probably twelve majors to inspect each private and put him through maze-marching. But I got friendly with several of them. They had a kind of shop at the top of Hope Street where they published books and pamphlets, and they included a couple of concert pianists and a tall, witty ex-diplomat called Micstowicz who was now a kind of consul and gave a lot of cocktail parties, sometimes with high-class intellectual conversation, and told me I should get a scholarship to Cambridge, which he made sound possible as well as jolly; and a little plump woman, Jadwiga Harasowska, who ran the shop and translated Burns into Polish and hated the Russians as much as she loathed the Germans, which I thought was understandable but misguided. She was glumly certain that her dear native land was doomed, and I often went up to the shop and sat for hours trying to persuade her she was wrong, but she smiled indulgently and knew she was right, and I used to go away gloomy myself because she sounded as if she might be right.

But I kept going back, and getting to know Norwegians and Swedes as well, in addition to all the natives I was meeting. I collected new people with the unquestioning intensity of a miser collecting cigarette-ends, even some I didn't like very much. I couldn't bring myself to discard any chance of new acquaintance, I wanted everybody and I wanted to be *persona grata* everywhere.

But something had to go. Suddenly one day I found myself revolting against the evening classes I had been collecting. I looked forward along the months ahead of me, with every evening accounted for in advance, and I couldn't stand it any longer. I just abandoned the whole thing and stuck to reading books for the filling of any holes left in my mind. The nett profit was about fifty words of Spanish and fifty of Italian, a jumble of notions about stage production and a headlong plunge into the string of books on philosophy and logic that Penguins were publishing at the time.

Life was full of chances to put on acts before new people. I travelled to the city by train, from the same station where I had once collected newspapers, but this time as a client with a season-ticket and a complacent glow when porters actually nodded to me. Part of my job was to comb the daily papers every morning for ideas, and I actually bought four papers at the station bookstall, a tremendously impressive thing among the young train set. I was mortified one morning when one of them, an old schoolmate, offered to exchange papers, and took my *Glasgow Herald* and handed me that week's *Rover*.

In the luncheon train I sometimes travelled with Big Bob and we pooled our recollections of the words of the latest pop songs. We were completists in the pop song game, we had to know the words of every song, even the ones we despised. If we got an empty compartment, Bob would sit with a newspaper on his knee drumming on it with his fingers for accompaniment while we sang duets, too engrossed to be self-conscious. I even started writing songs, but they never sounded up to Cole Porter, whom we revered as the Beethoven of the pop game.

Singing was about the only positive passion, apart from the universal appetites, that Bob had at the time. He drummed with his fingers and whistled and sang practically all the time, but it never irritated me, I did it too when I was with him and abandoned it and became another kind of character part as soon as I ran into my Polish chums or other newspaper people or my philosophy classmates. Then we met another enthusiast who didn't sing much, but could actually play the piano.

A pianist was a fat rich prize. To get somebody who could actually play songs to order, endlessly, was the nearest thing to being able to do it yourself. The pianist was David Alastair Nimmo. The insistence on the full name was the kind of eccentricity that I liked. He was thin and dark and worked with a food wholesaler's, and when I said he looked like Hamlet he burst with delight and shouted:

'Avaunt, avaunt, oh rump-fed ronyon, this is Henry Hall speaking and tonight is my guest-night.'

'Thank you and good night, Charlie Kunz,' I said. We were sitting in the Odeon Café in Renfield Street, the three of us, Bob and I having sneaked out of our offices in the afternoon each pretending to the other that he was so

120

high-up that he could come and go as he pleased, and David Alastair Nimmo recognized Bob from some dance they had both been at. He sat back in his chair with big, ham-theatre gestures, as if he was perfectly oblivious to anybody staring at him from other tables – he wasn't, but that made him even more of a Character – and said:

'Clasp me to thy heart with hoops of steel, sirrah!'

'I've only got this rubber band, oh gloomy Dane,' I said. I made theatrical gestures too. Big Bob said:

'See here, I don't zackJy latch on tuh this here tarryhootin, podners.' He had no acquaintance with Shakespeare, even less than we had. Sometimes we all talked carefully chosen American idiom, like hill-billies played by Bing Crosby. When Bob and I found that David Alastair played the piano, boogie-woogie a speciality, we did clasp him to our hearts, although he lived in the far reaches of Possilpark, away in the north of the city, and damanded demonstrations.

'But Possilpark is shore a mort a miles aways, gents,' I said.

'We can hire a studio in Paterson's,' David Alastair said eagerly. I hadn't even known till that moment that the big music shops in town had such things as studios to hire. It sounded like a big, man-of-the-world transaction. Strangers in the shop would think we were professional actors warming up for opening night; or musicians preparing for a St Andrew's Hall concert; or a song-writing team just in from America, when they heard us ordering a studio and saw us going mysteriously upstairs. But we couldn't raise one-and-sixpence among us after paying for coffee and Bob finally conceded that he had to get back to his office. 'I've got a lot of mail to sign,' he explained.

'He means begging letters,' I added.

'I sign my begging letters with a rubber stamp,' David Alastair commented loftily. 'It makes them look more illiterate.' I was totally won over by him, the ham theatrical manner and the Hamlet face and the piano-playing. We arranged to get money and meet the next day at five o'clock and fool around with that there old row of

121

ivories an' a mite of music-makin'.

But I didn't make it. Trouble came up in the office. We had picked up a story from a correspondent the previous week about a minor case at the Eastern Police Court, and it had been published because bicycle chains were new, and news, and the three teen-agers in the case had created a disturbance and were found with chains in their pockets when the police took them in. They had all been fined five pounds.

Now the family of one of the boys had written complaining that the story was inaccurate, that this one boy had never had a bicycle chain, and that he had been slandered in the story. My first reaction was a beautiful relief that I hadn't done the story in the first place, because I was making little mistakes in all directions about the office and it was nice to be innocent of real trouble. But something had to be done, and I was sent to see the family and try to convince them that the best thing for the boy was to forget the whole business, and that even publishing a retraction would just expose him to more ignominy. I took a tram out to Bridgeton at five o'clock just when the boys were due at the music-studio, and sat all the way going over my speech in my mind and feeling as confident as a murderer on his way to Scotland Yard for questioning.

The house was up two flights of a dark tenement stair, with that strange slum smell that I actually thought at the time was plain decay, but which I later discovered was the characteristic odour of ill-mannered tom-cats. There were only three doors on the landing, thank God. I always hated Glasgow tenements with landings that led into other weird corridors and dank uneven passages with doors everywhere, opening on to single ends so small that you can open the door without getting out of the box-bed. I pulled at the Green's doorbell, but the brass handle came out six inches without resistance and there was no noise from inside, and I knocked. A thin woman of about forty opened the door, wearing street clothes, and I introduced myself. She stared at me without understanding for a few moments, and then went back into the house and talked to somebody, and a very stout, short woman in her fifties came out. I went through the introduction again.

'Oh. Oh, aye,' she said. She had a kind, funny face and a lot of yellowish-grey hair blown out in all directions and her hands were black, with coal or soot. 'Oh, aye. Well, would you like tae come in? The place is a terrible mess, ah'm jist cleanin' oot the room fire.'

'Can I give you a hand?' I said craftily.

'Isn't that no' nice!' she said, leading me into the front room. 'Ah wish the men in this hoose were mair like you.' She wiped her hands on her overall and shook a chair till some papers fell off it. 'Jist you have a seat. You havnae came a' the wey fae London, have ye?'

'No,' I admitted. 'Glasgow office.'

'Oh, aye, ah didnae know they had wan. It's an awful loat a trouble for ye, a' the same.' Then she remembered what it was about and chid me, but without the least trace of malice. 'Here, that was a terrible thing tae print aboot oor Billy. It was that bit in the paper, Jean,' she added to the younger woman, who had sat uncomfortably on the arm of a chair and now nodded wanly, a pale negative soul. 'See if there's any tea left for the man,' the older woman went on, kneeling in front of the unlit fire and picking up a flue brush. I protested courteously, but the younger woman went away and fetched a cup and poured me some tea. The atmosphere was reassuring, it was going to be easy to win the old lady over. She poked and scrubbed at the fireplace and threw remarks over her shoulder while I drank my tea and looked sympathetic. She wasn't angry at anybody, just looking for justice for oor Billy, who turned out to be her grandson and not her son. That cleared up a puzzle about the boy's having a different name from Mrs Green. It appeared that although he had been with two of his chinas chirping at some girls and following them along Main Street, Billy hadn't had a bicycle chain, hadn't even been charged with having a bicycle chain and had been fined five pounds for nothing more than making a noise.

'Five pounds!' she said in disgust. 'Ye widnae have been surprised at ten shillin' or even a pound, but five pounds for that! As if he was a criminal or somethin'! He's a good boy, oor Billy. They policemen hivnae much tae dae wi' their time. But when ah saw that bit in the paper aboot a bicycle chain ah was right mortified, it's no ferr, so it's no.'

She finished with the fireplace at this point – there was a big electric fire blazing to heat the little front room – and at the same moment Billy came in. He didn't look desperate or vicious, but shy and silent when he discovered who I was. I held tight to my sophisticated role and although I was only two or three years older than he was, he was obviously impressed and anxious to escape. Mrs Green washed her hands and joined me in another cup of tea, while Jean still sat and nodded as an echo to her conversation. Bit by bit my smooth correct English wore away until we were all speaking the same tongue. I started to explain my mission.

She was sceptical, but I had no doubt I could talk her round, because the more I worked on the theory of dropping the whole thing the more I came to see the force of it myself. What had worried us was the possibility that she might want to sue, but there are some people who would just never think of suing anybody, and Mrs Green was one of them. She didn't like the law. She didn't break any laws, but to Mrs Green, policemen were tyrannical, hostile and whimsical, and they were agin innocent youngsters like oor Billy just because he happened to be there. Mrs Green was no fool. Policemen *are* different in slum districts. They suspect the population and the population suspects them, however law-abiding the population may be. I had the sensation of being on Mrs Green's side, and of Mrs Green's kin, and at the same time of being removed from the situation entirely, a stranger who spoke the language and came from another planet. Mrs Green had no reservations. She plied me with tea and was disappointed when I refused to have a full meal. She liked company.

I had declined to take my coat off because I wanted to get home for tea, but I was still sitting in it, panting slightly from the heat, two hours later. Jean had torn herself away at last, to cook some negative food for her negative husband's dinner, and Mrs Green and I blethered gossip and scarcely noticed she was gone. She was a very relaxing woman.

'Here, if you smoke you'll need a lighter,' she remarked abruptly over the second pot of tea. She produced a little cylindrical cigarette lighter and forced me to take it.

'Ah get them wholesale,' she explained. 'Buyin' an' sellin', ye see. Ah used tae have a stall at the Barras, but ah jist dae it fae the hoose noo.' I had never known anybody who actually bought and sold things deliberately. 'Here, dae ye take a drink?'

'Now and then,' I said easily. She brought a bottle of whisky out of the cupboard and started to break the seal. Whisky was already hard to get, and I tried to stop this rash act, but she brushed me aside.

'It's the New Year boattle,' she said. 'An' the less in the boattle, the less auld Green'll drink on Hogmanay.' As I sipped the whisky, I felt a warm sense of achievement. Two hours ago I had faced a libel suit. Now I was being plied with gifts and liquor by the plaintiff. 'Ah don't know how anybody can take that stuff withoot gettin' the boke,' she remarked, 'but you'll jist take it in moderation, no' guzzle it like auld Green. Oh, that's a helluva man, that yin. Still, he's the best ah've goat. Here, while you're here, you'll know a' aboot lawyers an' coorts.'

'A bit,' I said warily.

'Aye, better than that, mebbe you could pit somethin' in yer paper aboot the pig ma daughter's merrit tae. Oh, he's a bad rotter, he had oor Agnes black and blue the other week. He should be dampt well exposed, in fact he should be hung. Ah've telt him masel' ah wid swing for 'im if he laid a finger on her again.'

'But the polis are the boys for him,' I cautioned.

'Och, the polis! They're mair fit tae persecute wee boys chirpin' at some lassie that's led them oan in the furst place, them.'

'Ah, but ye see, we couldny print anythin' aboot this man,' I pointed out. 'Or he would be suin' us, unless it was proved in court.'

'By God, there's nae justice,' she cried. 'He should be hung, so he should! Jist an ignorant get, that's a' he is. It was a black day for oor Agnes, ah'm tellin' ye, when she goat that yin.'

She started to tell me the story of her loathsome son-in-law Jerry and her long-suffering daughter Agnes and I listened agape. Life as I had seen it was pallid and thin compared to this. Agnes had married her Jerry when she was seventeen, and after a few weeks of peace he had acquired the habit of coming home drunk and beating her up every few days. They had a single end a few streets away, and Agnes ran home in terror and tatters with terrible regularity to shelter with her mother.

'But she wull go back tae him,' Mrs Green sighed. 'We've telt her time an' again but she wull go back. It's nae time since auld Green gi'ed him a doin' tae teach him a lesson. He met the pig in a pub and battered hell ooty him.'

More than anything I was baffled by the character of Agnes, who kept returning to her savage husband and suffering his savagery. It was habit, I suppose. As incident piled on incident I formed pictures of the absent characters, Jerry big and rawboned and brooding like a D. H. Lawrence hero and Agnes white-faced and bowed and thin, and auld Green, the terrible avenger, a great horny-fisted patriarch. I was contemplating auld Green when the door opened and he came in. He was as short as myself, which is very short, and built like a toby-jug, red and grimy from his job at the gasworks. I couldn't believe in him. Mrs Green explained me, in flattering terms, and he shook hands with much satisfaction.

'That's the stuff – a wee drap a' whisky for the cauld,' he nodded. 'Keep your gutsy eyes aff it,' Mrs Green shouted. 'Ye'll have enough at Ne'erday, if you're no' drunk already, ya auld devil!'

'For God's sake act yer age, wummin,' he dismissed

her. 'When did ye ever see me drunk in the middle ae the week?'

'Bloody oaften!' He smirked sheepishly, and I got up to go. 'Here, ah'll jist see ye tae your caur,' auld Green offered. His wife was on to the trick in a flash.

'Runnin' away tae a pub before you're hardly in the door!' she condemned him. 'Och, don't seecken us, wummin,' he cracked back. 'Where's yer manners, lettin' a fella go an' loss hissel' lookin' for a caur? Come on, surr.'

'Don't you let him offer you a drink!' Mrs Green exhorted me. 'He's a real bad yin, that!' They were obviously not angry with each other, this was the way they talked all the time. Auld Green came down to the street to take me by the hand in case I didn't know how to get on board a tramcar, and he took me by the hand as far as the pub at the corner and hauled me in for a half-pint. He was such a jolly little man I wouldn't have thought of refusing although a half-pint after a whole glass of whisky seemed as much as I could possibly risk. He advised me to take care of myself and I would go far, anybody could see I was educated, and then he told me about his repellent son-in-law too, and without any fancy trimmings described how he had met him in that very pub once and belted him good-lookin. The barman frowned warningly.

I finally got away, with pressing invitations to visit the Greens again any time, with an agreeable glow of alcoholic warmth and a new cigarette lighter. I had every intention of seeing them again, I thought they were great.

My success with the Greens did me no harm in the office, and I did go back and see them whenever I was in Bridgeton with time to spare. By chance I kept missing the abused Agnes, but I followed her adventures with rapt concentration. Mrs Green always had tea on the boil when I appeared unexpectedly, and forgot after a while what I had visited her for in the first place. The third time I called on her, after a couple of months, I learned that Agnes had finally taken the wise step of abandoning Jerry for good and coming to live with her mother. But trouble wasn't over.

A fortnight earlier, Agnes had gone to the jigging with one of her old chums – auld Green insisted that she should put her futile marriage behind her and get some of the fun she had missed, and it was then I realized my picture of Agnes must be all wrong. She wasn't a thin bowed haggard housewife, but still a good-looking young girl full of life. She had enjoyed the dancing, and was walking home with her girl friend when they caught a hint of a commotion in one of the side streets. Anything like a fight was just the thing to finish off Saturday night excitingly, and they followed the noise. There was a crowd gathered outside one of the tenements, which Agnes saw was her mother-in-law's address. It wasn't a fight, yet, just an entertainment.

I still hadn't seen Agnes – auld Green and Mrs Green were telling the story between them, interrupting and contradicting each other. Auld Green told his version with pride to justify himself, and Mrs Green interrupted with tuts and insults, but she wasn't really ashamed of the story either.

Auld Green had been to a match and then to the pub. He was going home with a good skinful, and he stopped on the way to buy three 'special' fish suppers, a routine Saturday night treat. Then he found himself walking past the street where Jerry's mother lived, and it came upon him that the nauseous Jerry was living with his mother since Agnes had left him. Auld Green rolled up the street and shouted up to the first-storey window for the rotten cowardly nyuck to come down and get a basting.

'He was therr all right,' auld Green told me with relish. 'He came tae the windy an' showed his rotten face, as white as the bloody wa', ha ha! An' bigod, the next thing he was away an' his mither was there. So ah shouted up, "Sen' doon that yella-faced baster an' ah'll learn 'im tae knock women aboot."'

Jerry's mother never considered sending Jerry down for a second. What about Jerry's father? I asked, wondering if he was dead.

'Damn the fear a that,' auld Green told me. 'He was in

the hoose as well, but he keeps oota trouble. Mind ye, ah've goat nothin' again him, it's that mother an' that yella-faced pig a hers. By God, ah was ready fur 'im!'

'Jist askin' fur trouble, drunk an' disorderly,' Mrs Green snorted, not without affection. 'The best thing ye can dae wi scruff like that is kid on ye don't know they're alive.'

'He widnae have been alive long,' auld Green returned crisply. By this time Agnes and her girl friend were in the crowd, Agnes trying to remain unseen but incapable of going away before the end. When Jerry's mother realized she was getting a showing-up before the whole street, and that auld Green would never leave, she came down to face him out.

'Ah telt her ah was havin' nae quarrel wi' a wummin,' he told me. ' "Well," says she, "get tae hell hame an' stop disturbing the peace, you an' that daughter a yours, an' leave ma boy alane. He's jist a good boy thrown away, that's whit he is." '

The injustice of this inflamed auld Green.

'Him!' he shrieked. 'Him! That rotten bachle! Ah've seen mair spunk in a tuppenny rabbit, the swine. Ma lassie ruined hersel' when she took him. Come doon an' fight, ya swine!' Jerry was visible as a pale shadow behind the curtains, but he never came down.

'Away oota here, ya drunk auld pig!' his mother shouted. By this time there were maybe sixty or seventy people crowded round, and she lost her temper and tried to push auld Green out of her way to go back into the close.

'Only a swine like that swine Jerry wid hit a wummin,' he explained himself. 'But ah drew back an' let her have the three fish suppers acroass the mooth. By God, that shut 'er up!'

'Aye,' Mrs Green chimed in, 'an' got you the nick, ya sully auld fool.'

'Fined two pounds,' he said sorrowfully. 'Two dampt pounds an' ah never goat a punch at the swine. That's whit rankles.'

Mrs Green looked at me inviting me to share her disgust.

'Rankles tae hell,' she said. 'Ah'll never get ower the idea a they three lovely fish suppers flung away on that auld bitch.'

She was so upset that I burst into helpless laughter, and that started her, and in a minute we were all three helpless and spluttering. She was so tickled that she made no objections when auld Green fished out two screwtops and poured himself and me a pint.

'Ah don't know whit ye can think ae us, Cliff,' she said, wiping her eyes.

'You're absolutely terrible,' I moaned. 'Ah widnae be seen deid associatin' wi' the likes a you.' This started auld Green again, and he spluttered a good mouthful of beer on the front of his boiler-suit.

When I wasn't actually at the Greens', their whole life seemed unlikely and unreal. I told Bob and David Alastair Nimmo about the fabulous Greens, and although Bob cackled, David Alastair owned himself fascinated with them.

'I would fain meet these roystering peasants, coz,' he cried. We were sitting in another café at the time. 'Methinks they live the full rich life. Allow me to accompany you on your next expedition to darkest Brigton.'

Aye, all right, very funny, I thought to myself, and was ashamed to have dragged the Greens out for other people to enjoy and laugh at. The Greens wouldn't have minded in the least, but it was one thing for me to share their melodrama and another to talk about them as if they were quaint lovable types to be taken up as a kind of intellectual fad. I didn't think any less of David Alastair for wanting to inspect them in person, but I felt I should shut up about the Greens, and I decided I would never take David Alastair or anybody else to view them. He might have overawed them, and they would probably have laughed at his jokes, but I felt I had to protect them from anybody who thought of them as just a rollicking tale.

We did get round to renting a studio in Paterson's, and sometimes in Cuthbertson's in Sauchiehall Street, and often spent an hour playing and singing. The Merry Macs had just started sending their records from America with the new kind of close harmony singing, and without going so far as to read music, I began to take the harmony bit and left Big Bob the melody. It was getting to be an expensive ploy, because the studio had to be paid for and we usually ate tea in town when we were going for a session, and clubbed together to buy piano copies of the new songs, but David Alastair had started studying again at the Academy of Music, and he could sometimes get a room with a piano there for nothing and sneak us in looking like students. We were so impressed with ourselves we started talking about doing a Merry Macs act ourselves and going into the big-time.

Meanwhile, back at the Greens', things never got any more serene. I still never ran into Agnes, and sometimes I persuaded myself that auld Green and his wife had made her, and Jerry, and Jerry's mother, up out of nothing, but the tales of violence never flagged in their freshness. It still seemed incredible that the plump little auld Green could possibly be the fighting-mad terror of the stories, but he was patently a man who couldn't tell a lie. But it was Mrs Green who went on the offensive in the next chapter.

She had met Jerry on her way to the butcher's, and the unexpected meeting face to face provoked her unthinkingly.

'Ah swear tae God ah never laid a finger on 'im,' she assured me. 'No' that ah widnae of ah goat the chance. If oor Agnes was a bit mair like me that yin wid be in his grave by noo, the furst time he luftcd his haun. Ah jist stoapt him in the street and ca'ed him fur everythin, an' then he had the cheek tae insult me, so ah offered tae gi'e 'im ma message bag on the jaw.'

'You didny!' I said admiringly.

'By God'n ah did,' she repeated. 'An' whit dae ye think? The sowl ran away fur the polis!'

'Naw!'

Mrs Green cackled at the memory. About an hour later,

131

Agnes had come home and reported that Jerry was walking towards the house with two policemen.

'That's right,' her mother said cheerily. 'They're comin' fur me.' Agnes nearly swooned, but the policemen never arrived. Jerry had taken them round the neighbours to call for witnesses to the threats against his person, but the neighbours who had been standing by turned out to have heard and seen nothing at all. 'Barrin' his stupit auld mother,' said Mrs Green, 'that yin hasnae a friend in the wide world.'

It must have been nearly a year after I first met Mrs Green that Agnes decided she had had a long enough holiday from unholy matrimony. Her mother pleaded and auld Green went off his head, but she had made up her mind, and she went back to Jerry, who was sick of living with his mother by this time. Mrs Green was weeping when she told me. She was sure it could only mean more trouble, and I had to agree, but everything seemed calm and sweet, and it happened that I had no occasion to get to Bridgeton for several months again and almost forgot the Greens altogether.

When I was in the district again I nearly didn't look in on them. I had the guilty feeling that I had been using them for my entertainment, and it wasn't fair, and although Mrs Green always welcomed me like a son and heaped me with hospitality, she was getting nothing in return. I swithered and then decided it would be unfriendly not to say hello at least. I knocked at the door and got no answer, and I was quite pleased to turn away, when Mrs Green came upstairs behind me, red in the face and breathing heavily.

'It's you, Cliff! A cup of tea is jist what ah need, come on in, you're no' in a hurry, are ye? Whit ah've been through this day, in the middle a the sweep, tae.'

'The Irish Sweep?'

'Stoap the kiddin', ah've been having the sweep fur the kitchen chimley. Nae peace fur the wicked. But wait tae ah tell ye. Ah never thought ah wid live tae see the day.'

She hadn't been ill, just surprised at events. When she

132

took off her coat and hung it up, I saw she had her overall on beneath it, and her hands were black with soot as they had been the first time I saw her.

'It's That Yin again,' she explained as she put the kettle on. 'Ah thought wan hammerin' wid have sobered him, but there's nae improving scruff like that.'

'Wan hammerin'?' I asked, fascinated all over again.

'Oh, ye widnae know – where have you been, we missed ye, auld Green was jist sayin' the other day you must be on a foreign correspondent or somethin', it's that long since we seen ye.'

It eventually came out that Agnes's peaceful reconciliation with Jerry hadn't lasted long. Mrs Green didn't see her for weeks, and then a neighbour had told her that Jerry wouldn't allow Agnes to visit her family.

'Ah'm a peaceful wummin,' she insisted, 'but that was the end. Ah went roon tae Agnes's an' there wisnae a pick on her – he's been drinking the money again an' she was hauf-sterved. Honest, Cliff, everythin' went black, jist like the pictures. Ah gave that man – naw, he's no' a man, tae take yon fae an auld wummin – ah gave him the pastin' ae his life.'

'You mean you hit him?' I really couldn't believe it. 'And he didn't hit you back?'

'God help him if he had, ah' wid have had him in the jile for assault straight aff. Ah hut him wi' everything in the room except the chair, it was too big tae luft.'

'It sounds like fun.'

'Och, this is months ago. But did it learn him anythin'? Nut him. Then he fell an' broke 'is leg, an' hell mend 'im.'

The fall was on a later occasion, a thing that I had to straighten out for my own peace of mind. He had actually fallen off a lorry at work. Jerry was one of those people who work only sporadically and are prone to fatuous accidents when they do work, as a protest against degrading labour. He was in hospital for some time, and Agnes had a thin time without cash during a very cold month in the room they had sub-let in Gorbals.

A few days before Jerry was due out, Mrs Green had

133

bought some groceries and packed them in a box and asked a girl across the landing to take them to Agnes as a wee present. The girl came back tearfully after a long absence, still carrying the box, and reported that Jerry was back from hospital and refused to let any present from his mother-in-law into the house.

'That was this mornin',' Mrs Green explained, 'an' me in the middle ae the sweep. Ah didnae even wait tae wash ma hauns, ah jist put ma coat on an' took a caur straight tae Gorbals.'

In the interval, however, Jerry had been active. He was due for some dole money, and after chasing the girl with the food parcel, he sent Agnes to collect his cash, since he was still in crutches and couldn't walk farther than the pub at the corner. Then he must have got tired of waiting for her and decided to see about borrowing enough for a drink, because Agnes was coming back with the money when she saw a commotion in the main street from the top deck of the tram in which she was sitting. Agnes seemed fated to be confronted with scenes of drama and mayhem. Still retaining her simple pleasure in action, she got off the tram for a look, and this time found her own mother, so far from Bridgeton, engaged in a scene with her husband.

Mrs Green had actually met Jerry, by an accident terribly unlucky for him, on his way to the pub at the corner, hobbling on two crutches with one leg in plaster. Her outraged mother's instincts destroyed all restraint. Jerry blenched at the sight of her and tried to back away, but it was impossible on his new crutches. She delivered a few hard words, enough to draw a small audience, and then appealed to them to approve of her maternal anger. Jerry tried to bluster, but Mrs Green had caught her audience thoroughly. When she couldn't think of anything else to say, she looked up at Jerry's craven face and decided he was too tall to slap, so she jounced in and whipped one of his crutches clean away. Then she let him have it across the skull. Agnes arrived in time to see the old lady belabouring her son-in-law, with the crowd cheering her on, and with a final spasm of incensed

134

motherhood she splintered the crutch on him, threw the two pieces in his face, and walked away with Agnes peching after her, before any meddler had time to call the police. Agnes was so bewildered by the affairs of the day that Mrs Green sent her to the pictures with Jerry's dole money and told her to come straight home to Bridgeton thereafter.

'Do you think you've finally cured Jerry?' I asked her.

'The only cure fur that yin'll be a widden overcoat,' she gritted. 'Tae think ah should demean masel' at ma age hittin' that yin in the main street, durtyin' ma hauns on his durty crutch! That's somethin' else he has tae answer fur!'

'But it's nae use,' I said, exercising the licence of a member of the family. 'She'll go back. Oor Agnes is jist daft aboot sufferin'.'

'Over my dead body!'

'By God, that wid be some climb!' I said, and Mrs Green laughed till she shook all over.

'Anywey,' she said when she had quietened down, 'ah know how tae fix it. It's been in ma mind fur a while, and ah'm gonny dae it.'

'Whit?'

'Ah'm gaun oot the morra an' buy a talkin' budgie an' a radiogram.'

'Eh?' I said. 'But how is that gonny fix Jerry?'

'Och, tae hell wi' Jerry,' she abolished Jerry with an impatient flip. 'If other people can have a radiogram, we can have a radiogram. Anywey, it'll be nice against that wa', an' the budgie'll keep us cheery.'

I still don't know how a talking budgie and a radiogram affected the issue for good or ill, but so what?

Don't Call Me, I Won't Call You

Failure with Lily taught me nothing, fortunately. It wasn't enough to know girls in a crowd, a man needed to know one in particular, one of his own hunting. Looking back, I don't know what I was complaining about, I knew dozens. But for years on end, I remember, I felt I was getting nowhere in spite of that. I met another girl at a dance, and didn't quite manage to take her home, but as a matter of self-respect I had to follow up, because she had been prepared to speak to me, and I knew where she worked. The telephone was the thing. You could sound suave and tall and handsome on the telephone. I meant to telephone her the next day, but obviously you can't make dates without money in your pocket, a lot of money in case she smokes or gets hungry, and I kept spending my money. It was nearly six weeks before I thought I had enough for the job, about six shillings.

The way this worked out nearly put me off telephones for life. Six weeks was too long in the first place. In the second place she worked in a kind of warehouse place off Argyle Street where they didn't favour personal telephone calls. I had gone out of the office and called from a telephone booth to be certain of privacy, but the traffic and the noise outside made it hard merely to hear, and she kept her voice down to a mutter at the other end.

'You remember,' I coaxed her. 'The dance. Remember?'

'Oh,' she said unwillingly. 'Yes.'

'Well,' I said . . . and went into the rehearsed speech, but it was clear I wasn't getting across. I pictured some acid supervisor standing over her scowling, and wished I had the moral strength to say cheerio and hang up and forget all about it, but I couldn't, not after spending tuppence on a phone call and exposing myself. I had to get results. Standing sweating in the telephone box I knew I didn't want to see her again at all. She wasn't even very pretty. I would have been delighted if the line had gone dead and relieved me of the whole affair. I had made the effort and that was enough. But I heard myself blustering on and on and on, and her muttering resentful monosyllables and saying no, not next week, no, not the week after, no, no. Somehow we ended it. I went straight out and bought myself ten Capstan and a Penguin book about Russia by Bernard Pares off the six shillings and died slowly of humiliation. But there are some things about telephones that never strike you at the time.

About two months later, we were talking about telephones in the office one Saturday afternoon, in a lull between rushes of football copy. Five or six casual people came in on Saturday to help handle the football programme, and one of them, just new, worked the switchboard, which was also his regular job somewhere else during the week. He was recounting the entertainment value of getting crossed lines when he suddenly remembered the crossed line to end all.

'Ah was trying for a Central number, and here, ah got on to this guy tryin' to date this dame, but she wasn't havin' any. He says: "Do you no' remember me? We were at that dance –" Some dance or other they had been at. She hummed and hawed, and then she says: "Oh, that." You could tell this guy was not on, right away. But he kept on about this dance—'

He had total recall, and there was absolutely no chance of a mistake. He had landed on my line and heard every word. All the time he told the story I smiled stiffly and eyed him to see if he was talking at me, but we had never met at the time of the telephone conversation, and the name had meant nothing. He didn't connect the screamingly funny story with me at all. But it was so good that before this guy had finished pleading with this dame, everybody on our switchboard boy's office was hooked up to enjoy the programme. I had made my pathetic failure before a packed house. Never say anything at all on the telephone. Anything at all.

It was easier to look for fun that didn't involve this person-to-person horror. I decided I would write a terribly bitter novel that would show people, including Lily and the girl in the warehouse, that they had been under-estimating a great man, and I put in a lot of preliminary work, mostly on the draft of my speech for the Foyle's Literary Luncheon they would give me when it was published. Most of the time I was having a wonderful time. Big Bob and I worked out a slow-motion boxing act that paralysed the café set in Shettleston, and we went for long walks and practised singing like the Merry Macs and evolved long complicated jokes like visualizing a current radio programme called Music in Miniature, in which we conducted the band with half a matchstick and played imaginary double-basses two inches long. I was torn between the rosy prospect of becoming an overnight variety star and the even rosier prospect of being a celebrated man of letters, and sometimes I worked out timetables for a working day that would take in both, plus a Cabinet post. That would be a thing, I thought, a juvenile elder statesman with a bewildering command of public affairs and world reputation as a one-man Marx Brothers as well.

When Harry Roy's band came to the Empire and offered prizes for members of the audience to conduct the band, we telephoned each other deliriously, got home early to bolt our teas and went straight back to town to make our theatre debut. We couldn't get near the theatre, it was jammed, like nearly every theatre in Glasgow during the war. We bought an evening paper to see what else was on in town, feeling very dashed, and the first thing we saw was a crooning competition at the Locarno. We ran the whole length of Sauchiehall Street in terror in case the Locarno might be packed too. It was, but we got in, and ploughed our way with set, fanatical faces through mobs of dancers to get to the stage and get into the competition.

Bob sang some Crosby number, quite like Crosby, even with his pipe in his hand. He hadn't started smoking the pipe, but he liked to carry it as a prop and take it out and grip it when he felt like serious talk. I sang a rangy song of the moment called 'Starlight Souvenirs,' with a lot of long high notes, and handled the whole thing not unlike a boy soprano. We got friendly enough applause, but the fiver of the evening went to a girl who belted hell out of 'Basin Street Blues' and went on to hog two full choruses, brassy and raucous and really scruffy.

'Real back court stuff,' I said peevishly from the sidelines.

'She can sure sell a number, though,' Bob said.

'I hate her,' I said.

'A good baun, but,' Bob muttered thoughtfully. 'Boy, what a difference it makes standin' up in front of a real competent outfit.'

'Sure tootin,' I agreed. 'That luscious big brass noise makes a song sound smooth, real smooth, laddie.'

We danced with a few girls in a state of abstraction, thinking of how nice it was to sing in front of a big professional band, fame, money, music. Failure to win the five pounds was trivial. Going home on the bus we met two girls from Sandyhills and one of them said to Bob:

'What have you done with your pipe?'

'Why, I reckon it's right here in ma packet,' he said. 'Eh? How come you're interested in my pipe?'

'You would sing better without it,' she sniggered. Simultaneously we both flushed darkly.

'Och, you wereny bad,' she comforted Bob. 'Better than that dame that won it. Never knew the two of you went in for the croonin'.'

'Just practising on the scruff,' I said blandly. We took the girls to a café and bought them lime juice to keep them on our side in case they started telling the tale round the district.

There were competitions going somewhere almost all the time, but most often at the Locarno. The next time we went we had misjudged the date, and it was an acting competition instead of singing this time.

'God,' said Bob after we were inside. 'We're gonny have

to *dance*. Imagine comin' to the Locarno to *dance*!'

'It's awful common, innit?' I agreed. 'But I'm on for this competition. Come on, what can we lose?'

'Naw, I don't think I'll bother, Cliffie.' He called me Cliffie, a small source of irritation. It was over an hour to the time of the competition, so we danced and drank a slow cup of coffee. Now that I had resolved to try the competition, dancing was secondary in any case, but as usual I never seemed to find any human girls to dance with. They either said nothing and were impervious to talk, or they talked with such cultivated stupidity that it was better not to talk at all. I still don't know how other people find ordinary human beings with social talents in dance halls, although they must be there, because Bob found one, a nice one too; just slightly plump and dark, with a smooth well-rounded laughing face. I lost him for a couple of dances and then saw him sitting at a table with her. He waved me over, but kept on talking to her, rather loudly and fast.

'—and this is Pierre, my friend with the Free French Forces. The trouble is, he can hardly speak English. Do you speak French?'

'No.' She sounded crestfallen at not speaking French, and looked at me with that expression of dumb strangled friendliness that people give to incomprehensible foreigners and dogs. She didn't actually pat me.

'He's really a problem, but I'm doing my best,' Bob went on resignedly, the slob – anything to get a line that would catch a girl's attention, and I was the line just because I did Charles Boyer impersonations. Well, I didn't mind backing him up, but I liked the look of the girl myself, and I didn't plan to have any scruples about who saw her first, since it was actually my existence as a Frenchman that had got her to the table at all.

'Mamselle,' I said, and bowed low to kiss her hand. She liked that. '*Comme tu es adorable.*'

'What is he saying?' she asked Bob, who gave a charming shrug with his pipe.

'I 'ave say,' I chipped in, ''ow you are sharmeeng – so beauteeful ze smile, tres Parisienne.'

140

'He does speak English!' she accused Bob, and I hurried to save the situation by insisting Verree Not Much. Bob smiled in relief and went on talking to her. She was a student at the College of Domestic Science, or Dough School, and Bob was doing all right with her, being employed in Intelligence. He didn't actually say Intelligence, but he hinted wildly, and I was the evidence. With the ice broken, I started working my act hard, and there wasn't one thing Bob could do to snag me, because it all depended on me. It wasn't easy with my vocabulary limited to ten simple phrases, but I was getting the edge on Bob and getting him worked out of the conversation altogether when the girl suddenly jumped up.

'Oh, the competition!' she said.

'Oh? *Ah oui, il faut m'excuser*,' I cried, kissed her hand in a hurry and leapt up to burrow through the crowd. I heard Bob suggesting that they should skip the competition as I vanished.

I was just in time, because they were taking only eight men and four girls for the contest. Somebody had written a short melodrama of one page, with a heroine, a hero and a black-hearted villain, and the entrants had to try one line of the parts and be chosen for the performance by volume of applause. I was given a slip of paper with one of the hero's lines, and there was never a shade of doubt about it. I acted the three other heroes out of sight. The line was something like this:

'I would rather sell oranges, apples and honey pears in the gutter than betray a woman's honour!' I gave it laldy.

The three winners were taken backstage and given the full scripts to read through, then provided with a few simple props and brought out after the next dance to act the piece. We were also handed, in advance, two pounds each. I put on my props and pocketed my two pounds and went out to give the performance of my life, and I did, too. The play lasted about three minutes and was a big hit.

I couldn't help cackling as I went back to rejoin Bob. I was a success, I was rich, and Bob's pitiful pretence was exploded. He must be in a pathetic state of bluster by this time, and I could now start talking quick, poetic English to the girl from the Dough School and end up with every prize available.

'Hello, Cliffie,' Bob said sheepishly. 'Ripping good performance, what what?'

'Training and talent, that's all,' I said modestly. 'Did you enjoy it?' I asked the girl.

'Frenchman,' she chid me. 'Trying to fool people with a phoney accent like that.'

'I thought it wasn't bad,' I said airily. She patted me on the hand in a complacent way that was terribly irritating.

'You didn't fool me for a second,' she said. Bob shook his head and said:

'I warned you it would never work, Cliffie,' he said sympathetically. The deceit of it took my feet away.

'Well, night night, *Pierre*,' the girl said, and stood up. Bob stood up with her, and the last I saw of her was her back view on her way out with him. I didn't mind Bob selling me out, I would have done the same thing for him without compunction. I was mad at the girl for picking a nonentity when there was a talented, charming success available. On the other hand, I had two pounds, and applause ringing in my ears, and that's more than most people can bring home from a dance hall.

Smash Hit

Without ever actually doing anything to justify it, I was taken by people who didn't know any better as a theatre enthusiast and expert, and all this proves is that it is easy to acquire a reputation for nearly anything if you talk enough. If it comes to that, among some people I knew, especially in the ILP, where there were so many innocent trusting people, I even had a reputation as some kind of roué, and accomplished dabbler in black arts like sex and

142

drinking. I wished it were true. This is more comfortable than having a reputation as a saint. If people think you're a rascal, in that particular way, and at the same time you treat them with reasonable courtesy and don't steal anything from them, they feel they alone have called out the real good in you, and they can't help liking you in consequence. Anyway, sex and drink when tied up with the theatre seem romantic rather than squalid. Some of the separate compartments of life began to slop over into one another when I was asked to put on wee shows to raise funds for the Party.

The invitation came from the Bridgeton branch of the ILP, the most solid and celebrated corner of the faith and the home ground of Maxton himself. The branch had its own rooms, with a little hall at the back where a dance could be held – it was at a New Year dance there, in fact, that I met the girl who crushed me flat when I telephoned her for a date later. Nobody had thought of putting on intimate revue in the place before, but that's what I decided on; a few sketches, songs, a bit of music, monologues, and funny bits. I have hardly ever enjoyed anything so much, and mainly being accepted without question as the sole creator and master boss-man. It was easy to get performers and help because it was All For The Party, with a couple of bits of simple single-minded propoganda among the items. These were of no propaganda value, as it happens, because the entire audience would be members of the Converted, but it would please everybody and show that we weren't just frivolous stage types. One of the pieces was a long poem I wrote to be spoken in the person of Santa Claus, all about the horror of bomber aircraft. This went down tremendously.

The other was a one-act play set in an improbable café stuck on a Welsh mountain somewhere, perfectly terrible stuff about soldiers and pacifists with a ghost dragged feebly in to point a moral, which was that pacifism, like patriotism, is not enough. I found a drama-minded conscientious objector to play the hero, but the backstage bickering was frightful because he personally thought that pacifism *was* enough, and luckily we finally abandoned the play, which improved the standard of the show. I even got Bob into it, although the idea of socialism and pacifism filled him with horror and contempt. He was willing to sing anywhere, and did a solo act with one foot on a chair and elbow on knee and pipe in hand.

Then there was a burlesque version of *Macbeth*, incorporating the gravedigger scene from *Hamlet* for good value and working in plenty of joey-joey jokes and a big finish with Macbeth being called up for the HLI. The surprise spot was a Hell scene, just like the *Folies Bergere* but without the nudes, of course, instead a lot of sharp jokes about the kind of people who ended up stoking the everlasting fires.

It was a sell-out, opened and closed to an audience of easily a hundred and went with a bang, although the stage in the hall was only eight feet long and a foot high. There were no floats or tabs. We strung a clothes-rope across the hall just in front of the platform and Harry Sergeant, a Bridgeton member who was in a sense backing the show, borrowed a set of blackout curtains from an office and we hung these on rings from the rope and dragged them back and forth, from one side only. It still baffles me, but any kind of amateur show will get an audience in Glasgow and the audience will like it or tolerate it and come again.

The curtains, which were fine in theory, kept on sticking halfway so that the curtain-boy had to duck across the floor and pull them by hand, and got the second biggest laughs of the show. The biggest arose because that clothes line was being chafed gently at one end every time the curtain moved, and at last, while I was doing my Beelzebub and interviewing a Cabinet Minister, there was a small snapping sound and about forty yards of blackout cloth swirled down to cover the stage and everything on it. The show went on.

A bit of light relaxation in politics was a good thing because I was going before the Conscientious Objectors' Tribunal in a few weeks, a much stiffer test of a performance.

Dodging the Column

Rehearsing to be a conchie was different from rehearsing for a play, but it still needed rehearsal. Before the war and at the beginning of the war, the hearings of the Tribunals were given a lot of space in local papers, but as time went on they lost their novelty and their news value. Too many of the objectors said the same things to justify headlines and the Tribunals asked the same questions too often. These were the questions you could obviously rehearse. If this seems a funny way to go about demonstrating a conscience, the answer is that the Tribunals looked like a funny way of investigating it. How do you judge a man's conscience anyway, when the main effect of his conscience is to make him disagree with you? I don't know what the members of the Conscientious Objectors' Tribunals thought of conchies, but conchies didn't think much of them. Grant the Tribunals all the legalistic mechanism of fair play, and intelligent men to operate it, and you're still left with the fact that they were instruments created by the Government, and the Government was at war, and what nearly every objector thought about the Tribunal was that it was there to demolish any objections and get people into the Army. This was how the most reasonable of us felt about the Tribunals: they can be as fair and as reasonable as they know how, but for a start, they are convinced that we're wrong, and on top of that they're pretty sure we're malingering. How fair *can* they be?

And the answer to that is that the Tribunals did hand out exemptions to quite big numbers of conscientious objectors. But they turned down a lot more, and they probably made plenty of mistakes both ways. Among my own conchie acquaintances there were fewer dodgers than passionate martyrs. Some of us were pretty ridiculous, in fact, but to be a pacifist at all in wartime demands a certain amount of drama.

When it came to the bit, my mother was all for my being a conchie. She had a very simple practical attitude to war. She didn't want any of her family to get killed, no matter what for. I just had to be careful to soft-pedal the possibility of going to jail for my opinions, because she wouldn't have liked that either, although she would have stood it if she had to. I didn't actually want to go to jail, but on the other hand, nearly everybody wonders what it's really like being in jail, and conchies are about the only people who get the chance to find out without a stain on their records. I knew a couple of objectors who had done three months in Barlinnie, and they looked just the same afterwards. The experience sounded all right, in an eccentric way. Considering what some people in the Army had to put up with, jail was more silly than formidable.

The arguments for and against pacifism had been so well battered out that they were almost wearisome by this time. But the imminence of the Tribunal was unsettling. It had seemed so far away for so long, and now it was a matter of days, and I felt exposed and unprepared. It was too much to hope that the bench would hit me with any of the dead, stock questions: 'What would you do if you saw a German soldier raping your sister?' That wasn't a legend, some objectors actually were asked this. I lay in bed at night and rehearsed, not my answer, but the particular curl of the lip and the particular tone of tired contempt in which to deliver it. Alfie came home on leave from the RAF while I was in the middle of this phase, and took a still-baffled interest in my odd attitude.

'I know you're nuts,' he said dispassionately, 'and at least you mean what you say. But what the hell *would* you do if you saw a German soldier raping your sister?'

'Which sister?'

'Aw, don't be bloody funny.'

'All right,' I said, 'what would I do if I saw a Royal Marine trying to rape my sister? Declare war on the Royal Marines?'

146

'That's just bloody stupid,' Alfie exploded.

'How?'

'Have a pint. You've always an answer. I should know by this time to keep my mouth shut. Have you seen Elsie Thingummyjig recently?'

'I don't even know Elsie Thingummyjig.'

'I've got her phone number in my diary.' We stopped glaring at each other and talked about Elsie Thingummyjig. You make your point on the great moral issues and then talk about something agreeable.

Next morning I was late at the office because of some wartime transport crisis, and at lunchtime, instead of going home, I went across to a maidenly restaurant, decorated with china bunnies and bright yellow water-colour landscapes, for a healthy tuck-in at a tiny plate of *macroni au gratin*. Because of the transport breakdown, the place was jammed, a painful experience to me at that time. Lacking the training of early experience, I liked the *idea* of eating in restaurants and being poised and at home everywhere, but in the fact I squirmed in my heart when I had to face crowds of alien faces looking at me while I failed to find a place to hide, and that day was particularly bad. Finally a small table for two in a corner fell vacant, and I threaded my way to it wearing one of my fixed faces. A girl followed me and took the other chair.

Eating alone is a sorry thing for anybody. I always carry a book as the nearest substitute for companionship, to make me look and feel less lonely, and I propped it up and started on it at once. A person engrossed in his own affairs is a person of independence and therefore important. Besides, you get through a lot of good reading that way. It also saved me from having to look at the girl at the table, because of course, I wanted to look at her, she was a girl; and when you keep looking at somebody it puts you in an inferior position. I was so well buried in the book that I didn't notice much about her at all, right through soup and macaroni, and I started to become aware of her only while I was prodding blindly at a thin segment of Swiss tart. If I hadn't learned to distrust my fantasies I

147

would have thought she was actually trying to open a conversation. She looked round the room and kept returning to me, by clumsily managed accident, and now and then she gave a little cough as if to test her speech register. It went on for so long that I began to distrust my distrust of my egotism, and flicked a glance at her over my book whenever she looked away. She caught me at it, and smiled, a timid smile. I smiled back, not giving too much away, and then to my annoyance I gave a little cough, too.

'May I speak to you?' she said.

'Of course,' I said. The embarrassment and the aloneness and the performance with the book disappeared in a puff.

'I wonder if I could ask you something,' she said, very quickly. 'It's awfully embarrassing.'

It wasn't embarrassing to me, I was having the time of my life out of nowhere.

'It's probably less embarrassing than it seems.' I said smoothly. All I needed was a stethoscope round my neck. The girl brightened somewhat and told me that she had planned to go home for lunch, but what with the buses and the holdups and so on she had decided to eat in town, and now she had discovered that she had nothing in her purse but her bus fare, and nearly two shillingsworth of restaurant food inside her. It was so much like the kind of thing that happened to me that I never for an instant questioned her good faith. This was a plain case of a damsel in distress, a gift from the gods. And it was a mere unlikely chance that I had enough money in my own pocket to pay for her lunch. She was more embarrassed when this point arrived than she had been in telling the story. Her face flushed quite red, but I was too conscious of my own performance to take in any of the details except that she was a girl and she wasn't ugly.

'You'll have to give me your address so that I can send the money to you,' she said. I waved my hand derisively, but she stuck to the point, and after a little haggling I was able to do something I had often visualized. I opened my wallet and gave her my business card, newly printed only three days before.

'But there's no need to bother,' I said earnestly. 'You would do the same for anybody.'

'You'll never know how grateful I am,' she said. 'I must go. I'm late already.'

'Good-bye.'

'Oh, good-bye.' And she went. I was too polite to look round after her, so I didn't get a chance to see her ankles. Girls ought to have nice ankles. I didn't give the CO Tribunal a thought in bed that night.

Nothing happened on the next day, but the morning after that there was a letter for me at the office, marked Personal and double-underlined. Inside was a letter typewritten on octavo paper with an address in Mosspark printed in curly Old English lettering in pale blue ink in the top corner.

Dear Mr Hanley, it said, *I wish to thank you for your great kindness when I spoke to you on Tuesday, and my parents also wish to express their gratitude. It was most kind, and we would like you to know how much we appreciate it.*

Yours very sincerely,
Alice Smith.

She had done her best to say something more than just Dear Sir, Thank you, and she had been too delicate to mention the money in cold, brutal terms. There was a half-crown Postal Order pinned behind the letter, which gave me a profit of fivepence. But why all this insistence on parents? Was that to make it clear that she *had* parents, and wasn't a helpless orphan or a penniless adventuress who got free meals from strangers? Or had she dragged them in for the sake of padding the letter out a bit? It was nice to speculate, anyway.

'You're as blin' as a bat,' Big Eck said when I passed the letter round at the café that night. 'The bit aboot the parents means you've practically got your feet under the table already. You're *in*.'

'In where?' I asked coarsely.

149

'What's she like – skelly eyes?' he asked.

'No, she looks all right,' I said vaguely.

'Don't give us the patter,' Big Eck said. 'She must look like Dracula's daughter or she would never have picked *you* up.'

'She has a beautiful voice,' I said. I couldn't remember a thing about her voice.

'Bring her and let us see her,' he jeered. But he was impressed. It was a good thing to happen. After everybody had peered at the letter and held it up to the light and conjectured about the parents I displayed a carbon copy of my answer. This had given me some trouble. At first I was inclined to answer in the same cool formal tones as her letter, to avert any further embarrassment, but after three or four attempts I decided on the gay, airy note. I lost the carbon copy last time I flitted, but the gist of it was that I was the one who had cause to be grateful for the chance to perform a heroic rescue in this unromantic age and that I was sorry I hadn't had the chance to stop any runaway horses for Miss Smith while I was at it, but maybe, fortunately, as I was out of practice with runaway horses, and so on. It was a much longer letter than hers and I was pleased with it.

Her envelope went under the microscope next. It was made of different paper from the letter, and the stamp had perforations across the face, which meant that she had taken it from her office stamp-box and worked in one of those money-conscious offices where they perforate the stamps, as Glasgow Corporation offices do, to discourage pilfering, I suppose. All this told me was that like most people who have privately printed stationery, her parents always ran out of envelopes before they ran out of paper. It always happens because even if people order the same number of envelopes as sheets, they use the envelopes for paying bills and use up the stock faster without touching the paper. But the envelope had a name and address printed on the back flap, and this had been painstakingly x'd over in a typewriter to cover it completely. It came out with a little light rubbing and squinting from different angles. It was a merchant firm of some obscurity in Hope Street, quite near my own office, and this gave me a telephone number to add to what I knew about Alice. It was difficult to get a picture of the parents although I had taken the impression that she was an only child. They would be gracious, graceful people, in a well-ordered house, preferably with a lot of money. Her father would be grizzled and shrewd and good-humoured, and her mother would be slender and handsome and still attractive, with gentle hands and a deep, serene smile. Maybe I should just ditch Alice and try to date the old lady, in fact.

In any case I didn't have the patience to wait for another letter, which might not come. I gave my answer time to arrive, and the next day I waited till the boss was out and I could count on an hour clear of interruptions, and telephoned her office.

She answered the phone herself, but I played it foxy and asked formally to speak to Miss Smith.

'This is Miss Smith,' she said, both a question and an assumption in her voice.

'Hello,' I said.

'It is you, isn't it? How did you find out my telephone number?'

'The trained detective mind,' I said, indulgently.

'Your voice sounds much deeper on the telephone.'

'This is my baritone day.'

Her boss must have been out, too. We spoke for about forty minutes, and I arranged to take her to the pictures on the following night, since that was the night I got paid. There was no question of humming and hawing. Big Eck was right. I was in, and the possibility of refusal never occurred to me. On the next morning again, Friday, she called me back and invited me to tea before we went to the pictures. This fitted so well the conventional legend of the entrapment of innocent bachelor boys that I put up a conventional struggle, but curiosity was stronger than apprehension. Anyway, I wasn't even twenty yet. And no matter what Big Eck said, I had done what people were supposed to do. I had found a girl of my own, without

151

introductions, without living next door and without getting slapped. I kept wishing I could remember what she looked like.

Cats are People Too

When Jimmie came on leave that weekend he was brown like an Egyptian and looked as tough and healthy as a killer wolf. I telephoned Alice at once to cancel our next date, since the minimum duty of a home bird, I reckoned, was to be available for drinking or blethering with returning travellers. There was nothing different about Jimmie since his last leave except that he had made more friends and enemies. His references to the war at sea were always indirect and elusive except in relation to personalities. All the people he met were bigger than life compared with the two-dimensional characters that occurred in my own life, and they all had unexpected peculiarities.

The stories about these people were never thrust on you. They trickled out in ominous, suggestive little droplets at unpredictable moments that always drove us to cross-question him and demand more details, and these were supplied often unwillingly until recollection gripped Jimmie and carried him away. For months before he went into the Navy, he had worried us with passing references to an engineer who worked beside him and whom he called the Penguin.

Eventually he explained that he called the Penguin the Penguin because the unfortunate man had no legs, just feet starting straight out of his pelvis. 'He has to get special biler suits made for him,' Jimmie explained compassionately. 'They're jist a kind of blue peeny and he fastens them in the middle at the bottom wi' a safety peen.'

The Penguin was an amiable, well-integrated individual

152

except on Friday at five when the work skailed and the men went to the pub at the corner for a pint. The three barmen worked like slaves to serve the five o'clock rush, and man after man got his pint or his hauf, but the Penguin never got served.

'He gets oot ten minutes early because it takes him longer to scuffle doon the street to the boozer,' Jimmie added, shaking his head in sorrow. 'But it's to no avail, an accursed fate is working against him. When he stauns up at the bar, his heid is six inches below the coonter. The barman's face goes ashen when he hears the voice squeakin' for a hauf, an' the pub empty, an' mutters tae the boss that it's the Ghost Drinker of the Cromwell Arms coming back to haunt him for the short measure he got back in '92. Then the mob comes in an' he serves them with trembling fingers and guilt clutching at his pasty-faced heart.'

All this is the mere legitimate embellishment of the story-teller, a manner of speaking rather than an attempt to mislead. You accept that the basic facts are accurate. Then, said Jimmie, two sets of knuckles would appear over the edge of the bar counter and the Ghost Drinker would squeak for a hauf, his squeak choked with rage and thirst. And as the barman kept serving pints to other, later customers, the only sign that the Penguin was there would be the sudden whitening of the knuckles as his fists tightened with fury, until at last they scrunched through the mahogany and the Penguin fell back clutching two chunks of splintered wood, and still unnoticed by the shuddering barman.

It wasn't a story at all, simply a little piece of observation from real life, as Jimmie hurried to point out. His passion for observing real life made it impossible to gather anything in the way of war experiences from him. The Navy at sea was just a convenient place in which to observe. He did tell me, sitting over a pint in the Kirk Hoose, that his destroyer had run into such dirty weather in the Mediterranean that everybody on board was as sick as a pig, and he demonstrated how the Commander had read a burial service and vomited simultaneously. The wind had blown away the funnel cowl, and the rain poured straight into the engine room until they strapped the youngest OD aboard across the top of the funnel as the only handy makeshift to keep the water out. After that they reached the Indian Ocean, and varied the diet and the monotony by catching flying fish in buckets.

I found this hard to believe, but Jimmie refused to give any explanations at the time. He mentioned flying fish once or twice during the weekend and it still sounded unlikely. The weekend must have given him time to recall the missing details. Or, as he said, the memory of flying fish was wrapped up in a harrowing story that he had been Trying to Forget. It was certainly a shocking, cruel story.

Jimmie himself (he told me) invented the sport of catching flying fish. The seas in the Indian Ocean were so high that fish flying from one wave-crest to the next often landed smack on the deck or bashed their brains out on the side. More of them cleared the ship altogether and hit the water safely on the other side.

Jimmie took a bucket on deck, and after an hour or so on rope-soled shoes, developed a slick technique of leaping sideways along the deck with the bucket at arm's length to field the passing fish. The game became the crew's passion.

It was at this point that the Engineer Officer's cat came into the story. It was a black, lean, sycophantic cat that sucked up to officers and despised ratings, and every rating on board counted a day well spent when he had landed a boot in its ribs. But nobody thought of anything more deadly than a boot until the cat strolled on deck one Sunday and watched coldly while half the crew leapt about with buckets catching big, juicy flying fish, or more often failing to catch big, juicy flying fish. The mechanics of the sport were being mulled over slowly in its cold little mind, and when it had worked the trick out, it suddenly appeared among the bucketeers and joined in.

Nobody could compete with the cat. It had four legs and could do a sideways leap of twelve feet, and eight feet in the air at the same time, and every time it leapt, a flying fish shot into its open front end and thudded against its closed back end. And at the same time, it could catch a fish and dodge three vicious swings from sailors' buckets.

'I had nae personal objection to the cat,' Jimmie recalled, 'apart fae flinging a depth charge at it once or twice I never lifted my hand in anger. But an old three-badge killick brooded on it, an' one day his mate lured the cat wi' a sardine, an' the killick suddenly rushed on deck from concealment an' booted it straight into the Indian Ocean. It sank with its face turned to the ship an' an expression of diabolical malevolence directed at the three-badger.'

'A dampt shame,' I said tearfully.

'Aw, it got back,' Jimmy silenced me. 'As soon as the news went round, the crew rushed on deck wi' buckets for a rich harvest. The three-badger caught the first fish – a great big long yin, flying at unprecedented speed. He had the bucket pressed against his chest, an' the impact sent him hurtling across the deck tae the other rail, his spine broken in three places.'

And when his mates crowded round, they saw that it was no great long flying fish that had killed him; just an ordinary flying fish, with the cat gripping its tail. The cat got out of the bucket, curled its lip and edged backwards to the safety of the Engineer Officer's cabin. That night it was flung overboard in a steel box. It appeared on deck an hour later, spitting iron filings and giving everybody on board a wide berth. The cook rammed a skewer through it, and it reappeared on the following day wearing a small bandage and the Purple Heart.

The whole thing had sickened the crew of flying fish. They now spent their leisure murdering the cat. At Bombay, while the Engineer Officer was ashore buying five cases of sardines, a party of desperate men trapped the cat, smothered it in fuel oil, stabbed it, rammed a spoonful of rat poison down its throat, and heaved it over the side for the last time.

They threw it over the wrong side, and its limp body

struck an iron rung of the dock ladder and hung there until consciousness returned. With failing strength it clung to the ladder, under the ship's hull and out of sight, throughout the long ugly day, until it heard the beloved footsteps of its master thudding drunkenly along the gangplank and aboard. Rung by rung it hauled itself up, boarded again and dragged itself to his cabin. The Engineer Officer was sitting in his cabin counting the sardines when he heard what sounded like a faint knock on his door. He ignored it. It sounded again. He stood up with an oath and opened the door. For a second he saw nothing.

Then, as he stepped back into the cabin, the cat clutched the doorway with its front claws and hauled itself erect on its back legs, reeled for an instant and then gathered its fading forces in the tradition the Navy had taught it. Its right paw lifted in a Navy salute.

'AB Pussycat reporting for duty, sir,' it croaked, and fell dead into the cabin.

Courting is Pleasure

It was like trying to juggle a dozen balls at once, just keeping a hold on everything, around this time. All the things I was up to were trivial enough, but I couldn't in my greed give up any one of them. There was still football and hockey at the playing fields and now that the nights were dark early, a game of cards or a talk in the railway carriage afterwards, and interesting things to talk about and the chance of an occasional squabble with one of the jingoistic bloc from the old school who were all studying to be gymnastic teachers and become PT instructors in the Army and kill Nazism stone dead with physical jerks. It was nice to have some people to dislike totally.

Then if we were ever going to hit the big-time like the Merry Macs, Bob and I had to keep trying out the noise of new harmonies and meeting Alastair David Nimmo for try-outs round the piano. I started growing a moustache and enrolled for piano lessons at the Athenaeum. A lot of my jobs at the office were tending to run over into the evenings, and I liked to keep some time free on Thursdays and Fridays to visit *Reynolds News* office to talk to John Bell, nearly the last and certainly the biggest of the Old School of journalism, because he knew so much about everything and was always ready to talk about it. There was still the ILP, and the Tribunal looming nearer and nearer. In a despairing bid to fill up the loose minutes of the week I saved up two pounds and sent away for a guaranteed course on How To Grow Tall. It demanded thirty minutes of agony each night and morning. There was Alice as well.

After the first time, I suggested another date, and after that we fixed another. There was no negotiated contract or anything. So going steady was something you just drifted into for lack of opposition. It was an odd kind of steady, of course. The only night we deliberately arranged anything was Friday, and even this was complicated, because Friday was one of the evenings I liked to go round to talk to John Bell at five o'clock, and that usually ended in an invitation to Cairn's pub in St Vincent Street and the talk could go on for hours.

John in those days was a fixed institution in Glasgow journalism, a bit like the Arc de Triomphe and about the same size. I had heard of him long before I met him, from other people in newspapers and from people in the ILP, since he was an old ex-ILPer. The world is full of them. When he showed that he liked talking to me I felt I had graduated into full manhood. He was tall, about six feet, but his height was scarcely noticeable because he was enormous in all directions. To look at he was just a big fat man, in fact, probably addicted to over-eating and maybe over-drinking. His face was so big that his cheeks bulged over his collar, he had a wide soft mouth shaped like a girl's and his eyes, looking tiny in his great face, glinted behind black-rimmed glasses like Billy Bunter's. When he talked I sat like a mesmerized rabbit.

It would have been hard to picture anybody less like myself, at five feet three and eight stone four. When he was coarse it came naturally from his huge person. When I was coarse it sounded like something I had read. But apart from being coarse when he felt inclined, he could talk anybody rigid about football, which struck me as a particularly dull talent, and do the same with economics or history or music. He exasperated me by admitting indulgently that Chopin was talented, but a young man's composer. I didn't even know what he meant. But I had to defend Chopin or be a mere poltroon. I wanted to champion all the champions of progress, in music, too. Kay Cavendish was running a disc-jockey programme at the time under the title, 'It Ain't What You Do, It's the Way That You Do It' – mostly of new American bands and singers.

'Surely that's worth doing – giving music something new by a fresh approach,' I implored him.

'The premise is false,' he boomed at me – his voice was so powerful that he could have called any of his acquaintances in Glasgow by throwing the telephone away and sticking his head out into Buchanan Street. 'It *is* what you do that matters.' Then he would smile a fatherly indulgent smile that was winning and maddening simultaneously and wait for me to utter some fresh idiocy. Talking to him, in his little office or in the pub downstairs, gave me a potent feeling of being alive with every pore. Without making any effort he always found himself holding court in the pub. He was a kind of king of every pub he chanced to patronize. The old friends who drifted over to talk to him were as likely to be professors of moral philosophy or classical composers as football fans, although there were an awful lot of football fans. They came to talk or to have arguments settled, since John knew everything about every game of football ever played. And in the middle of some obscure tussle over a forty-year-old Cup Final he would straighten me out on the relation between the quantum theory and the music of

158

Bach, which he played on the piano himself with great skill and sensibility.

'I think you're all wrong about being a conchie, Cliff,' he said amiably one Friday night in Cairn's. 'It's no practical, boy. It's no practical.'

But while I was ready to admit every word from his lips as a gem of wisdom and experience, I wasn't disciple enough to shake in my own faith.

'Somebody has to do it,' I said. 'The bomber canny cure whatever's wrong wi' the world.'

'Can Hitler?'

'I'm insulted, John,' I said. 'You're suggesting I *like* Hitler.'

'Away ye go, boy, don't put words into my mouth. But don't kid yoursel' about the Germans – they're dangerous.'

'Including your wife?'

'Ach, don't annoy me, Cliff. If Marian was in Germany now she'd be locked up, or deid. I know the Germans, boy.'

He did, too. He spoke the language fluently, had spent long holidays and worked as a tourist courier in Germany before the war, and his wife was a handsome German girl, with Jewish blood.

'Did I ever tell you how I met Marian?' he cackled. 'There was a crowd of us on a conducted tour and she was conducting it. Well, walking through the streets of Berlin I took out a fag. It was the last one in the packet, and I threw the packet away. She didny think I noticed, but I saw her pickin' it up, an' by God she walked three miles before we passed a litter box she could throw it in.'

'Well, what's wrong with keeping the streets tidy?'

'Nothing! Everything's too bloody tidy, that's what's wrong. It's the German nation, Cliff, believe me, boy. You can get so keen on tidiness an' order that you'll do any damn thing you're told. Have you no' had enough to drink?'

'No.'

'As long as you don't blame me you can drink the pub dry. Did I ever tell you about the pal of mine – pal! I was his best man. Didny see him for five years after the weddin', an' then his wife glared at me an' dragged him away. He told me later she had taken an awful scunner at me because once or twice when he went home wi' a skinful he had said he had met me. Never saw the bloody fool. I felt like punchin' his nose.'

I smiled brightly. I had told my mother the same thing more than once or twice. But at least she didn't know John.

'You were talking about the Germans,' I diverted him.

'Ever tell you the time I was in a park in Berlin an' there was a gate wi' a plank laid across it, an' a notice sayin' "Out of Order?" The next gate was a mile away, so I stepped across the plank an' on to the pavement. Hadny gone three yards when a fat German polis ran up an' ordered me back intae the park. "It is forbidden to leave by this gate," he said. An' don't think he was kiddin', that's the way their minds work. Do you know he wanted me to step back across the plank, walk a mile to the next gate and make my exit there? The law is the law, boy.'

'So you went back in?'

'Not on your damned life, boy. Hee hee hee. I pointed out to this squareheided comrade that if it was illegal to *leave* the park at that gate, the illegality couldn't be wiped out by the commission of another misdemeanour, namely, re-entering the park by that gate. Cliff, you don't know them as I do. He wanted me to walk on the pavement to the next gate, walk inside the park there, and then walk out again! Always polite, remember. But the law is the law.

'By this time a crowd had collected, an' there's nothin' the Berliner loves like a good argument about the law. Once it was goin' good, I quietly walked away an' left them shoutin' the odds at one another. An' *that's* why the Germans are dangerous.'

'Or fine, if they're led in the right direction.'

'Have you no' noticed they have a talent for bein' led in the other? If Hitler had never lived they would have invented him. Never mind, maybe you're right about the

Tribunal. You'll get on all right at it anyway, you're an argumentative wee bastard. Good luck.'

John's most fascinating quality was his refusal to be blinded by any dogmas, even his own. 'I'm a utilitarian,' he used to say. 'If a thing'll no work it's nae use. Do you know what I've come to believe in? The Inevitability of Gradualness.'

But when he got on to politics he took such an individual outlook that no label would fit him. Sometimes he would give a crystalline Marxist analysis, and the next minute he would say:

'When the comrades talk about "economic man", boy, I just want to go intae a corner an' make a rude noise. What the hell are you an' I up to right now? Is talkin' about Beethoven economic sense? When I take the chair at Union meetings, is it for economic reasons? Tae hell wi' that, I would be better off economically lyin' in bed an' lettin' somebody else take it. Tell you somethin', old Henry George had as good an idea as anybody – the Single Tax. Half the Comrades have forgotten it, or never heard about it. But however you look at it, all wealth is in the land. Get the land an' you've got the lot.'

The only things he was stubborn about were everything he happened to be talking about at a given moment, and the overwhelming superiority of Shakespeare, Beethoven, Brahms and Bach to anybody who had followed them. I thought he was pretty rotten about Chopin, though.

Unhappily, John and Alice were in sealed separate compartments of what was like two different lives. If I was seeing Alice on a Friday night I had to skip John because seeing him, I would want a drink with him, and I didn't want to meet Alice with drink in me, even the two or three half-pints which were all I ever wanted to drink, then.

The parents were nothing like my picture of them. Mr Smith was thin and slight, with thinning fair hair merging into grey, a rather sharp nose and pursed lips. Mrs Smith was a wee plump Glasgow body with roly-poly fingers. But my feet were under the table all right. Mr Smith was the manager of a grocery shop, a useful thing to be during the war, and the table was laid with a gentle contempt for the shortage of eggs and chocolate biscuits. They lived in a Corporation house pretty much like our own except that the furniture was newer.

Alice didn't have skelly eyes. She had green eyes both set straight, and light brown hair, and her face was well-boned and nice, especially her teeth, because her mouth was broad and thin-lipped, and it spread out and curved right up when she smiled, and showed her teeth and made two deep dimples in her cheeks. Her eyes crinkled when she smiled too. Her forehead was narrow and high, and she wore her hair plain, with a wave over the temples and a little roll down on the neck, and the rest brushed straight and shiny. She didn't say very much when we had tea or supper with the parents. Most of the conversation was from them to me and back again.

Although noticing things about the Smiths, the ordinary things you notice about people, I didn't come to any conclusions about them or pass any judgements. It was their house, after all. It must have been nearly the first time I was taken into a stranger's house and sat at the table on purely social grounds, and they were kind to me, although I felt a better idea would be to be away somewhere in the dark getting to know Alice.

Mr Smith wore zipp-up boot slippers in the house, and did a lot of quiet thinking with his head tilted and his eyes half-closed between bouts of conversation. He had a European map on the wall above the wireless, with coloured pins stuck in it, nearly as much fun as a model railway apart from being a nice way to fight wars. My heart sank slightly when he fixed himself to the radio for both the six o'clock and the seven o'clock news, but it was a reasonable enough thing to do and I knew a lot of people who felt like traitors if they missed a single bulletin. Mrs Smith and Alice sat dutifully silent during the news. Mrs Smith fidgeted somewhat in keeping an eye on Alice to see that dad wasn't disturbed. My own rapt silence was taken for granted, I was a man.

Then Mr Smith and I would digest the war news, and

162

after wolfing the poached eggs and chocolate biscuits he would tilt his head and get ready for a high-level strategic conference with me, me being a reporter and therefore well in with Churchill and the German High Command both. I got quite good at the game, especially since Mr Smith's long pauses for thought with his head tilted, gave me plenty of time to work out the logistics of blockade and invasion. We never argued. We just exchanged opinions and then considered them judicially, as one general to another.

'Mind you,' Mr Smith would say, 'Mind you, Cliff – and this is just between these four walls. *Anything* might be careless talk. The food position's going to get much worse before we're finished. Well, you probably pick up bits of information yourself, in your career. But tinned food? I see it from the inside, and if you believe me, vanishing, pouf! We'll be tightening our belts.'

'Oh, no, Alec!' Mrs Smith would say. 'Do you really think that's true, Cliff?'

'Of course it's true,' Mr Smith would tut impatiently. 'I don't know who should know if I shouldn't know.'

'What's wrong with you, Alice? Cat got your tongue?' Mrs Smith would break off coyly. 'You've hardly said a word since Cliff came in.'

This silenced Alice entirely, of course. She would reach for another chocolate biscuit and throw me an agonized smile. Mr Smith would deliver another considered judgement on the food position. It didn't interest me personally at all. I liked good food, but I liked any food. I always figured I could live on chips or raw turnips if I had to. Wartime moans about food wearied me because they didn't mean anything to me.

After a while Mr Smith would terminate the discussion with a look at his watch and the wireless and say:

'Well, I've enjoyed our wee chat, Cliff. It's time we let you young people off on your own, you'll be wanting to enjoy yourselves.' It sounded foreboding.

'It doesn't look as though you'll get much chat out of Alice tonight, Cliff,' Mrs Smith would say, as if Alice was deaf or absent. 'I keep telling her not to be so shy, but does it have any effect? Water off a duck's back.'

Alice talked quite rationally away from the house, though it was true she was quiet as girls go. I had a coat with wash-leather linings in the pockets, and on cold nights we always walked with hands clasped inside one of the pockets. I don't recall that we learned much about each other at first, everything was a joke. We sat in the back seat at the pictures and kissed when the screen went dim. What I do remember is that the back row in the local pictures had seats two or three inches higher off the floor than normal, to allow for the heating pipe running along underneath them; I couldn't get my feet down to the floor, in fact. In trying to settle comfortably I crossed my legs and groped with my feet to tuck one toe behind the heating pipe, and without warning developed a cramp as big as an egg under one thigh. Madeleine Carroll was on the screen at the time, it must have been almost her last film. A pain shot along my thigh and I let out a sharp high yell. We passed from that to hysterics.

There were difficulties, naturally. Mosspark is a long way from Sandyhills. It was all right on Fridays, when I went there straight from the office. Three nights a week Alice took evening classes in book-keeping or something, and often on these nights I would spend the early evening at the playing fields and duck out of the railway carriage, looking complacent and mysterious, at about half past eight or nine, and catch two buses to meet her after the class and take a walk. It was practically a foreign country she lived in. Glasgow is like that. People don't know any districts besides their own unless they have business or relatives there. The idea of going to live anywhere in the city far from Sandyhills would have struck me as nonsense. Paris, New York, Brazil, yes. Maryhill or Knightswood or Mosspark, absurd. I was only now getting to know any other corner of the city at all.

Late nights I took for granted. Now I had nothing but. I almost always managed to miss the last tram and walked into town or all the way home, hours of trekking. It gave me time to think, or sing to myself, and no matter what the hour, there were always other people walking home or walking somewhere. It was an energetic wooing with a lot of interruptions. Sometimes we walked by the railway and stopped for a session, or danced a few steps. But we always ended up huddled comfortably behind the Smith's coal-shed in the back garden, and although we kept as quiet as mice, Mrs Smith called Alice to bring me in for supper after a maximum of five minutes.

It wasn't that she wanted to interrupt. Her only aim was to keep me warm and well-fed and happy. And somehow she saved an egg for me.

Here was another small difficulty. Although I could eat anything else, I had never been able to stomach eggs since I was about eight. The big mistake was in concealing this on my first visit to the Smiths, but it would have been churlish to turn down such a rarity as an egg so proudly served, so I expressed my thanks too well, and I was on eggs for life. Most evenings I could force the hellish thing down and keep it down until I was clear of the house, but there were times when I had to smile casually and excuse myself and get into the bathroom to be sick, with the taps running to smother the noise because it was an unusual kind of house with bedrooms upstairs, but the bathroom downstairs beside the living room.

It was all right being out till all hours at night. My mother was resigned to it, and she showed a lack of inquisitiveness that startles me now in recollection. But she did nag about my pale face and an occasional spot, an unheard-of thing to appear on my rude cheek. The eggs did give me pause, but the long walks home were healthy, after all, I told myself.

Dad Wouldn't Like It, Beloved

We had a tiff one night. It was my fault, and I could have stopped it at any moment, but to my surprise and horror and fascination I heard myself carrying it on. It was partly irritation because Alice was so hard to have a quarrel with. Partly it was irritation at a relationship that wasn't moving anywhere. It was pleasant to kiss in the pictures, and pleasant to snuggle beside the railway, but it was all innocent and anti-Russellism. I never stopped to think that Alice might feel like more dangerous advances. Sometimes I half-hoped she would make them herself, but I was never candid with her about that. She was too nice. Instead I got irritated and huffy and didn't go back to the coal-shed to get dragged in for supper. We rarely saw each other at the weekends, but on Monday it was my day off from the office and I telephoned her from a phone box and apologized and told her I loved her and meant it. I felt better afterwards.

That night I met her after her class and got bang in trouble again. We were walking slowly by the railway, and not intending to go back for supper and waste precious minutes of privacy, when she said woefully:

'It's awful to think you'll be away to the Army next.'

'I won't be away to the Army at all,' I said. The subject had simply never come up.

'There's nothing . . . wrong with you, is there, Cliff?' she muttered into my ear, and squeezed my shoulder apprehensively.

'No, I'm as strong as a pit-pony. I'm a conchie.'

'What?'

'A conscientious objector.'

'Oh, Cliff.'

You would have thought I had just announced the passing of a beloved granny.

166

'Don't die,' I told her. 'It isn't fatal.'

'But you never told me.'

'Does it make any difference?'

'No, no!'

'Okay, then.'

'But, Cliff.' She kissed me for a while. 'I don't know what Dad'll say.'

'What the hell does that matter?'

'Don't swear!' She slapped me fondly. 'He's awful down on people like that.'

'Hasn't he got any wee coloured pins for conchies on his map?'

'That's not nice. Dad did his bit in the last war.'

'Good for Dad.'

'Don't you dare talk like that.' But she was half-hearted in her defence.

'Do you want me to go and do my bit?' I asked her cunningly.

'No. No, I want you to stay here forever.'

'I'd freeze to death,' I said. 'Never mind about Dad, he'll get over it.'

'But we can't tell him!'

'Why not? I'm not going to have an illegitimate baby or anything.' At this she slapped me fondly and chidingly again, and I thought briefly, should I pursue that line and see what develops? Instead I gave a patient lecture in pacifism, which she loved.

'You're really very brave,' she said.

'Don't kid yourself,' I said, 'but Dad's bound to find out, so you may as well tell him, or I'll tell him.'

'He wouldn't believe it, after all your talks about the war and everything.' This was a sharp blow. There had been plenty of openings to tell Dad before then, and I hadn't taken any of them. It was too easy to go on playing his strategy game and avoiding any real talk. Alice persuaded me not to say anything to Dad until I had to.

'But what do you have to *do* to be a conscientious objector?' she wanted to know.

'I have to go to a Tribunal next week,' I told her. 'If they like me I don't have to do anything else. If they don't

167

I have to join up or go to prison. I'll go to prison, of course.'

'You can't! Cliff, don't be crazy!'

'You can send me a file pie, Alice,' I comforted her. I felt quite sentimental about going to prison, for the moment.

Whose Conscience is This, Anyway?

In preparation for my Tribunal appearance I shaved off my moustache, in case it irritated the bench. It was fair and feeble. I wanted to look honest and sincere. Merely *being* sincere isn't enough. There were other shrewd dodges. One was to write practically nothing in the form they handed conscientious objectors when they registered for military service. The safest thing to write was: 'I object to war on ethical grounds'; or even better still, just: 'I object to war.' To go into any long explanations merely gave the Tribunal a basis for cross-examination before the hearing even started. Another sound scheme was to steer clear of religion and the Bible. They often had a professor of theology on the bench, and there's an outrageous thing if you like, a professor of theology trying to argue teenagers out of their dislike of war. Applicants were allowed to affirm at the opening of the hearing instead of taking the oath, and unless the objection was on religious grounds, this was also a sensible move in that it helped to cut out one line of questioning.

There were so many good tricks, in fact, that everybody should have got off. The Tribunals can't have been all that bad, because many people actually were exempted from soldiering. And the mere existence of the Tribunals was a good thing. Not many other countries at war have ever been prepared to be bothered with individual consciences.

The hearing was called for two in the afternoon, in one

of the courtrooms in the County Buildings, a dark-panelled room with a highly polished mahogany counter for the bench. It was a bright cloudless day in the late autumn, with dusty blocks of sunlight lying near horizontal across the room and recalling droning classroom afternoons when the teacher's voice faded to a remote buzz under the buzzing outdoor noises of summer. It was an effort to think and impossible to remember.

The questioning was courteous and interesting, no hypothetical discussions on rape. The Chairman was a sheriff, tall and high-boned. His face recalled some character actor in films that I couldn't place, and it was irritating not to be able to concentrate on this speculation. 'Moral and ethical grounds . . .' he was saying, '. . . surely . . .' I gazed up at his face and involuntarily tried to put it against the background of a film. '. . . decision reached by a democratic majority . . . ?'

'There are some questions so important – too important—,' I heard myself saying, '—so important that people must decide them for themselves . . . too important to be surrendered to anybody else, even to a majority.'

'That's a reasonable statement as a theory . . .' He was giving the matter serious judicial thought. 'But in cases of survival . . .' a long, leisurely debate went on and on and on. There was nothing fiendish about it. The other members of the bench must have joined in, but I hardly noticed them. The Chairman was the antagonist. There were moments of abrupt clarity when I felt that it might be possible to convince him, to make him see the light, but there was never time to press forward, always another searching, quiet question, another change of subject. It wasn't unfair, only tiring.

'It is wrong, you say, to conscript men to kill other conscripted men who themselves are not responsible either for the fact of war . . . Is it fair to say that you would have no moral objection to men engaging voluntarily in civil war?'

'. . . Less immoral, perhaps. In a civil war, a man has at least chosen his side according to his conscience, and the man he faces has chosen too, though . . . they have probably chosen the wrong way to settle the question.'

'And what do you say of the case of outsiders who might intervene in such a war, on one side?' He really wanted to know, it seemed. It was not a trap, I could smell the Spanish war from afar.

'In such a case the outsider has weighed right and wrong without compulsion, and regardless of nationality.'

But we were thinking of different things.

'But if the intervention is an act by an outside Government, using its own disciplined soldiers?'

There was a long silence while I tried to track back and readjust.

'You don't object to civil war?' another member of the bench chipped in helpfully.

'Which civil war?' I stammered. 'The question is a little hypothetical.'

'Would you not say that ethics are hypothetical things?' he asked with mild triumph.

'No. Yes, in a way. It's a confusing question.'

The Chairman craned forward, a long swooping movement.

'We appreciate that this is an ordeal,' he said. 'Would you like to sit down for a few moments?' I stared at the varnish on the bench and shook my head. If I sat down I wouldn't want to get up. What I would like to do is ask *you* sods some questions and demand the answers.

'The point of the question is, whether . . .' I can't remember what the point of the question was. After something under an hour I was finished. Jimmie Carmichael, the Bridgeton MP who was then a Town Councillor, and one of the First War pacifists who hadn't changed his opinion after growing beyond military age, was in the court in the official role of my Friend. A Friend, who could not be a lawyer, was permitted to give moral support, but not to coach or answer questions, and was allowed to speak as to the applicant's character and previous convictions. His testimonial didn't interest the bench so much as his revelation that the applicant's three

170

brothers were all serving in the Royal Navy.

'Do you find life difficult at home because of this?' the Chairman asked me, tickled and wondering.

'No,' I said. 'I have the most cordial relations with my brothers. They don't find my opinions odd.'

He found that odd.

We retired to the public benches to hear out the other cases and wait for the decisions to be handed down. Then I was angered. The Tribunal didn't spend an hour on anybody else that afternoon. The six other objectors were all religious objectors, and they were trapped and trussed neatly and slickly; mostly, as far as I could see, because they weren't as glib or as used to debate as I was. The third of them was genuinely inarticulate. The theologian's questions baffled him.

'I've been brought up wi' my uncle,' he said earnestly. 'An' I believe in the Bible, an' it's wrong to kill.'

'Yes, yes, but answer the question?'

'It's wrong.'

'Please answer the question.'

'Well. Ye see, I've been brought up wi' my uncle—'

The uncle intervened from the back of the court to try to explain. He was silenced acidly. The bench returned to the boy. It took them less than two minutes to lose all patience and tell him to stand down. The uncle came forward to speak, conscious of a black mark already against him.

There was no point in the uncle saying anything. The boy had failed to answer the perfectly simple questions. By God, I thought, if you're simple you have no right to a conscience. You do have to give a performance. The bench retired and people stared at one another hopelessly in the courtroom. They returned and read a brisk list of names. Rejected. Rejected. Rejected. Every applicant was rejected. I was baffled and furious. But I hadn't heard properly. I was exempted; the sole exemption of the day's intake. It's the bunk, and anybody who presumes to judge any stranger's conscience on ten minutes' acquaintance is a fool.

171

The boss was brusque and silent at the news. He had done his bit in the First War, too. My mother was as proud as hell. Alice didn't know what to say when I telephoned her.

'Aren't you glad?' I asked her.

'Yes . . .'

'Och, to hell.' I hung up. With grim satisfaction. It's nice, martyrdom.

Glasgow must have spawned more than its statistical quota of conchies. The legend of Red Clydeside and the workers' forums and the pre-war hunger marches had to have some effect. The place was crawling with them, relatively speaking.

Most people thought life must have been bright and cheerful in Switzerland, during the war, when every other country around was blacked out and bombed and hungry, but it wasn't quite true. A Swiss friend told me recently that his countrymen felt as neurotic as coots during the war because in spite of their neutrality the war was pressing all round them in their minds, and the knowledge of misery and death in other countries gave many of them an uneasy feeling of getting off too lightly from the twentieth century. A lot of British conchies had the same feeling.

One I knew volunteered for duty with the Fire Service in London as soon as his exemption was granted. The official recognition of his conscience wasn't enough.

There was another one, Cally Jackson, who wasn't content to wrestle with his conscience. He carried it about on his back with the blood dripping from it. When he met you, he would have a great groan and stare out of pink-rimmed eyes.

'Ah wish tae hell they would come for me the day,' he would say. 'An' get it ower wi'. Prison would be better than this hingin' aboot.' But he was totally exempted at the tribunal. He was worse if anything after that.

'Ah *know* ah'm in the right,' he would groan. 'But is it fair? Look at people like Tash an' Joe gettin' sent overseas. Maybe they'll get killed. Whit right have ah got

172

tae get aff? Even although ah know ah'm right.'

'Tash an' Joe are all for you,' we would tell him.

'So they say,' he would mutter glumly. He left his job and volunteered for farm work, in search of discomfort to ease his soul. In three months he had rheumatism.

'Ah don't mind that,' he said. 'Ah'm bloody safe – naebody's shootin' at me.'

Tash came home, he hadn't been sent overseas. He was stationed somewhere in Yorkshire having the time of his life. Cally used to look at him when he came back on leave the way a man looks at a tenant in the death-cell. Then he slipped quietly away and volunteered for the Army. They turned him down. He eked out the rest of the war digging spuds and feeling like a murderer.

War is hell, all right.

One Has a Duffy at the Auld Chantin' Gemme

The close harmony business was beginning to shape up. Travelling to work on the train with Big Bob gave me two rehearsals a day, and we were away beyond the parallel-thirds stage. I was experimenting with dominant seventh harmonies and contrary motion, and we thought we were just about ready for the big-time. The affair of the Dough School girl at the Locarno was long since forgiven because it had turned out to be a disaster. When Bob took her back to her digs that night he met her friend, who at once started to cut in and steal Bob away. He was rapturous with self-esteem until he started noticing something odd and intense about the friend. It took him a month to suspect dimly that she was a Lesbian, and without waiting to check up, he fled in terror from both of them.

173

We were all set up for a large-scale talent competition at the Locarno anyway. We had bought sheet music and practised with David Alastair at the piano and we were quietly confident. We called ourselves the 'Low Notes'.

On the afternoon of the contest I was sent to Motherwell on a story. I chased it with the sweat streaming down me and both eyes on the clock, and sat on the bus back to town sick with apprehension as time flew by. There was a traffic jam outside the bus station, and trams were lined all along Sauchiehall Street. It didn't occur to me to take a taxi. I ran the whole length of the street and staggered through the doors with about ten minutes to spare before the competition started. Bob and David Alastair were chewing their nails in the lobby because they both sang melody in the trio and it wasn't going to sound very harmonic that way.

When we got backstage it became clear that we had plenty of time. The MC allocated us a number well down the list and there was nothing to do for half an hour but listen to the opposition.

It was nothing to worry about. Some of the singers were actually in tune, but not much more than that. We dismissed them brutally as our turn got nearer and we all started to sweat. We had argued a good deal over the song we should sing, and finally settled on 'Tangerine' because we had arranged a big, high, loud ending for that. Number Eleven went off to good-natured applause, and the MC announced somebody called 'We Three'! There was a silence while we glared at each other and demanded to see the list again. Then we realized he meant us. We came on from the side and clambered up through the orchestra to the piano.

After that there were no difficulties. David Alastair, cold and poised, knocked out the four-bar introduction and we pasted the slats out of 'Tangerine', with the plain ending as written; a half-chorus solo on the piano to let David Alastair show off, and then the last eight bars in chorus, with the big extended ending. We could hear our own noise through the big, expensive amplifying system,

174

smacking the back end of the hall and bouncing back at us, and it sounded fine. So did the applause.

'Chuck the contest,' I said to Big Bob on the way back through the orchestra. 'That's enough. The winners. Money. Fame. Stop the show. Everybody go home.'

'Reck'n that wus real smooth, pardner,' he agreed. 'Where's yer bloody Merry Macs noo?' Conscious of the glances of approval or idle curiosity from stray members of the public, we sat at a table near the dais and waited for the other unfortunate contestants to go through their agony until we might collect the prize. There were three to follow us. We heard out the first of them quavering 'Because'. Big Bob gave me a sorrowing glance and imitated a man thrawing a chicken's neck.

Then a scruffy little boy of about eleven was ushered on the stand. His arrival created a furore of ohs and ahs and we glared at him with hate in our hearts. He had a long discussion with the band leader about his key, and evidently didn't get anywhere, because he eventually stepped up to the mike and launched out on the 'Rose of Tralee' unaccompanied. The pianist picked up the key and joined in. At the second bar the singer flipped up three semitones, and the pianist groped about behind him. By the time the pianist had readjusted, the boy had fallen back about two full tones. He didn't sing more than six consecutive notes in one key, but we were still worried. Crowds love scruffy juveniles, especially when they're really bad. And there was a five-pound note going for the heat.

'They canny pick that,' I said. 'There's a law against bloody child labour.'

'He's probably a forty-year-old dwarf,' David Alastair opined.

'My God,' Big Bob wailed. 'Look!'

The last contestant was being led out. He was being led with passionate care, and musicians were getting up and moving their chairs to let him pass. He was poking before him with a white stick.

'It's a swindle!' Big Bob moaned. 'You canny beat a

175

blind man – it's impossible.'

'Maybe he can't sing,' David Alastair suggested hope-fully.

'What the hell difference does that make?' I asked him. 'He's blind, isn't he? We're ruined.'

'Maybe he'll fa' aff the platform an' break his neck,' Big Bob offered. We looked up eagerly, but the blind singer wasn't co-operating. Once he had touched the mike, and adjusted it with professional fingers, he squared up to it and handed his stick back to whoever was handy, and next second he was quavering out 'Bless This House', with his head thrown back and his face turned up to catch the light and make sure everybody saw it. It was as nice a bit of exploitation as I hope not to see, and we were dished. Crosby could have done a double act with Gipsy Rose Lee and it would have meant nothing after that. Even the choice of song was a blow below the belt. We sat slumped in misery at the unfairness of the world and decided to give up show business for good. When the band leader came over and patted Bob on the back he got no response at all.

'We'll come on crutches next time,' I said cynically. The band leader smirked sympathetically.

'Not a bad act boys,' he said. 'Do you live locally?' Bob nodded.

'Would you be interested in a few Sunday concerts?' the leader asked us.

'What – for money?' we asked.

'Well, not for nothing.' We surrounded him grimly, unbelieving. 'Come and see me Tuesday week,' he said. He was a thin-faced Cockney with rimless glasses. 'Should be able to fix up something, boys. Not many harmony acts about these days.'

We sneered at the blind man on our way out. We were going pro. Over a cup of tea we thrashed the whole future out. Sunday concerts were all right as a beginning. We could do them and still stick to our jobs.

'Would you go fulltime?' Big Bob asked diffidently.

'Durn tootin',' I said. 'How about you?'

'Sure.'

176

David Alastair wasn't so sure, but we soon talked ourselves into a state of reckless enthusiasm. I could hardly wait to see the boss's face when I told him I was resigning to go pro.

My mother thought I was daft, but she didn't worry because she also thought it would never come to anything.

'Do you think I'm *frightened*?' I asked her in irritation. 'This is a *real* prospect – fame and wealth!'

'Och, away an' don't be daft,' she said.

That Friday David Alastair was called up to the RAF. Three days later Big Bob caught a chill in his kidneys and took to bed for a month. With one thing and another, we never got back to see the band leader again.

These are Prison Bars, Mac

One night I was sitting in a tram from Mosspark to Argyle Street counting my money and feeling like Uncle Vanya when the driver shouted upstairs: 'Heh, is that you?'

I shouted back uhuh, and he shouted back: 'Ah thought ah knew the face. Faur fae hame, urn't ye?' I was sitting upstairs out at the front. After thinking it over I went down to see who he was. I didn't know his name, but I knew his face, so I gave him a cigarette and sat on one of the lower steps while he drove through the blackout.

'Seein' a burd hame?' he asked me, and I said:

'Aye, an'll probably have tae walk fae Argyle Street.'

'Ah'll chinge the p'ints an' take ye right hame. Naebody'll know.'

'Aye, right,' I said. 'We can keep the caur in the back green for the night.'

'Gaun steady?' he asked. I said uhuh again.

'Ye picked a helluva place for it, Mosspark,' he muttered. 'Back a beyond at this time a night. Thinkin' a gettin' merrit, masel'.'

'You're no',' I said politely.

'Well, tae tell ye the truth, ah'm no', but she is, so whit can ye dae?'

'Flee the country,' I suggested.

'Fat chance. Ah'm for the high jump this time. Canny see a wey oot at a'.' He meant it.

'Is she pregnant?' I asked him sympathetically.

'Naw, naw, nothin' like that. Ah never got that faur.'

'Well,' I was puzzled. 'Just say ta ta an' that's that.'

'Ach, it's no as easy as that.' He wanted to tell somebody. 'She's nice all right – ah quite like her, nothin' wrang wi' the girl. Her aul' wife thinks ah'm the great wee boy as well. They would feel terrible if ah jouked it. The aul' wife's been buyin' us dishes an' everythin'. Ye canny be rotten wi' people.'

I was incredulous with horror.

'But you must have started it – ah mean, you must have *asked* her.'

'Och, hell, ah never mentioned it. It's the girl. She's daft tae get merrit. Ah took her oot a few times, an' went up tae her hoose, an' that, next thing ah know she's ringin' the bloody bells an' savin' up torn paper for confetti. She's nice, mind ye, we get on all right.'

'Well, tell her,' I said. 'If you don't want to get merrit, you'll jist make her miserable for life.'

The most horrifying thing was his matter-of-factness.

'Ah've tried a few times tae tell her. She jist starts greetin'. Ah hate that. You know the kind of thing, starts greetin' an' askin' me if ah love her. Well, whit can ye dae? Ah love her all right – well, ah like her all right. Quite nice-lookin', tae. She's too nice for me, in fact.'

'An' are you jist gonny get merrit like that, for life?'

'Well, ah mean tae say. It's no' ma idea, but look at it this way – it's bound tae happen some time, innit?'

'My God,' I said.

'How's your burd in Mosspark?' he asked me. 'Got the aul' hooks in ye? She must, if you go the length a Mosspark tae see her.'

'Naw, nothin' like that,' I said easily. 'Jesus, ah'm jist a boy. Hardly oota school.'

'Dae ye think ah'm drawin' the pension? Still, you can talk your wey ooty it. That's ma trouble, nae good at the talkin'.'

'Write your dame a letter, then.'

'Ha ha!' he laughed out loud, delighted. 'Write her a letter when she lives in Dennistoun. Ah pass her hoose every day. It's a cable ah'd have tae send her – tae Bombay or some place. Ach, it'll no' be sa bad. She can cook, that's wan thing. Ah'll be all right for ma chuck.'

I thought, when I left him in Argyle Street and set out to walk the rest of the way home through the night, that other people must be more heroic than I was. Or insane. To be edged into marriage because some girl's mother liked you? Surely it didn't happen in life!

I had a long way to walk and a long time to think, and the farther I walked the more morose I got; not on my account, but on behalf of all the millions of people in the world who drifted into misery laughing when a few unpleasant minutes could get them out of it. That thought lasted me sentimentally as far as Glasgow Cross, and the Tron Steeple donged midnight at me as I passed. Between Glasgow Cross and Barrowland half of my mind was speculating idly on what I would do if somebody shot out of a close and attacked me. From Barrowland to Bellgrove I thought about Alice, and as nobody shot out of any closes, I kept thinking about her the rest of the way as well.

Our little difference on the day of my tribunal appearance was patched up; or rather, it wasn't patched up, it was welded. We didn't see each other for a few days, and I was busy enough with other things not to mind very much. Then Alice telephoned. She wasn't sure whether she should apologize or demand to know what was wrong with me, and I felt such a beast that I apologized. Then she apologized. In ten minutes we were bleating at each other and swearing never to quarrel again. On our dates after that I didn't go to the house. I met her and we walked or went to the pictures. I escaped the egg diet and quite often caught trams home instead of walking.

Everything was fine. I never asked her why I wasn't going to her house and she never told me. After about a fortnight, however, the old routine clicked back into place, eggs, chocolate biscuits and everything. It was just a little quieter in the house. I got the impression that Mr and Mrs Smith divined that we had had a tiff, and were anxious not to inquire into it in case they started it again. But that night, the night I was walking home from Argyle Street, Mr Smith hummed and tilted his head longer than usual after the six o'clock news. Then he blushed, and forced himself to look at me, and said:

'So we'll not be losing you to the army, Cliff?'

Everybody – me, Alice and Mrs Smith, hung in a tight silence for a second.

'Ur, no.' I said gravely. The silence loosened at once and Mrs Smith went on pouring tea and breathing.

'Well,' Mr Smith said. He was in a painful embarrassment, but he knew what he was going to say, and he tried to smile naturally while he said it. 'I always say I can respect a man who sticks to his beliefs.'

'Well, thank you,' I said. Alice looked at the table and the window and her hands and the teapot. Mrs Smith, released from tension, cried out in affectionate scolding:

'I must say I never dreamt for a minute, Cliff! Never dreamt. Of course, *Alice* would never say anything, trust Alice. And you always looked so fine and healthy.'

'Mm, I am,' I said.

'Well, you're quite right,' she cried. 'I just said to Alec, he'll tell you himself, I was just saying, it's terrible when you think of the number of conchies going about and not admitting it. That boy down the street, no you don't know him, that boy down the street, *he's* got himself into a nice safe job in Rolls Royce, big money and everything, Reserved Occupation. He's just as big a conchie as anybody but he'll not admit it.'

'He isn't really a conchie, then, is he?' I suggested reasonably. She made a contemptuous gesture with her hand.

'He's out of the army. If that's not being a conchie I

180

don't know what is. Except he'll not admit it. He thinks nobody can point the finger at *him*.'

'Oh, I don't mind fingers being pointed at me,' I said patiently. I took it as an insult to be bracketed with the boy down the street, but there would be no profit in trying to explain that to Mrs Smith.

'Nobody'll point any fingers at you in this house,' Mr Smith told me with an agonized smile. 'After all, that's a person's own business, if Alice doesn't mind I don't think it's anybody's business.'

Eventually Alice and I escaped.

'You see, it's all right,' she said.

'Uhuh.'

'Well, it is, isn't it?'

'Yes, Alice, it's all right.'

'Of course, I haven't told anybody else, Cliff, honestly, don't worry about that.'

'Why not?'

'Because I won't tell anybody else, that's why not.'

'I mean, why not tell anybody else?'

'Well, it isn't anybody else's business, is it?'

'I suppose it's everybody's business. If I'm getting off easily, people are entitled to know.' I wasn't being bitter or facetious, but Alice disposed of that remark with a loving and impatient sound, refusing to indulge in my child-like maunderings. We didn't go back to the house afterwards, so I did catch a tram halfway home. Now I was playing back the record in my head.

The whole thing was ridiculous. The Smiths had been as nice as they could be, but a hundred years wouldn't be long enough to explain to them that I wasn't in need of sympathy or secrecy. They were willing to accept me despite my shameful secret, and I didn't have a shameful secret. I would never be able to communicate with them on that point. And Alice's loyalty plunged me into gloom as I found myself striding along beside the grey silence of Janefield cemetery. She would never tell anybody, of course. She had probably told the girls in her office that I was in Intelligence, or some other heroic caper.

If Alice doesn't mind I don't think it's anybody's business. That was what Mr Smith had said. Where did he get that stuff? Wait a minute, play that bit of the record again. If Alice doesn't mind I don't think it's anybody's business. If Alice . . .

Why should Alice mind? What did he mean? The oftener I said it over to myself the thicker I felt the prison walls closing round me. I abandoned working from the stated evidence and made up my mind that the reason why the Smiths were ready to fly in the face of convention and respectability and patriotism for my sake was because they were ready to forgive a lot in a son-in-law. And walking past Janefield I knew that I didn't want to be anybody's son-in-law – not anybody's at all. I was too young to die. I covered the last stretch from Parkhead Cross at a good six miles an hour, with the hounds of hell behind me.

That week one of the girls who played hockey at the school had a twenty-first birthday. It was too late to arrange anything fancy, so we all decided to throw a party in the old railway carriage. We brought cakes and sandwiches and lemonade, and I cut a key out of a piece of pasteboard and painted it with aluminium paint from Woolworth's, for a surprise. We played football and hockey as usual, but it was dark early, and we crowded into the carriage and ate the feast by the light of three candles. The feast didn't last long. We made some little speeches and everybody was very gay. After that there was a discussion about the remaining part of the programme, and although the carriage was an awkward place for an ordinary party, with nothing but fixed wooden benches along the sides and across the ends, we blew out two of the candles and had kissing games, mostly one game, the one where the girls sit on the boys' knees and move round to the next boy every ten minutes.

Nan, the birthday girl, was radiant with affection for all mankind at her party. She wore her hair piled up to keep it off her face for hockey, and her eyebrows were permanently arched up too, giving her a look of unbelief and surprise. She looked a real scatterbrain, and she was. She was very slim and neat and light on the knees. After a while I started pulling the pins out of her hair.

'Does your mystery woman let you do that?' she cooed at me, out loud. There were shouts of glee round the carriage.

'No, she's totally bald,' I told Nan.

'She's a man!' somebody shouted.

'No-o,' I said slyly.

'Prove it! Bring her for inspection.'

'Aye, bring her. We're wan wummin short anywey!'

'Shut up, you're all jealous,' Nan chid them. 'You could never bring her from Mosspark, could you, Cliffie-wiffie-wiffie?' she moaned into my ear.

'Who said anything about Mosspark?' I queried.

'You're being spied on!' somebody shouted.

'*We* know!'

'Is she a widow? Widows are rerr!'

'She is not a widow,' I answered back into the dark. 'My widow lives in Perth. She has a title and a castle and she showers me with costly gifts.'

'Hurray!'

'Give us a knock-down to the widow!'

'You should have brought your mystery woman from Mosspark to my party,' Nan said, waggling my nose in her fingers. 'I'm jealous of her.'

'All is over between us,' I told her. 'Never mention her name in my presence again or I'll squeeze you to death,' and I squeezed her to death and felt unfaithful and dastardly happy.

Next time round I got the tall girl, who was not quite as light as Nan but not heavy either, and really beautiful, with clear skin and dark brown eyes and soft lips. The whites of her eyes glinted in the dark reflecting the candle flame. She was so obviously taller than me that she wasn't eligible, but in the dark in the crowd that was irrelevant.

'If you were my height and I was your height I would marry you,' I said glibly.

'So would I,' she said. I touched her mouth with my

fingertip and she shuddered slightly. It was a great party.

On the Friday of that week I met Alice and did one of the most brutal things of my life, and it was even more brutal because I had planned it in detail, and I kept looking at myself and admiring my performance and telling myself how honest and brave I was. I cried off the idea of going to the pictures and we went to a café, to talk. For five or ten minutes neither of us said anything, and then I started my prepared speech, which was that there was no use in going on because we weren't suited to each other. I wasn't paying too much attention to Alice while I said it, but I realized afterwards she must have anticipated it, from the way she sat silent and made it easy. She was so quiet that I wandered off the script and stammered, at a loss for words. But she didn't protest or argue, the way I would have done.

'I kind of had a feeling,' she said.

'I feel mean,' I said, and by this time it was true.

'You don't need to,' she said. 'If you had been mean you wouldn't have turned up at all.'

'I couldn't do that,' I objected.

'It's all right, really.' She wasn't pale or trembling or anything. 'I'll just have to think of what to tell the family.'

'You don't have to tell them anything.'

'Well, they're bound to ask, aren't they? Hm. Mum'll say it was my own fault, of course. It must have been my fault.'

'It's my fault,' I said indignantly. She shook her head and didn't say anything. I didn't know what to do next. I had rehearsed my little speech, and even tried to prophesy Alice's answers, but I hadn't thought of the next move. She saved me again by making it.

'I'll walk you to the car stop,' she said. I nodded, and she took my arm in the blackout outside. I squeezed her hand. We stood and let three trams go before I finally went, and she smiled and waved to me from the stop. I sat on the top deck with my thoughts in the conventional turmoil, vaguely angry because I didn't feel nearly as noble and honest and brave as I should have, and Alice had given a nobler performance than mine. But on top of that I felt prodigiously free. It would never have worked, I told myself, and that was the truth at least.

There was that impassable mental gulf between me with my odd notions and the nice, kindly, un-understanding Smiths. There was the lack of excitement, the kind of excitement I had felt abruptly with the tall girl in the school carriage. And on top of that there were those damned eggs.

A Wee Refreshment

'You'll always be in trouble,' John Bell said, 'if you don't learn that when you see a drunk, your move is to run, boy, and leave him to rot.'

'But that's inhuman,' I objected. 'Maybe he's an innocent character, led astray, there but for the grace of God go I kind of sod.'

'Immaterial, boy. Run, do not walk, to the nearest car stop, alone.' He bent his wide lips in a pouting, professional grin in his great bulging face, defying me to argue with his vast experience of life. Working till nine or ten or eleven every Saturday night, I nearly always acquired a helpless drunk on my way home. Real drunkenness has declined a lot in Glasgow since the days when half the population blew its wages on a Friday night and took home a half-bottle on Saturday night to cure the Sunday hangover, but a lot of people still take a skinful, and most of them managed to find me in those days. They drove me to a panic. I was sure each one was heading for a fatal accident if I personally didn't carry him to his doorstep. The worst kind were those who were so drunk they couldn't even talk.

'Listen, boy,' John said kindly. 'You'll learn. I used to be the same. Did I ever tell you the time I met Willie

Paterson – we were boys at John Street School – the time I met him on the top of a Brigton caur on a Saturday night, too puggled to see his fingers fornent his face. Wurra aul' Zhohnnie, goo' aul Zhohnnie, he was kind of chantin'. So I got a good grip and took him off the caur – he would have been lost anyway out in Auchenshuggle if somebody hadny poured him off. 'Sall right, boy, he kept mutterin', Ah know ma wey hame. But I had to be the Band of Hope boy, took him right to his door.

'Know what happened? His wife came to the door and fell on me. "You're the pig that's been leadin' ma poor man astray!" That's what comes of being a good Samaritan. Be a Levite, boy. Pass by on the other side. And if it's your turn, which it damn well is, it's a pint.'

I didn't accept John's callous philosophy until the same thing happened to me in precise detail. I collected a drunk on the Saturday night bus who turned out to live round the corner from my mother's. He was so staggered that I had to take him right to his door and ring the bell, and a few seconds later I sustained a ringing clout across the ear from his exasperated wife. She offered no explanation for this, but I gather she had reached the same conclusion as Mrs Willie Paterson. It's hard all the same to ignore a drunk completely. Another Saturday night I shared a compartment with one on the late train to Shettleston. He lay muttering and snoring in a corner till the train stopped at Carntyne, and then he stood up and opened the door.

'Zis Clydebank?' he asked me.

'No – Carntyne!' I said, shocked, since Clydebank is a long way from Carntyne in the opposite direction, at nearly midnight on a wartime Saturday night and the last buses to everywhere long since gone.

'My God!' he said, and shambled out on to the platform with his arms waving. 'Where the hell is Carntyne?' I never found out what happened to him.

'But the old drunken days are gone and forgotten,' I pleaded with John Bell. 'I mean, Scotsmen don't drink any harder than anybody else nowadays. It's just a legend.'

'That's right,' he said, 'That's right, Cliff,' and patted my arm genially. 'I've said the same thing a thousand times. Last time I was at the NUJ conference in Southport. Do you know Southport? It's one of those coast resorts in Lancashire where they carelessly built the sea forty miles from the promenade – the tide goes out practically to Nova Scotia. So the city fathers have built themselves a toy sea beside the promenade – a boat lake about the same size as Lock Katrine.

'Well, we had a good night on the Saturday at the hotel, and got to kip about 3 am having drink taken, and I mean taken, boy. But I was having an argument with a London delegate about these Scots drinkers, and particularly these Glesca drinkers. "You're just an ignorant provincial nyaff," I told this citizen. "You'll get worse drunks in London or Liverpool than you ever get in Argyle Street." So one thing borrowed another, and he bet me a quid that the first real drunk we saw at Southport would be a Scotsman.

'We took a walk for the imitation sea breezes on the prom on the Sunday, me and this misguided Cockney comrade. And there we saw a helluva commotion – the whole population hangin' over the prom laughin' its melts out at what transpired to be two men in a boat away near the horizon on this grandiose paddle pond. They were tryin' to change places, and boy, these boys were drunk.

'"There you are," I said to the Londoner. You could see what the boys were – wee tight serge suits, big boots – Durham miners, or Mancunians through for the Wakes. The lad was fishin' out a quid from his wallet when we heard a voice across the lake – the voice that breathed o'er Eden, Cliff.

'"Aw, fur God's sake staun stiddy an' see's a haud ae the effen oar!" So don't tell me about Scotch temperance. boy, it cost me a good quid that day. An' what the hell was *any* Scotsman, drunk or sober, doin' in Southport in April?'

It is still true that the Glaswegian tends to do everything to excess. It must be the mixture of the old Highland Calvinist and the shanty Irish. The Calvinist either shuns the demon drink totally or he attacks it without quarter. And the Irishman likes a hoot, there's no doubt.

In my lust to be a real, arrived man I followed the Glasgow tradition when I found myself in drinking company. A half of whisky and a half-pint of beer to chase it. You throw the whisky back whole and then hold the whisky glass up carefully to let the last warmed drop fall into the beer, for no reason except ritual. People get drunk quickly and royally this way, but not so quickly as the wine-bibbers. The wine man is out for a drunk rather than a drink.

In my youth I saw some of the last jake-drinkers, the desperate characters who had arrived at methylated spirits as the cheapest and quickest route to blindness, but they died out during the war. I heard about the lads who ran coal-gas bubbles through a bottle of milk to give it a kick, and the others who wined off diluted Brasso. I never saw them although I did know a man who favoured eau-de-cologne as a regular tipple.

And I once knew a man who briefly operated an illicit still in a ground-floor tenement flat in Parkhead. The cheek of this dumbfounded me. You can understand a man setting up the pot behind a Skye Mountain, or even on the Wee Cumbrae Island, but a distiller who sets up in business in Parkhead is a real individual. The only complication in his apparatus was a tube consisting of about two thousand wooden bobbins, the kind they wrap cotton thread round, which led from the still to the open air some yards away from the kitchen window, to carry the distinctive smell of alcohol away from the house. He risked only one making before he dismantled it and stared the neighbours right back in the face. The reason why I knew about this venture was that I had a friend who was lucky enough to be offered a glass of the cratur. He fell maudlin drunk instantaneously, and when he wakened next day and drank a cup of weak tea, he fell maudlin drunk again, and kept going helpless every time he touched any liquid at all for the next seven or eight days. It was very inconvenient.

The wine is nothing like that today, and will not leave its devotees either blind or insane. It's a fortified wine legitimately made, in Britain, with some far-fetched chemical resemblance to port and sherry. It's cheap, and a couple of bob will buy a thumping beaker over the bar counter. When you chase it with beer you are really going somewhere, though you may not be fit to recognize it when you get there. Only a few Glasgow pubs specialize in this wine trade. At the other end of the scale you can buy a glass of claret or Burgundy over the counter, and people do.

Drinking with the family had a lot of the atmosphere of a Sunday school picnic, although we didn't have tinnies round our necks on pieces of white tape. When Harry or Jackie or Jimmie came home on leave I naturally went out for a drink with them, usually to the Kirk Hoose, which was a coaching stage before my mother lived in Shettleston. It was called the Kirk Hoose because the parish church originally stood beside it. Sixty years ago the parish minister started negotiations to buy the land and close the pub because the congregation were in the habit of having a noggin on Sunday on their way to or from the kirk. Whatever happened, the pub was never closed. It was the church that moved up the hill out of harm's way, and the Kirk Hoose is still there.

Our trips there were like Sunday school outings because we had no intention of getting drunk. We just liked the atmosphere and the talk and the taste of the beer. By this time David was in the Merchant Navy. He and Jimmie both had a fondness for exotic native souvenirs – Jimmie had long ago promised David that he would bring him home the skull of a m'Bongo m'Bongo warrior. He brought home a pith helmet instead. David turned up once with a fez, and then an assortment of linen tropical hats. Jackie produced a forage cap of the Spanish Republican Army. One summer evening when we had the unlikely coincidence of the three of them all home at the same time, we were leaving the house for a stroll up to the Kirk Hoose when Jackie tried on the pith helmet in front of the hall mirror. The three of us looked at him. We didn't discuss the thing. We just found the other hats and picked one each. My mother rushed to the door after us.

'Take those stupid things off!' she demanded. 'People'll think you're drunk, or tramps, or something.'

'We ur drunk tramps,' Jackie grinned.

The regular barman started when we lined along the bar at the Kirk Hoose. We eyed him gravely without saying anything, and at last he said: 'Well, gents, what'll it be?' He never mentioned the hats. We felt that we had added to the colour and life of Shettleston. We took our pints to a table in the corner and sat down, but kept our hats on. We were proving something that seemed important at the time. If four clean, respectably-dressed people do something outrageously odd without betraying that they think it's odd, people will conclude it must be all right; there must be a good reason for it.

The customers rolled into the Kirk, looked at us, some of them said hello; they got their drinks, and then looked back, and we smiled affably, and they smiled back and turned away wondering if they had forgotten something.

It might have been the same summer night the barman started shouting Time barely after nine o'clock. Closing time was halfpast nine, but they started shooting the customers out early during the war, and it grated on us. I was facing a new pint, and I could never drink great quantities of liquid in a gulp. I left half of it, and we bought some bottles of beer to take home for supper. This in itself was a social innovation in Sandyhills. It's a respectable, perjink wee place, and although most people in it like a drink, they would have considered it a mark of depravity to cart an unashamed armful of screwtops through the streets. Jimmie didn't see life that way, and we all agreed with him. We made it so obvious that the most perjink neighbours were forced to notice it, and we felt we were removing the Victorian stigma from the honest pint.

This night I came from the Kirk feeling bitter and aggrieved.

'I canny drink a pint in a wanny,' I said. 'Eightpence worth of beer lost forever.'

'I didny leave any of mine,' Jimmie said thoughtfully.

'But you're a quick drinker,' I said. He leered at me and started to unbutton his loose raincoat with one hand. The other hand was in the pocket-slit of the coat. It was clutching a full pint measure, with the head foaming and not a drop spilled.

'I'll drink it in peace,' he sniggered.

My oldest brother Harry was in the Navy now too. My four brothers-in-law were in the forces; Mattie's husband Bill in the Regular Navy, Mary's husband George in the RAF and Johanne's husband Johnnie in the Navy. Flora was married to a regular RAF man. In various random groups according to leaves the family made a formidable rank along the bar of the Kirk Hoose. They were good days, in between other things.

It was impossible to tell what kind of war Jimmie was in, since fantasy merged so easily into fact. Jackie had lost his ship at Dunkirk and was washed up on the Belgian coast. He gathered a group of six other strays and after failing to persuade a Belgian fisherman to lend them a boat, had to sail back to England with the unhappy fisherman tied up in the locker of the launch. He lost a chip off his shoulder and had a troublesome series of bone-grafts afterwards, in time to be ready for the Norwegian invasion, where he saw dreadful sights and was left with the odd sensation for some months that he was poised in space watching himself going through the motions of life. But even when he described this seriously to me, cheerfulness kept breaking in.

Alfie, my piano-playing schoolmate, crashed in the Atlantic on duty with Coastal Command and was reported missing. He beached some days later on a golden shore fringed with palm trees, and took it that he had drifted round Cape Horn and landed in Tahiti until a Wren marched briskly across his line of vision. He spent a riotous few days in the Scilly Isles where he had landed, and came home glowing with new experiences. Then he transferred to Bomber Command and was reported missing again, and that time he didn't come back at all.

Hugh, the effortless winner of jauries and football and girls, was in Bomber Command too. A classmate once said of him that he was so jammy that if he jumped oot a windae, he would fa' up. He was the child of the gods. And he was reported missing too, and never came back. I never got accustomed to death like this; it seemed too absurd. My brother-in-law Bill was serving in the *Curacoa*, convoying the *Queen Mary* from New York on a sunny Sunday morning when there was a confusion of understanding and the liner ran amidships into the little ship which was sailing in zig-zag ahead of her. The smaller ship went down in pieces and the *Queen Mary* couldn't, under wartime sailing orders, stop or even slow down for survivors. We were stupefied with grief.

David spent nine months in New York waiting for a ship to be refitted. He drank in Greenwich village and became half-engaged to an American girl and lived the life of Riley, and brought me back a luxurious brief case with all my initials on it in solid gold. He was afflicted with the wanton generosity of the family and the house was loaded with such trinkets as rawhide whips and Indian sandals. I never knew until he left the sea that he had hated every minute of it.

Life is a Gamble, if You Can Find a Bookie

A vet, or a stable boy, or a jockey, or a foreign spy, knew somebody who knew Big Bob, and wanted to put him on to a good thing. It was a horse called Red Letter, and it had done badly in its two races to date, but it was a dead cert for its next appearance at Stockton, and it would be running at thirty-three to one. The prospects were so hush-hush that Big Bob had to tell me. That's the way to gamble, I reckoned; know somebody who knew. But after all these years I didn't know where to lay a bet.

The old crumbling cottages in Shettleston Road were long demolished, the cottages with a microscopic shop stuck in one of them and the wee man who took thruppence each way or sixpenny three-cross-doubles. Bob's father was experienced in posting bets, but I didn't know how to go about it, and the suspense was unbearable. For the first time I started to comb the racing programmes in the paper, and a fortnight later Red Letter turned up at Stockton, and at thirty-three to one too. The race was on the next day. It was Monday and my day off and I had an unbroken pound note ready to turn into a fortune.

Just in time I realized I knew a bookie. Stevie. I had met him one night months before in the Kirk Hoose, where he was drinking very little and looking sad and alert. At opening time I hurried up to the pub and bought myself a half-pint of beer and waited.

He didn't turn up, and I was chary of inquiring about him, but I still had the pound and I couldn't keep on drinking, so I started asking questions and eventually ran him down in another pub nearer Parkhead. He remembered me all right.

'I want to back a horse, Stevie,' I said nervously.

'Don't be daft, son,' he said. 'Gam'lin's a mug's

gemme.'

'Aye, I know. But I just want to back this one horse. Red Letter, at Stockton tomorrow, thirty-three to one.'

'If it's thirty-three to wan it canny *run*. That's nae wey tae bet. Long shots are nae good tae anybody.'

'Will you take the money?' I insisted.

'That's ma business, son. But ah don't want tae take it – honest, you're makin' a mistake.'

'I can afford the money, Stevie, never mind.'

'It's no' that at a', come on, noo – whit'll it get ye? Gam'lin'? It'll ruin your life.'

'I know,' I said. 'Red Letter, a pound to win.'

'Aye, aye, haud on tae your money for a minute. Ye see, you jist don't know about gam'lin', son. My God, ah laid ma furst bet when ah was twelve – ah used tae take lines tae the bookie for ma faither, an' wan day ah got a tip, an' took a bob an' put it on for masel', in ma faither's name. A double. It came up for mair than a fiver.'

'Hotsy totsy,' I said. 'That's the kind of thing. Red Letter, here's the dough.'

He didn't seem to hear me.

'Ah was that frightened at the thought ae a fiver ah couldny get the courage to collect the winnin's. But the bookie met ma faither an' haunded the money tae him. Ye know, the auld man came hame an' gave me the leatherin' ae ma life. "That'll learn ye tae gam'le on hoarses!" he bawled at me. If ma mither hadny stoapt him he would have kilt me stone deid.

'But it was nae use – ah had tasted blood. Ah was done fur. Ah've been a gam'ler ever since. If ah had loast that bob ah might never have laid another bet, an' made somethin' ae masel'. For God's sake, you're a decent young fellah, son – you've got education, an' brains – ye'll make somethin' oota yersel'.'

'Sure,' I said. 'But I just want to make this one bet. Red Letter, at Stockton.'

'Look! Look at me! Whit the hell am ah? A naebody – a bloody wreck, if you knew the truth. Ah've had thousands,

194

gam'led the lot. Ah'll have thousands mair, an' whit the hell good will it dae me?'

'I'm different,' I assured him.

'Ye think that. But honest, son, ye don't *know*.'

The pound was damp with sweat from my hand, but Stevie went on and on. Every Glasgow bookie I have ever met since has the same patter. Gambling horrifies them. All I knew then was that when Stevie was talked out, he was going to take my pound whether he liked it or not. But as he went on and on with his story of doom, it grew harder and harder to agree with him and still press the bet on him. Completely unconvinced, but over-mastered, I went home half an hour later, with my pound still in my pocket. Red Letter won by about two hundred lengths the next day.

Maybe I was lucky. Maybe I would have turned out to be a bloody human wreck if I had backed it and won, but I don't believe it. Gambling is too much of a bore. All I know is that I could have used £33 and it's gone forever. Later on I got into the habit of spending a shilling on the football pools every week, and that struck me as the dastardly limit of the reckless life for me, but I got tired of filling in the coupons. Something carefree without red tape, like the French National Lottery, would be handier for my type of idiotic timid gambling. I won three prizes in that when I was in France on holiday, nearly fifty shillings altogether.

The Glasgow shovel shops are the thing for serious gamblers. There's been a lot of official talk about legalizing cash betting, and it hasn't got to the Statute Book yet, but Glasgow is a jump ahead of the law. There are about 200 betting shops operating around the city today, paying the tribute of a regular fine for breaking the law and carrying on soberly in between times.

Some of them are old vacant shops in mean streets. The first sign I had that they existed at all was in a side street in Gorbals when I went into a grimy little shop for cigarettes and found twenty people standing glumly listening to a loudspeaker. There was no shop counter and no shop stock. Instead, there was a kind of ticket window in the back wall.

The better-class joints have chairs and television sets to keep the customers happy between results. The bookie I met in one of these was a third-generation operator, with a university education in science, a Jaeger sweater and a bedside manner.

'The television set is a bad thing, of course,' he said thoughtfully. 'It makes the place too much of a rest-home – it isn't really good for people to get into a betting shop and then linger on and on – bad for them in the sense that it encourages them to gamble too much. But what can you do? If one shop has a television set, the others have to follow suit or lose trade.'

I had been planning to write a newspaper piece about betting shops, and he was delighted to co-operate.

'Of course the shops are illegal,' he agreed. 'But the climate of opinion has changed – the legislation will come almost certainly, and in the meantime we pay the fines and look cheerful. We pay the fines of any customers found on the premises too, of course. Bad for business if innocent customers get fined or kept in prison overnight just for patronizing us.

'This isn't a shovel shop, by the way. Winnings are held until after the last result of the day. I don't approve of the shovel system, personally – don't know why they call it shovel. Maybe it's shuffle. The shovel shops pay out right away after each race. Well, it stands to reason it's bad. It encourages the clients to lay their winnings on the next race and have a bet on every race on the card. Gamblers have to be protected against themselves, and it's up to the bookie to protect them. They are our livelihood, after all.'

The gambling shops have a running commentary service laid on by telephone line by Exchange Telegraph. The whole thing is very businesslike, and the Dean of Guild Court has to give its approval to premises for use as betting shops, although the law says they don't exist. The funny thing is that while the shops are flourishing, the Glasgow greyhound tracks which ten years ago were declaring dividends of thousands per cent are falling on tougher and tougher times. The customers are vanishing. And a lot of them must be vanishing into the warmth and the television of the betting shops. But the shops need the tracks to provide races for the customers to bet on. So the shops put a few pounds in a kitty every week to keep the dog tracks from going bankrupt. It all helps to preserve the purity of British bloodstock or something.

The Purest Diamond

In 1957 they ran an X-ray campaign in Glasgow to attack what remained of the ancient scandal of Glasgow's tuberculosis rate. More than two-thirds of the whole population queued at the X-ray stations, a number that staggered the most hopeful officials.

The campaign's biggest success was to persuade people in Glasgow to call tuberculosis tuberculosis. They called it poor health where I came from, as the old Celts talked about the Góod Folk, in the hope that by using the right name they would be left in peace. It was in the same class as syphilis in respect of horror and shame. I can remember my mother casting dubious eyes on one or two of my childhood friends and warning me that they didn't look as if they were 'in good health'. They just looked peely-wally to me.

It's easy to say that tuberculosis was the poor man's disease, but the shame and secrecy that wrapped it were more fundamental and superstitious than the shame of mere poverty. It must have been some lingering remnant of the underground Calvinist theory that deadly sickness was a judgement on sin, original or inherited, and tuberculosis was elected as the particular judgement since syphilis was too disgraceful even to think about in secret.

But it was always somebody else, somebody fairly remote, that it happened to, until the time I was working on night shift as a sub-editor on a daily paper and looking round in despair for a way to change the pattern of life. Working at night gnawed at me. It was pleasant enough at the time, but it made the weeks and months fly too evenly away, and then the years. It was pleasant to be free during the day while other people worked, but disturbing to be starting to work while other people went home for the evening. It would be wrong to exaggerate this. There is a kind of stoic satisfaction in renouncing the routine pleasures of society, a histrionic satisfaction if you like; but histrionics do wear thin when they don't vary. And sub-editing a newspaper is a fascinating business until the basic tricks are learned. After that it's routine like any other routine.

At least I was trained in coming home late, in the small hours. At one or two or three o'clock in the morning the city streets would still be populated with the strays of the night; late dancers and late drinkers passing through, and loafers and drifters living their lives and holding their society round the coffee stalls; the scruffy petty crooks and the low-lifers looking for the money for a drink or a bed, and the drab little colony of prostitutes who represent Glasgow's commercial vice and make sex seem like such a lousy idea. On fine nights if I missed one of the night trams or if I was on the graveyard shift I would walk the five or six miles home.

Sometimes I would carry a walking stick to persuade myself that I might be set upon somewhere along George Street. It made a good ringing sound on the pavements. The walk never became automatic or monotonous.

Walking at night through the city is a kind of drug that sharpens the senses and releases the imagination. I wrote dramas and acted them in my head and felt unconquerable or unbearably sentimental watching the clear cold outlines of things under the moon, the pale flat highlights and the sharp black still shadows.

So I wrote a drama in my head and crept into the house one morning at six o'clock and wrote it quickly before it could fade, and the next day I went to see two friends to arrange to do something about it. I had never quite escaped show business. At some time or other I found myself lured into a concert party that had been started as an offshoot of a tennis club in Tollcross. The members couldn't agree on whether it was worth going on with and I was invited to pass judgement on it. Without actually going so far as to join the tennis club, I found myself writing extra material and doing funny pieces and acting as compère for the show. It was put on in a minute church hall in Shettleston, with every seat packed and customers sitting on the radiators, and the public acclamation was so loud that the concert party started to get bigger than the tennis club and got carried away with itself. There were actually only three or four people in the whole show who had anything like talent, but they had enough to keep it moving and infect the enormous cast of supers.

It was two of these talented chums I went to see that next day. One was an old school acquaintance, Alec McDougall, a pianist and wit, and a conchie to boot. The other, Jack Diamond, started out as a singer. He was a celebrated boy soprano in his time, in fact, and won big festival firsts with automatic precision. By this time he was a tenor, and his voice was startlingly beautiful and sensitive. He played the cornet in a brass band on the side, but that never arose.

He was a long thin boy with a thin tragic laughing face, and he must have been funny from birth, but he was only now spreading out as an amateur comic. He wasn't a synthetic joke-teller, he was just funny, and there's no way of explaining that kind of funniness. I was doing impersonations, but I was doing them as a kind of cold study, while he used to throw off impressions from nowhere, or turn into characters that had occurred to him from the blue, characters that didn't exist until he thought of them.

The natural droll is the most difficult of all men to describe, because he did things and said things that wouldn't have been funny done or said by somebody else. Sometimes I would see him on an early morning train going into Queen Street Station. The compartment he travelled in was always crowded with teenage girls who wanted to listen to him doing things like reading the morning paper or telling them about his boss. On one such morning when I was on the train too, they landed in a compartment already occupied by two morning-weary middle-aged businessmen trying not to notice that the day had started. They, the two strangers, gave the girls a lack-lustre scowl and put their newspapers up to hide. Jack looked fairly bleary and early-morning himself, but when he said something commonplace there was something about the sound of his own voice that reminded him how ridiculous everything was, and he immediately began to imitate himself. The two middle-aged strangers shrank farther behind their papers, but by the time the train got to Queen Street, fifteen minutes later, they were indignantly, unbelievingly choking with mirth.

The thing I had written was a burlesque thriller serial I felt could be sold for radio, but I didn't want to sell the script. I wanted to present the BBC with the whole show in a parcel. The hero was a private detective who couldn't detect, the villain was a surrealistic character dedicated to villainy as a calling, and the third character was the hero's Glasgow assistant, who didn't think much of dangerous adventures and always had to get home to his granny's for tea at five o'clock. We met in one another's houses on my nights off and rehearsed till it went like lightning. I had cast Jack as the detective, but after the first rehearsal he made the assistant a bigger thing than either of the other two characters, and we switched the roles round to let him do it.

I had years ago met Moultrie Kelsall, the drama producer at the BBC in Glasgow, when he encouraged me to write plays that I never got round to, and I took the script up to sound him out about it. He read it over sitting in one of the corridors they use for lounges at Broadcasting House in Glasgow, and then persuaded me to try it on the Variety Department instead. We fixed a time for an audition, and the three of us turned up at Broadcasting House feeling uncertain and angry.

'We need a lot of sound effects,' I said to Howard Lockhart, who was running the Variety Department. 'It doesn't sound like anything without them. Can we have them?'

His voice came through the studio loudspeaker from the control room.

'. . . be all right, we'll imagine them. Or you can indicate them as you go along, if you feel it's necessary.'

We looked at one another in despair. We needed sound effects badly.

'. . . ready if you like to try it now,' came the voice. We glared up at the control room and somebody nodded kindly behind the glass panel. I shrugged my shoulders.

'Tring tring,' I started. 'Hello?'

The action limped along for a minute or so, the point where the villain's eight hundred henchmen sawed the floor away from the detective's office and the heroes plunged into the underground burn beneath the building.

Jack gave a long dying yell, and then leaned forward and carefully enunciated:

'Splash,' in a low, intimate tone.

'. . . a minute. That's great. Just like that. Better than sound effects,' the voice boomed out of the loudspeaker from the control room. 'Funniest thing I've heard in years.'

We were well away. We never did use the studio sound

effects, although we sometimes came to the microphone later, when the show was running, with odd bits of stuff tied round our necks with string, for rattling or thumping or scraping when some special noise was necessary. In the second instalment I wrote in nearly as many sound effects as dialogue.

There were seventeen or eighteen subsidiary parts, which we shared among us.

People should really have early struggles when they decide to take up broadcasting, but whether it was a dull move or not, we were in at the first shot. There were snags, of course. There was no place in broadcasting schedules for a fifteen minute serial. *Canny Reid* was finally fitted in as a spot to ballast a half-hour discoveries programme, and cut to seven minutes.

'It makes us look like amateurs, kind of,' Jack said. 'My Gawd, how I *loathe* amateurism. It's that common herd, they give me the jandies, I swear I absolutely swear. Hell. See, I swore.'

'Money is better than amateurism,' I said.

'Hee, hee,' he said.

'Have you read the contract?' Alec asked me. 'If you miss a broadcast they can send you to Devil's Island for life. See it – this wee row of dots at the bottom. It's printing.'

'Sign it quick,' Jack said. 'A vacation in the tropics, chaps, free board and floggings. We're in. Stars. Ah'm buyin' a big automatic autograph-signin' pen. It works that quick you can gi'e folk your autograph before they have time to escape.'

This discoveries programme was scheduled to be recorded on Sunday afternoons in a cinema in Paisley, so that there was no difficulty about getting time off for the shows. We had always imagined performing our little serial in an empty studio without an audience, and we resented being put on a stage like a music-hall act, but we soon found we were wrong, and that everything sounded better when there were people there to laugh at the funny bits, especially as they did laugh. We still didn't like being involved in an amateur-discoveries programme, but as we got into the thing the resentment became less a matter of dignity and more one of sympathy for the discoveries, who turned up from all the corners of Scotland every week with bright rosy illusions that fame had come to them, and trailed back to the corners of Scotland every week to go back to their jobs and never be heard of again. Everybody outside the entertainment business has naif notions about this fame business that they would discard if they thought for just a moment. They imagine that one broadcast or one turn on the Empire stage is practically stardom, and never stop to reflect that as audiences they hear hundreds of people broadcasting without remembering their names or expecting to hear them again. The discoveries business is a particularly callous kind of exploitation. It's cheap and easy to organize, it produces a lot of really terrible entertainment and it has nothing to offer its victims but a short exposure to the public and a long turn of disappointment. The big stars who started as discoveries would have become big stars in any case, without getting mixed up in any discoveries nonsense.

During the run of the programme, we got used to seeing the parade of one-timers and putting them at their ease with all the smooth confidence of old pros with three broadcasts behind them. We didn't forget them all. One of the doomed acts that turned up in the third week was a singing sister act, and one of the sisters was so nice that Alec kept a hold of her after the broadcast and married her. I was ready to get married myself, but just at this time it didn't seem likely. The difficulties had started, though I hadn't realized it, at that birthday party in the old railway carriage when I first kissed the tall girl with the dark hair. Later we fell into an easy kinship with the excuse that short men and tall girls had a common bond in their lack of averageness. She was well sought after, and I found plenty of girls to keep me interested, but the flavour wasn't in them, and we finally dropped the excuse and started to go steady, in the face of a lot of opposition from a lot of quarters, including Big Bob, who had known her longer than I had and was beginning to entertain serious feelings about her. By this time she was working in Edinburgh and we had decided for the seventh or eighth time to forget the whole thing, but it was impossible to forget it.

By the second instalment of *Canny Reid* we felt we were getting grip of the radio business. We were familiar with the corridors and the attendants and the clean quiet smell of the studios at Broadcasting House where we had Sunday morning rehearsals before travelling in two busloads to the cinema in Paisley for the show. The orchestra liked our material, and some of the lines in the script were being adopted as catchwords among the studio attendants. We had the same cheerful illusion as the transient discoveries that success was in the bag, and maybe that was something, after all. In spite of odd arguments and resentments, a BBC series is always an amiable community. But Jack wasn't on top of his form, although he was good. Little things worried him irrationally. When I wrote the scripts, I wrote them straight off with three carbon copies, on blue-tinted paper I had bought cheap, and he developed an attachment to it. He was insistent about using this draft on stage instead of the final script of the complete show that was mimeographed on foolscap sheets by the BBC.

At the fifth rehearsal he turned up looking pale and even thinner than usual, and sickly worried in case anybody should think he was ill. He was ill, all the same. He had to call off the sixth show and go into hospital for observation. We carried on with the help of another regular in the show who accepted the part apologetically and made a good job of it without being Jack Diamond. After the sixth show was over I took a train to Edinburgh to do something about my own personal life.

Although the audiences were still laughing their heads off at *Canny Reid*, and other broadcasters liked its calculated lunacy, the listener research returns for the show were poor and orders were given to close it after the eighth week. It was just on the New Year and I had five days off. I brought New Year in in Edinburgh, and on the third of January I came home with the dark-haired girl to see about getting married. A couple of days later Alec and I went to visit Jack in hospital. It was a hellish experience.

The thinness of his face now was the thinness of skin stretched tight over bone with no flesh between and his eyes were huge and moist back in the sockets. And something in him made jokes impossible. The source of jokes itself had dried up.

'You shouldn't worry, Jack,' I insisted, feeling lost and God help me, resentful at his unshakeable gloom. 'You're in the best place for getting fixed up.' He shook his head bleakly and impatiently.

'You'll feel brighter after a few weeks' rest,' Alec tried to comfort him. 'I'll never feel brighter,' he answered. The incorrigible drollery was completely gone. He had the single-minded despair of a frightened child, and I knew that it was only the temporary depression of illness.

'I'll be writing a sequel to *Canny Reid*,' I said. 'For the summer.'

'No,' he said. 'No.' And then his voice broke and he said: 'I know. There's somethin' here that shouldny be here.' And to our horror, tears started up and flowed down his cheeks and he rolled his head over on the pillow to hide them. There was no comfort for him. But he apologized in a weak voice and told us not to worry when we were going away.

They Should Subsidize It, It's Good for the Country

I felt I should have had a lot of money to launch into marriage, but money would never behave rationally with me. Most of the money I had made as a tiny radio star had vanished agreeably in weekends in Edinburgh that I couldn't force myself to regret. Some people are masterful with money, and I suppose it's a good idea. At that time I still thought that one day I would be. Now I know it's something you have to be born with. It's like having a neat little house with everything in good repair and always some sherry in the sideboard in case of unexpected guests. Now I know the kind of house I live in will always have a bit falling off that I mean to fix some time, and if any guest is unexpected he can take his chances or bring his own sherry. I've drunk ours. Once I kept a bottle of whisky in the sideboard for nearly a month, but there's a limit to what flesh and blood can stand.

We had always been resolved on a quiet, simple wedding in any case. Anything in the nature of conventional ostentation wearied me. Since there was no money around, we could have it our own way. My mother and my sisters refused to believe we could be so disgraceful, but as the days went on you could see the realization dawning in their faces that I actually meant a quiet wedding when I said a quiet wedding. It dawned like that cloud the size of a man's hand, and they were perfectly disgusted. I made an appointment for eleven-thirty on a Saturday morning in the registrar's office at Parkhead, and as far as I was concerned, that was everything taken care of.

'That's nae weddin' at a',' my mother protested. 'It's

no' decent.'

'It's legal,' I said cheerfully. Whenever we started arguing about this I always found myself giggling, like somebody who is being tickled against his will. I knew I wasn't going to change my standpoint or retreat, and I knew my mother would never stop trying. I didn't want to be unkind about it, but I didn't mean to be influenced, either, and whenever she returned to the attack I started tittering helplessly. It must have been very irritating.

'What's the use of arguing?' I would splutter. 'I'm stoney broke!'

'Stoney broke!' she would echo in disgust, dismissing that paltry argument. 'Stoney broke!' And she would shove me impatiently. This would make me titter even more, and she would shove me again. Soon she would be shoving me all round the house while I spluttered and laughed helplessly until I was sore. Jimmie and David would look on patiently.

'Help me!' my mother would scold them. 'Make this stubborn toad see reason!' This would start David tittering too, while Jimmie would point out that if I was broke, I was broke, and what the hell was the use of a fancy wedding anyway?

'I give this family up,' my mother would end up disgustedly. 'You've got nae pride.'

'That's right.'

I had found two unfurnished rooms in Hillhead, at the west end of the city, just on the banks of the Kelvin; a new and alien land. The only regrettable thing wasn't the absence of a fancy wedding, but the lack of any furniture to put in them. The thought of this embarrassed me. But since I hadn't had the foresight to have a lot of money, there was nothing to be done about it. We would be rich in time anyway. But a member of a big family is never entirely without means. My mother donated a bed, and there was an ancient and forbidding wicker three-piece suite my father had once brought from Madeira. It was agony to sit on, and on quiet nights it creaked spontaneously

207

throughout the hours of darkness, but it looked all right. I had a bookcase full of books and the loan of a wireless, and Anna had some century-old heirloom china and a little box with six knives in it. At nine o'clock on the Saturday morning, when my mother was still incredulous and horrified, a lorry came to do this nice light flitting, and Jimmie took control of it and insisted on paying for it while I brushed my shoes. At eleven o'clock I caught a tramcar to Parkhead to meet my bride.

'You'll have to take a taxi, at least,' my mother cried in despair. 'What for?' I asked her. 'Am I lame, or something?' But she was so flabbergasted by this deliberate callousness that I telephoned the local taxi man and asked him to meet me at the registry office after the wedding.

'I'll be there, don't worry,' my mother said. 'Don't you dare,' I told her. 'There'll be nothing to see.'

The wedding group consisted of the principals, and an old colleague and friend from my reporting days, and Anna's young sister, looking tense and stricken. We hit the registry office in nice time and were taken to a pleasant little room at the back, with a carpet on the floor and an electric fire going, for it was a cold January. There was nothing grudging about the ceremony. The registrar gave a well-pointed little speech assuring us of the significance and validity of a civil marriage and wished us well, and proceeded to the business with quiet and very forceful formality. I could sense Anna's sister feeling solemn and weepy and fighting back a fit of the giggles.

The best man produced the ring, which was an heirloom from Anna's mother, and I started to fit it on. It wouldn't go past the top knuckle, of course, and after a short struggle I heard myself muttering: 'Just keep your finger bent and it'll stay there for the meantime.' We left the office thoughtfully and found my mother and my sister Johanne waiting for us outside, beside the taxi.

'Thought you would get away, eh?' my mother cried triumphantly, and emptied a pound of confetti inside my shirt. The tension was released, everybody was happy.

The four of us climbed into the taxi, with passers-by glancing round incuriously, and Johanne shouted through the cab window: 'Roosty pockets! Hard up! Hard up!' At least we didn't miss that ritual. I dug out all my change and heaved it out on to the pavement, and we rolled away waving while my mother brandished a penny and laughed and sniffed all at the same time. We had lunch in a private cubicle at the Royal, with a flask of wine, and then the happy couple caught the McBrayne's bus for a five-hour trip through a snowstorm to Tarbert Loch Fyne while the best man took the best maid to the afternoon show at the Odeon. It was so cold on the bus that we huddled under a rug with our feet tucked up and opened a case and drank the half-bottle of gin I had packed for emergencies, neat.

'Well, here we are,' I said in the darkness near Lochgilphead, and guzzled a shot from the neck of the bottle. 'Squalid, innit?'

'Putrid,' my wife said. 'Hurry up with the bottle.'

It wasn't traditional or even romantic in the conventional sense. It was merely strange, partly because there was none of the strangeness we might have expected. But it wasn't squalid or putrid; it was a time for breathing, an end of uncertainty. After the snowstorm, the sun shone in January in the Highlands and we had a village to ourselves, unvisited by any other stranger. But we left for home before the week was over because we weren't sure that we could pay the hotel bill for a whole week.

There was plenty of space in our living room, on all sides of the furniture. We had yards of some white material that we draped over boxes and suitcases so that they might easily have been bits of furniture as long as you looked at them from one angle, like a stage set, and we both went out to buy a pound of frying steak and a pound of onions. While it was frying I unpacked my books from the wooden box they had travelled in, and set two places on top of the box, as we didn't appear to have a table. It was then we remembered we didn't have a fork either, and it's quite difficult to eat fried steak with two knives instead of a knife and fork, but it tasted good. After the meal I strolled along Great Western Road to a cluttered hardware shop and asked for two forks.

'No,' I said, thinking that we would probably do a lot of entertaining. 'Make it four.'

'Four forks,' the girl said. 'Eh, will it be just *using* ones?' Using ones were one-and-thruppence each. They lasted a long time, till the plating wore off to show the brass, and then the brass started to wear off too.

Life in Hillhead was life in another Glasgow. A hundred years ago it was new territory being pioneered by the fat city merchants, and the old terraces still have mounting blocks for carriage passengers and horse-riding ladies. But the city has been pushing out to swallow it, and the fat merchants have trickled farther west and beyond the boundaries or have quietly disappeared. The grand houses are slowly evolving into nursing homes and hotels and service flats, but the place is still genteel and proud of itself, as of course every village in Glasgow is. Hillhead was particularly like a village, with the Kelvin separating it from lesser places in the city and quaint little rows of terraces and architectural follies and odd, hidden streets joined one to the other by secretive flights of stairs; and through it swept the Great Western Road, which was and is still a fine noble boulevard and a splendid spectacle by day or night.

The people were perhaps more correctly-spoken and perhaps worse-mannered than elsewhere in the city; especially many of the matronly souls who carried the air of the old, plutocratic Hillhead with them and were disgusted with the way the world, and the old place, were going. I supposed they had been brought up to expect the best, and they were damn well going to get the best, especially the best places in bus queues and bakers' queues, if they had to use their elbows and feet to do it.

But perhaps it was the strangeness of the place that made this more obvious than it was – it's always easy to pick on the bad habits of people when they're foreigners.

And we had never lived so close to other people before. There was another married couple in the house where we lived, and we lived alongside them on terms of curiosity and courtesy and bewilderment. We never discovered their names, but we called them Joe and Ethel, and every morning at half-past eight, because we never rose at a respectable hour in the morning, we would be wakened by a noise from their bedroom that sounded like somebody dragging a loaded tin bath across a tiled roof. Other people's domestic noises are the most mysterious things on earth. Ethel was friendly and completely without any kind of expression, and spoke in a Belfast accent as thick as pale cream cheese, in a breathless monotone. We shared a kitchen, and she kept a loving friendly eye on any cooking that Anna had to leave temporarily. Her favourite trick was to turn the oven up in case our baking might fall while it was unattended, and four or five times we ate a black candy stuff that Anna claimed had set out to be meringues.

At the end of the first week the Inland Revenue gave me thirty pounds in income tax rebate, and we spent it all on a big plum-coloured carpet. The old lady in the flat next door congratulated us on buying it.

'Did you see it arriving?' I asked, puzzled.

'No,' she said, 'I don't hear you walking about on the floor any more.' We didn't walk about on the floor. We crawled on it, to feel the thick pile. Often we listened to the wireless stretched full out on the carpet just to be sure we possessed it, and that it wouldn't fly away.

I had given up sub-editing for a writing job, and I was back at work four or five days when I had a telephone call from one of the lads of the old concert party days.

'Congratulations on your marriage,' he said.

'Aye, good-oh,' I said.

'Have you heard any news?'

'What about?' I asked him.

'About Jack Diamond.'

'No,' I said, 'I must get up to see him.'

'Oh. I thought you might not have heard. He died yesterday,' he said.

It must have been what they used to call galloping consumption, for he had sunk as a man doomed within weeks of the diagnosis; a great talent and a wonderful spirit stolen from mankind by a disease that Glasgow was by way of having a corner in.

The Thin Red Line

A writing job isn't the same thing either as fame or the top of the tree, but it's better than working. After a period of despair and disillusionment it settled down to a situation where all I had to do was fill a space every day with seven or eight hundred words, and once I had rid myself of the haunting fear of every sensitive columnist that three more days will see the last idea on earth used up, I found for the first time a kind of freedom that goes with few jobs in this world, since I could do anything I fancied and call it gathering material. This is not quite so cushy as it sounds because the material has to be gathered somehow, and the readers have to like it, but it is a good life, on a good paper. And it is nearly the only job in the world in which you can get to know people and look for stimulating conversation for its own sake, in your working time. The city was full of racing drivers and auctioneers and scholars and tramps and cranks that I pursued and collected like stamps.

Passing the Strathendrick bar one day I bounced off John Bell, the first time I had seen him since I was married. When he realized that, he dragged me straight back into the bar. There was a restless little man with him, about my own size, with a leathery Irish face and a shy smile and dark burning eyes.

'It's Harry Keir,' John boomed at me, 'and now you can tell your mither you know an artist.'

'You'll be an artist yourself,' Harry said, in a friendly tone that was searching and discomfiting.

'No, I'm a paid hack and bum,' I said. 'For money.'

'It's the great thing, the money,' Harry said.

'Especially if this paid hack and bum has enough to stand his hand,' John said at me.

'Ah, you're an artist, though,' Harry insisted. 'You've got the face, hasn't he, John? I can see the thin red line inside you, burning you up.'

'It must be the radishes I had for breakfast,' I said, flattered but uncomfortable.

'Ah, you can deny yourself,' he said earnestly, but cheerful all the time. 'But if it's in you it's bound to force its way out. An' I don't know – maybe you're right, Cliff. Deny it an' live a happy life. God knows art's never done anything for me.'

'Gentlemen,' John Bell said, pouting his lips in his bulging face in a smile of derisive affection for all humanity, 'you are both shooting the bloodiest awful bull it has ever been my misfortune to have to listen to. If you don't shut your faces I'll treat you to a post-mortem of the Rangers-Hibbs game.'

'That's the voice of sanity,' Harry told me confidentially. The fitba'.' He grinned at John. 'You're a big overbearing bastard, John.'

'Have you never seen Harry's work?' John asked me. 'No.'

'Your education hasny started, then,' John said.

'I'll start it right away,' I said.

'I think you're a man that'll like some of my stuff,' Harry told me. 'No' that you need to flatter me, you understand, Cliff. It varies, you know. But I think it's got

213

maybe a touch of honesty.'

'You'll never make a salesman,' John said. 'See Harry's stuff, you'll like it all right, Cliff.'

So I met my first real artist, and I did like his stuff, not only because I liked the artist. Meeting people like that was one of the joys of the job. Harry's charm was odd and original, for always he had this earnest, penetrating manner and at the same time a happy tolerant feeling in his gravity, and his mind was always churning over and over and over like my own, but although he was probably fifteen years older, he was more restless and impatient than I ever was. He is what people call a proletarian artist, which means in Harry Keir's case that he draws and paints what he knows best and that is the warm, sprawling, reckless life of working class Glasgow. He works with a fearsome speed and intensity and his little workroom is stacked with scores and scores of his pictures, thrown off in a white heat and left aside while he looks for something else to use himself up on.

When I first met him he was drinking not only regularly, but heavily and often too heavily, and looking at his own behaviour in a mixture of disgust and wry amusement.

'Some of my best pictures are scattered in pubs across the face of the city,' he once told me. 'By God, Cliff, what a fool a man can be in the drink!' He speaks in a sweet accent with a trace of Irish brogue.

'I've sold a picture for ten guineas, landed in some pub I don't even know the name of on my way to deliver it, and given the same picture to the barman for the price of a whisky. When I think of it, it's enough to make me weep, but what's the use of weeping? It's life, Cliff, life. A man is a damned fool and an artist is the damnedest fool of the lot. You just do what you can, an' God help you. Unless you're an artist with a business head, like Bill Crosbie. There's a man that's taken care of himself, an' a good fellow at that. Ah, but what's the use? The leopard canny change his spots. Anyway, that's the test – does a barman understand the stuff? Never mind the damned critics and the arty vultures, Cliff, it's the people that count.'

Many of the pictures Harry was producing at the time, most of them in pen and wash, lit up what was most gallus and reckless in the Glasgow character. I have one on my living room wall of a sleazy old down-and-out who played jazz on the bagpipes outside Glasgow's pubs, with two scruffy unwashed urchins staring up at him and the steamy yellow light from the pub windows streaming out over him with the smell of liquor and stale sweat that would have made better propaganda for the Band of Hope than any of the hand-coloured anatomical sections the teetotal fanatics ever hung up on their easels. There's another one of the Ancient Mariner with the albatross hanging from his scrawny neck, and it has that Celtic sense of doom and horror that makes buyers uncomfortable because it strikes so close to the bone.

It always impressed me deeply that a man could live with this overmastering sense of tragedy without evasion and yet be cheerful and generous beyond reason. Once or twice Harry came with his wife Elsa to visit us, which usually meant that our two wives spent the evening by the fireside while Harry and I went out to drink, and although I could easily take a drink, and often take too much, I could see that Harry had a more urgent thirst for it than I ever had. There was no conquering it. And yet drunk or sober he was always the same amiable generous character, hostile to nothing but humbug and his own failings.

He had the great advantage of a wife who was talented herself, but was primarily dedicated to nurturing his talent; a good life for a rare type of woman. But there is nothing static or entirely predictable in this life. A couple of years must have passed during which I didn't run into him at all, and when I did, he had joyfully thrown off the drink and was working harder than ever. He chuckled over it, as youthful and ageless as always although he had come through a grave illness.

'I told the doctors I was finished with the drink, you

know, Cliff,' he said. 'One of them kind of laughed a bit at me – we got on fine, he and I, he used to say he wished he could get a hold of what I had in my head – he said: "We've heard all that before, Harry – everybody says it." But I said to him: "All right, you've heard it before – but you haven't heard it from me. I don't care what anybody else has told you. I've just decided I'm tired of drinking. There's no sense in it any more. I've used it up and I'm finished." Ho ho! He didn't want to believe me. But it's true. I like pubs – you understand, they're the greatest places on earth for pure character. But I canny be bothered with the drink. I'm not sick of it. I'm just finished with it.'

And more years than that have flowed under the bridge, and it turned out to be nothing but the truth. Not that he lost his other old bad habits. He turned up one morning with a great flat parcel under his arm and opened it out to show a misty landscape I had rashly admired six months before, and had a nail banged in my wall and the picture hung before I could start haggling over the price, and then flattened me with a look at the mention of money.

'I'm finished with the picture too,' he said. 'I had to paint it, and now to hell with it, I've got other things to do, at least if you've got it you'll look at it. Do you like it, Anna? Aye, I quite like it myself. It's got something. I did that damned well, that feeling of emptiness. I'm painting better than I ever did, but it's a hell of a life for a woman when a man's working hard. I'm telling you, Anna, you'll have to put up with a lot when this man gets started.'

'I'm leaving it nice and late,' I said. 'I've been lying fallow for over thirty years.'

'You're a wise man, Cliff. But I can see it, it's boiling up in you.'

'That's raw onions,' I said.

Who the Hell are You Calling a Celebrity?

Harry Keir is the outstanding living limner of the strange essence of Glasgow in art. The other is better known and as great in his own way, although he was born in Ayrshire. I was at the Playhouse Ballroom one night passing an hour with Harry Hines, a clever gallus Cockney who runs a dance band under the name of Doctor Crock, and a Glasgow girl who turned up from somewhere asked me:

'Do you know Bud Neill?'

'Very well,' I boasted.

'Did you know him before he was famous?'

'No, just within the past few years.'

'I can't be bothered with that,' she said. 'I get tired of people who know celebrities but they didn't know them before they were celebrities.'

'Awa' an' bile your heid,' I advised her.

'What do you mean by that?'

'You ask Bud Neill – he didny know me before I was a celebrity either.'

'Are you a celebrity?'

'Have you never heard of George Bernard Shaw?'

'Oh.'

Bud Neill came of a comfortable Ayrshire family, but according to various stories he has told me in my cups, he spent the first seven years of his life in Tibet, as a husky dog. Later, when doubts were cast on his ability to pull a sledge, he left Lhasa in a fit of pique, fitted with a two-stroke motor, and crossed the Sahara Desert in a cement-mixer.

'That was before I joined the *Record*,' he explained. 'From the Dalai Lama to the Dalai Record, ha! You didn't know that, boy, did you?'

217

'I did,' I muttered thickly. 'I was the second dog on the left.'

'That's ma boay!' he shouted.

I met Bud while I was writing an unsuccessful radio series for Stewart and Matthew, the husband-and-wife comedy dancing act who graced the old Dave Willis Half-past-eight shows at the King's Theatre and are now stars with the fabulous Fol-de-Rols. Charlie Stewart was a boyhood friend of Bud Neill, and also incidentally of Eric D. Clarke, another Ayrshire character who came to Glasgow to do his comic artist and has been doing it and getting more and more boyish with it for over twenty years. Bud turned up in the King's Arms one afternoon when I was having a drink with my stars and mulling over the murderous notices we were getting in the *Evening News*. The artist was already a kind of cult among all social and intellectual strata in Glasgow.

In fact, he worked as a bus driver, funeral undertaker and various other things before he started to draw cartoons in earnest, and was invited to join the staff of the *Evening Times*. His daily cartoon wasn't a joke in the sense that any other artist of the time was drawing jokes. It was just a bit of Glasgow, often meaningless on the surface, and whoever on the *Evening Times* first thought of taking him on must have had more perception than most newspaper editors, which wouldn't be hard. He was the first evidence of new, indigenous Glasgow humour since J. J. Bell and Neil Munro. After the first jolt of incomprehension, Glaswegians started to tear open the *Evening Times* to gobble the latest Bud Neill titbit, as salty and esoteric and Glasgow as a black puddn' supper. How do you explain the art of a man whose finest product was a squashed drawing of two shapeless things against the background of a square tenement, with the caption:

'Haw Jennifer! Ma kirby's fell doon a stank!'

It can't mean anything at all, never mind anything funny, to anybody whose ear hasn't been attuned since childhood to the weird harsh variations of Glasgow's language.

He was tall and thin, in smart careless clothes with a trace of American accent; a face composed of bold planes of bone under a fine dome head covered with straight fair thinning hair; he wore gleaming false teeth and rimless glasses, and could have been a successful insurance salesman from a Frank Capra film.

'Hallo, Charlie,' he said when he came into the King's Arms. 'Ah heard your show last week. It stank.'

'You're delicious when you're doing your diplomatic routine, Bud,' Ann Mathew said. 'Have a glass of glass, ground fine.'

'I saw your cartoon in the *Times* yesterday,' Charlie told Bud. 'You can draw nane.'

'But tell us something we don't know!' Bud said, leaning back from the waist and smiling his happy, maddening smile. 'Ah've been tellin' people for years ah canny draw – of course ah canny draw. Ah'm jist a . . . a rotten-joke merchant. Quips for clothheads.' He laid his hand on the bar and spoke with patient emphasis. 'But I *know* I can draw nane – I'm not an impostor.'

'You're just a lovable, honest louse,' Ann suggested.

'That's ma darlin'!' Bud said, in delighted admiration. 'You understand me, Ann. Ah love ye.'

'Ann's been takin' lessons in morbid psychology,' Charlie chuckled.

Bud switched into a careful oratorical style.

'Now don't take my, eh, candid and hee hee, essentially incompetent – no, illiterate – criticisms as a personal affront. They're purely objectionable.'

'That's all right, Bud,' Charlie assured him. 'You just think I'm as funny as a sair heid.'

'That's ma boay!' Bud responded, laying his arm across Charlie's shoulders. 'It's probably just the stinking script they gave you. Good to see you, Charlie.'

'This is the script writer,' Ann said with an evil smile.

'You're doin' a great job, boay,' Bud said instantly, cackling to himself. He clasped me to his heart at once with hoops of steel. Since that odd day he has kept swimming in and out of my line of vision unpredictably and ominously. He lurks with his family somewhere safe and remote in the country, and exists only as a legend for most of the year, but in irregular seasons he appears without warning in Glasgow looking thoughtful and harassed and searching for something to keep him off his work. His range of acquaintances is wide and catholic, and he keeps picking up more people as he goes.

It's true that he can't draw, in the same way that James Thurber can't draw. The recurrent heroine that waddles through his work is a dream, or a nightmare figure, of the shrewd, sentimental, unlettered Glasgow wifie sunk on thick ankles and clasping hands under sprawling bosom designed for wedging over a windowsill for a good hing, and she rises to the level of poetry when her inarticulate hunger for beauty drives her to sigh: 'My, ah like rid herr. Rid herr's rerr.'

'Ach, poetry ma bottom,' Bud said when I accused him of it. 'Honestly, now, you don't think that's *good*? Well, it's all right, I suppose. Who knows what's good? Still, if you say it's good there must be something in it – something that in my preternatural ignorance, ha, that's good, something that in my preternatural ignorance I have not as yet detected. Detected, is that right? My vocabulary is somewhat inchoate tonight. I must be sober, or something equally horrible.' He leaned back for a better look and glinted joyfully through his Glenn Miller specs.

He had just arrived in town on one of his unannounced social orgies, found me staring vacantly across my desk and carried me unprotesting to a place where he was sure he could get a drink before the pubs opened. On the way he remembered he had promised his wife Mary he would have a haircut.

'Nice and gentle, son,' he admonished the barber, flashing him a warm loving smile. 'Don't shave it to the bone – make me look intellectual.' The barber shot a look of inquiry at me which I ignored. None of us had had a drink yet, and if a customer wants to speak his mind, who deserved that more than a barber? After a few snips, Bud held up a hand under the cloth.

'Cease, desist, brother!' The barber hesitated, his insolent confidence undermined. Bud reached out for a hand mirror and held it up above his head.

'Naw, naw,' he chid the barber. 'You're lettin' the old cranium show starkly through.' The other customers were twisting in their chairs to see who it was that had the nerve to tell a barber off. The barber ignored Bud and turned to me again, and his sullen face was asking the question: 'Is this animal insane, and if so, dangerously insane?' I returned his gaze stonily.

'He likes his hair cut,' I said reasonably, 'the way he likes his hair cut.'

'That's ma boay,' I heard Bud muttering, and then, to the barber, 'Don't worry, you're a good kid, pay no heed to my maudlin mutterings. Just don't *scalp* me, that's all, boy.' And then a great white grin burst out of him at his own impertinence. But he got his hair cut the way he wanted it. He ruined everything by tipping the barber a half-crown. The barber sidled over to me while Bud was hurling himself into his coat.

'Has your friend had a couple?' he muttered out of the side of his mouth. I eyed him coldly.

'Not a drop.'

'Who is he?'

'His name is Bud Neill.'

A great light spread over the barber's face.

'He's the great boy, int he?'

'He knows what he likes,' I said, not wishing to be shirty. The barber leapt forward brandishing a clothes brush.

'Everything all right, Bud?' he asked eagerly.

'Well, you should know,' Bud said. 'What do I know about hairdressing? All I can do is put myself in the hands of the expert. Sure, it's very chic. Chic.' He grinned sheepishly at me. 'Get the French accent, boy.'

His cartoons had just moved from the *Evening Times* to the *Daily Record*. The specimen of that day I have forgotten, but the scene was a pet shop, and there was a notice hanging above the counter reading:

'Budgies Repaired.'

'You don't really think that's funny – or original, or artistic, do you?' he asked me. 'Aw well, maybe it is. Maybe I'm really great. Maybe I'm an egghead, like you. I don't know. Sometimes I think I should go back to the bus-drivin'.'

'Uhuh,' I said.

'I'll have you know I was a good bus driver,' he protested. The talk comes out of him just like that.

'Well, the country needs bus drivers,' I agreed.

'It can damn well need them. Look, that fruit-shop's got mushrooms. Does Anna like mushrooms?'

'She loves them.'

'Come on we'll buy half-a-stone an' take them up as a surprise.'

'Who on earth could eat half-a-stone of mushrooms?'

'Us,' he said, surprised. We didn't manage to finish them all; there must have been a pound or two left over.

The Rich Free Life

Anna and I were visiting my sister Mary one afternoon on the way to the grocer's, and before she even had the kettle on she looked at me sideways and said:

'What do you think of this daft idea of David's?'

'Which one?' I asked warily. It sounded like a crisis in which I wanted no involvement.

'Och, he's talking about leaving home and living in some kind of studio. Has my mother no' told you?'

'Not a cheep.'

'She will,' Mary said forebodingly.

'Good,' I said. 'I hope you've got chocolate biscuits, I'm hungry.'

'I always wanted to live in a studio,' Anna said half-wistfully. Mary waved her hand in impatience to find we weren't expressing the proper sentiments.

'It would have been different for you, Anna,' she said, tutting.

'Why different for me?

'Well, at least you have the talent – and you could cook.' Anna raised her eyes heavenwards at the perpetual accusation of artistic talent, which people are always making with no evidence to go on, though it isn't unfair, either.

'Well, David can cook,' I countered. Mary turned on me in exasperation.

'Och, you're as bad as he is,' she accused me. 'The very idea!' She rinsed out the teapot and put the tea in. 'It's that Mackie that's got his noddle full of trains and rails.'

'More likely David's got Mackie full of trains and rails,' I said easily. Mackie was an art student and contemporary of David's and not the most forceful character in the city. He was at the Art School on an ex-Service grant. David was working as a film cameraman with a documentary company by this time.

'Well, whoever's to blame, it's terrible,' Mary went on. 'What in heaven's name does he want to leave a good home for? You'll have to talk to him.'

It was a family crisis all right. David and Mackie were burned up with the ideal of freedom in an arty bachelor establishment, and the family was perfectly revolted. There was some vague idea of holding a family conference, like a Dodie Smith play, to discuss what should be done, but whether there was actually a round-table meeting I can't make out. At any rate, I was unanimously elected as the spokesman who might have influence with the mad young fool. I was perfectly useless for the job, because I couldn't stop laughing when the case was put to me.

'You would think he had had enough of living on his own,' Johanne put it to me, 'after his time in the Merchant Navy.'

'Well,' I said, 'nobody complained when he left home for *that*.'

'Don't be daft, that's different. He doesn't *have* to go this time.'

'Well, maybe that's why he wants to,' I said, getting impatient myself. Johanne made a despairing sound but I had the feeling that she was putting the case against David more out of a sense of duty than from any violent disagreement with him. The rest of the family was united in real horror.

'What's worrying everybody,' I said to Johanne, 'is that he and Mackie will have their girl friends up for orgies.'

'Well,' she agreed, 'do you think they'll no?' At this I started laughing again and got useless.

'If they can persuade the girl friends,' I managed to say.

'They'll persuade them all right – *art* students!' This drove me to even more helpless laughter. 'You don't want to see David getting into any trouble.' She insisted on being realistic.

'He isn't an infant,' I said.

'That's just the trouble.' She laughed as well. 'You smart young things areny as smart as you imagine.'

I had to stop myself from laughing like a fool when the subject came up with my mother, because she was honestly hurt at the idea of her last-born spurning the parental home and the care and affection he could get there; but she put the case in practical symbols too.

'He'll no' get proper food,' she insisted.

'Well, he'll come crawling back soon enough when he's hungry,' I tried to soften the blow. 'He just wants to try

224

his wings.'

'Huh, wings!'

'It'll be good training for when he gets a wife,' I suggested.

'What kind of wife will he get? Somebody he's ashamed to let us see!'

The family felt that I had failed them entirely. It was useless for me to try to plead that everybody should have a period of life away from home, just on general principles, even from a good home – especially from a good home, in fact. Men grow up in their mothers' houses and most of them go straight from there to their wives' houses, and nobody objects to that transfer, as long as they're still in the grasp of the law and a good woman to keep them under control. I was all for David's daft scheme even if he starved a bit. Probably most family crises are the same. Each one is the end of the world, but after the deed is done, life adapts itself and goes on. The family threw its hand in and David and Mackie set up their bachelor establishment studio in what had once been a noble L-shaped room near St George's Cross. Its nobility was long vanished. Not to overload the language, it was a ripe slum room in a ripe old slum house, with a good view of another row of slums from the window.

'Dead Rive Gauche, innit?' David said smugly. 'It smells jist like the auld bit Pauris.' They distempered the walls in terra-cotta and added some slick bits of small modern furniture to the crumbling objects that went with the room. My mother held grimly aloof for nearly a week and then consented to visit the new place, suppressing tears of vexation and shame at the meanness of it. David and Mackie, of course, saw nothing of shame or vexation in it. Another pair of art students had the room downstairs, and they all took a Bohemian delight in the domestic struggles of their authentic slum neighbours. Like all young brothers, David was an arrogant whippersnapper. He took to giving us lordly advice on interior decoration and straightened Anna out generously on cooking. The

225

spaghetti Bolognese era had just dawned.

'*Naebody* can make Spaghetti Bolognese like mine,' he announced insolently. Whenever he was making a claim with inadequate grounds, he increased the Glasgowness of his speech to make it sound more convincing. 'Nut even the Italians.'

'You'll die of carbohydrate poisoning,' I said dispassionately.

'Nut a chance! Bags a protein in ma Bolognese. You jist hivnae got the flair fur it. Stacks a protein.'

'Where?'

'In the auld Bolognese, that's where. The auld garlic.'

'Garlic!' my mother wailed.

'Garlic is a civilized food,' David insisted, defensively.

As Mary's house was the nearest family outpost to the slum, she had to provide a useful service of lending cups of sugar and watching David anxiously for signs of nutritional decline. Although she had been so passionately against the studio project, she actually got a big kick out of it. There was always something unbelievable happening among David's neighbours; an occasional wife-beating, bailiff's men popping in and out and husbands clashing with their wives' fancy men.

Anna was in hospital being delivered of our first child when David and Mackie and their mates downstairs threw one of their big housewarmings, and I went along with Fergie, Anna's brother. The studio was tidied, in a way, and chairs and boxes had been brought up from downstairs for the guests. There was an enamel bucket on the floor before the fire.

'We're experimenting with rare exotic wines,' David said, in the voice that was meant to forestall horrified protests, but which merely aroused dire suspicions. We had heard about these wines. Most of them were the British vintages. Not exactly port-type, more of a port-type *type*. Different brands kept coming out every few weeks, with disquieting names like Auld Mercat and Diva, but they all tasted the same. The emergence of new brands looked like a trick to keep trade going after the clients had tried the old names and got the horrors.

'Not Diva,' I said to David, trying to sound brave.

'Tush tush,' he said.

There were other guests there already, friends and friends of friends, and that's always dangerous. There was an assortment of girls, headed by an aggressively built blonde with beautiful legs and an expression of dumb nubility. There was a small young painter who had actually lived in a garret in Paris and was modest about it. There was a thin actor who had had a job in some unlikely Midlands rep company that same year, and who wanted everybody to sing folk songs, or Hebridean mouth music. There was a thin girl with a nice face and absolutely no sex appeal at all who had recently inherited a cooked-meat shop and had an Austin Twelve of her own. There was a little short-sighted girl who made hand-flung pottery. Somebody had brought along an out-of-place University Arts graduate who was politically-minded and kept looking round the party as if he expected everybody to take him for a genial father-figure indulgently tolerating the pranks of his kiddie-winkies. There was also a poet, with a pale face and adenoids, which I thought was carrying tradition to excess, with a big thumping name like Fife Cairngorm or something. I sat down on a sofa arrangement beside the short-sighted pottery girl, and she blinked into my face in a friendly way and tried to climb on my knee without letting me notice what she was doing.

'Eh, did you bring any likker?' David asked me pointedly. I handed him a bottle containing some whisky.

'Potency fur the auld bit punch!' he chanted to Mackie, who by this time was kneeling beside the enamel pail stirring something inside it. Before I could prise the pottery girl off, David poured the whisky in on top of whatever was in the pail already. Mackie uncorked a dark bottle with an ugly green label and emptied it in after the whisky. For the first time I noticed a collection of empty beer-bottles, gin-bottles and other things including a cider flagon, tucked away in a corner beside the fireplace. One of the downstairs students came in with a trayful of mixed cups and glasses and two jam jars.

'Grab a utensil and dip in!' cried the genial host threateningly. The adenoidal poet dipped a cup and drained it with unpleasant greed, but failed to drop dead clutching his throat. The pottery girl left me and came back with two cups of brown liquid with stray curls of foam swirling round the surface. It didn't taste very good although it smelled alcoholic in the most general sense.

'The beer was a mistake,' David shouted judiciously above the rabble. The spectacular blonde sat on his lap and ruffled his hair, a gesture he ignored.

'Who's that?' I asked the pottery girl.

'Who? I can't see from here. The blonde? That's Jo. She works in a shop,' she said.

'Is it you that owns the Austin Twelve?' I asked her.

'No, it's Lily. She's here somewhere.'

'Keep your eye off Jo,' David shouted at me, and then to Jo. 'That's ma brother. He's merrit. An' PREGNANT!'

'Are you married?' the pottery girl asked, enthralled.

'Yes, and I'm old,' I said. 'Which is Lily? Does she lend people her Austin Twelve?'

The supply of the stuff in the pail lasted well, partly because it was so nasty, but the party got noisier. The actor, Paul, sat on the floor in front of us and rested his elbow on the pottery girl's knees and looked up at me looking vital.

'Do you like mouth music?' he said.

'No, I sing by ear,' I said wittily. The liquor in the pail must have been worse than I realized.

'It's easy to sing,' he said eagerly. 'Hin han horo doro hin pan horo doro hin han horo doro oich oa doro!'

I made an effort to join in, but I couldn't think of any words except heedrum hawdrum.

'That's great,' he said. 'Just a minute.' He pulled a harmonica out of his pocket and started to play it lovingly, and badly. There were encouraging shouts from other guests to chuck it or get bashed to death. The pottery girl got off me and tried to do some kind of reel in her bare feet, but Mackie shooed her away from the area of the pail, and she vanished round the corner of the L part of the room and danced by herself, falling over things now and then. Some time later I went out to search the dark landing for the toilet, and found the young artist from Paris already there, rolling his forehead back and forth against the wall in intervals of being sick, and crooning calmly to himself.

'*Je . . . le . . . regrette . . . tant . . .*' he was saying, '*d'etre malade pendant . . . votre . . . aimable . . . soiree.*'

'*Pensez nothing de it,*' I assured him, placing him to one side so that I could get in and shut the door.

'*Mais au moins je n'ai pas été malade sur votre tapis,*' he was crooning to the wall.

'*Vous etes un vrai gentleman,*' I said. 'You may not be very elegant, but the true mark of breeding is to be sick quietly in the right place.'

'*Merci,*' he moaned. 'I'm sorry if I've spoiled your lovely party.'

'Welcome, any time,' I said, a little thickly I noticed. I passed David at the door on my way back, and he whispered to me, 'Keep your mouth shut, but there's a bottle of real drink planked for efter.'

'Where?' I whispered. 'In case you faint or anything.'

'In the gramophone.'

Next time I took stock, somebody had shrewdly borrowed Paul's harmonica and hidden it, but he had another smaller one in another pocket, and he was still optimistic about starting up a mouth-music group. The pottery girl was doing something stooping down and stamping which apparently was meant to represent walking the tweed. Nobody paid any attention to her. Then the door opened and there was a scattered cheer for a short, dumpy person in a grey fisherman's sweater, dirty dungarees and black half-calf boots with the trousers tucked into them. He was wearing glasses and blinking through them, his cheeks naturally puffed out like those of a small apprentice Father Christmas so that his eyes were squeezed up above them. He had a small old-fashioned beard, but the bits of his face that were shaven had a three-day stubble too.

'Good aul' Link!' somebody shouted. 'You were the only thing that was missin'!' Link answered with a friendly little short-sighted smile, his head lifted as if he was about to say something, but he didn't.

'My God!' I heard Mackie moan from behind me. 'Hide the beds, quick.'

'Who's Link?' I asked him.

'Jist Link. Everybody knows Link. He must have been thrown oot 'is digs again.'

Tipsy hands were urging Link towards the enamel pail and pressing cups of liquid at him, and Link was responding with a fine show of modesty and reluctance.

'I didn't know you had company,' he cried in a high-pitched little voice, very precise but with a faint stammer. 'I hope I'm not de trop, hee hee hee!' He allowed himself to be forced to a cup of the stuff from the pail and smiled round in innocent delight.

'He's bloody well no' sleepin' in ma bed,' Mackie muttered resentfully. Mackie himself was tall, a little over six feet, and shockingly handsome, with a mane of black hair and a gaunt young face that betokened a burning intellect and a character annealed in the crucible of life, but somehow he kept ruining the effect by speaking. You couldn't help feeling he did it deliberately.

'You can kick him out,' I argued, not very interested.

'Link? Kick Link oot? It's like kickin' a daud a flypaper oot. He sticks. Ugh, ah'm fed up wi' this party noo.'

I had a nagging urge to find Lily and get a look at her Austin Twelve. I had never known a girl with her own car before. But I found myself wedged in a seat at one of the windows with the University man who was interested in politics. The rest of the party seemed to have gathered round Link, who was crying some anecdote in his high voice and convulsing them. Mackie was lounging on the fringe of the audience scowling.

'I'm Alastair Aitchison,' the University man said portentously to me. 'You're in the Press.'

'Oh, is that where I am?' I answered dully. I wondered why it had got so stuffy. 'Let me out, somebody.'

'I'm interested in newspapers,' he ploughed on. 'In their political influence.'

'Non-existent,' I told him, trying to catch what Link was saying that was so funny. 'Look at Roosevelt,' I said.

'Well, look at Roosevelt,' he repeated, thrown off his stroke.

'All right, we'll both look at Roosevelt,' I said. 'Move over and let me see him too.'

He made a gesture indicating that he appreciated my frightfully funny patter, but that we really must get down to brass tacks. It was obvious that there was no escape from him.

'My cup is empty,' I said pathetically.

'You can have half of mine.'

'But that's Communism,' I objected. He lit up and fixed me with a crusading glare.

'You know,' he said, 'it astonishes me to find misconceptions like that even in journalists who are supposed to be well-informed.'

'Oh?'

From the group at the fire there was a burst of drunken mirth, and Link said what sounded like: '—so I paid the auctioneer the five bob and carried the mummy home over my shoulder. My mother screamed and screamed and wanted me to throw it in the midden, but I said: "We could keep it under the bed." But she wouldn't have it in the house, so—'

'Communism doesn't mean share and share alike, give one coat to thy neighbour and so on. It's a purely economic theory based on national ownership of the means of production.' Alastair Thing intoned into my ear. 'Plus the dictatorship of the proletariat and a number of

231

other elaborations I don't need to go into at the moment.'

'Good,' I said. 'Come on we'll listen to the mouth music.'

'Are you afraid you'll get converted?' he asked me, with the suggestion of a sneer. The poet individual with the pale hair and pink-rimmed eyes had interrupted Link during a pause and was trying to recite one of his poems.

'Give us Eskimo Nell!' David shouted coarsely, cuddling the blonde absent-mindedly. The poet individual swung round on him with a tight, liverish face.

'Maybe you don't appreciate poetry,' he snapped, 'but some people appreciate poetry. You can at least have the manners tae haud your wheesht whilst ah declaim!'

The pottery girl paused in her tweed-walking to peer at the source of the voice and cry: 'Wheesht, everybody – it's Lallans! Spiel awa', ah'm harkin' at ye!' I heard Mackie, already sunk in gloom, groaning a long groan.

'There'll be nae Lallans in ma hoose,' David bawled in deliberate provocation. 'Speak Glesca or you get flang oot!'

'Heah, heah,' came from Paul, the actor, in his mincing stage English. The poet person was still standing up and breathing in short jerks through his nose. 'Who's fur coffee?' David cried to the gathering.

Everybody was for coffee except the poet, but he had lost his audience. Mackie stood up and said to David: 'Ah'll get the kettle an' staun at the cooker, an' you can put the penny in the gas. But for God's sake keep quiet this time.'

'Ah'm always quiet,' David answered huffily. 'Everybody else'll have tae shut up as well, or we'll never get the kettle biled.'

'They'd be better shoutin' an' singin',' Mackie protested. 'That'll cover us up better.'

During the discussion that followed this odd exchange, my political chum started on me again.

'I'm standing for the Town Council this year,' he said with painful casualness. 'Why don't you come to one of my meetings? You might pick up something – a good angle, maybe.'

'I would rather be tied up for the night in a bag of starving rats,' I assured him. He laughed uneasily.

'You probably think I'm rather young for a professional politician, but Labour is the party of youth,' he said. 'After all, Pitt was Prime Minister at twenty-four.'

'Pitt was a twit as well,' I said. I was beginning to enjoy myself. I realized in a flash of drunken lucidity that I had never spoken to anybody before in this tone. The recollection of the millions of bores I had suffered from mere courtesy rose in my throat and I felt I was turning over a new, nasty, appetising leaf. 'When will you be fifteen?' I asked him.

'No need to rub it in.' He gave a fake booming laugh. 'Actually I'm only twenty-eight.'

'Youth?' I hooted. 'Youth? You should be merrit wi' five weans at your age.' Mackie brushed past us with the kettle.

'A bloody professional teenager,' he threw at Alastair, who flushed deep red and stammered for a word. Mackie shouted from the door at the party to keep up a racket, but a suspenseful silence fell as he and David crept out on to the landing, during which one of the downstairs students explained:

'It's hellish. There isny wan bee family in the hoose that ever puts money in the gas except us, an' there's only wan meter for three cookers. Listen tae the silence! The bees are sittin' wi' their ears tae the keyholes!'

Quite distinctly we heard a match being struck by Mackie at the cooker on the landing outside, and quite distinctly, the creak of the stairs as David crept down to the meter in the hall.

'Talk, quick,' the downstairs student said. 'Sing, dance!' But we were too interested in what was going on outside. From somewhere downstairs there was a sharp click. Then another. David had put the penny in the slot and was turning the knob click by click in the hope of doing it silently. There was a short curse from Mackie on the landing, and then another match was struck. More clicks. And then the unmistakable clang of a penny dropping in the resonance chamber of a gas meter. And instantly a deafening noise broke out in the building, with feet pounding and doors slamming upstairs and downstairs. The walls trembled. Mackie came back into the room in a matter of seconds, nearly weeping with rage.

'Ye canny beat the sods!' he shouted. 'They're fryin' chips on every ring in the hoose! There isny a peep left in the stove.'

David came bounding upstairs.

'Sorry folks,' he said suavely. 'Wur neebors have detected the presence a money in the meter. They had their scouts oot the minute Mackie lufted the matches.'

'What? No coffee?' Paul the actor wailed tragically.

'We'll try again when the sods go tae bed,' Mackie said glumly.

'Ach, it's nae use,' one of the downstairs students said, 'When they think there's money in the hoose, they pit the weans on a night shift tae listen fur the gas meter.'

'Aye,' David agreed, with modesty and pride. 'They know when we've got company fur a cultured booze-up, it's bonanza night at the stove.' Somebody suggested sending out a delegation to buy fish suppers instead, and during the babble that followed, I said unpleasantly to Alastair:

'You're wastin' your time here. Away doonstairs an' drum up the Catholic vote, if you aim to be a Labour councillor.' And instantly I was sorry I had spoken, for one of the downstairs students looked across at me sharply, and I remembered he was a good Catholic. I winked at him, but I felt that a wink was inadequate.

'What's this?' Alastair pounced. 'Religious prejudice?'

'Och, away an' spew,' I said, defeated and disgusted with myself. 'But somewhere else.' He gave me up.

Before the fish supper discussion had time to get settled, some people started to leave. Link had managed to get the

234

only armchair, and he was sitting in it looking relaxed and settled, with his half-calf boots off and his feet rested halfway up the mantlepiece. David exploded in rage and pain.

'Somebody's stole the Isolabella!' he seethed. I was at his side at once. 'Look,' he said, and pointed at the open lid of the radiogram. There was nothing inside but a turntable.

'It was that political pig,' Mackie said, but he looked aggressively at Link, who smiled with his little eyes crinkled up and said, without moving his feet from the mantlepiece: 'I never touch sweet liqueurs. I find my palate disagrees with them.' He evidently took it for granted that he would be suspected, and accepted the suspicion without resentment. The party brightened up from what was becoming a lethargy. Everybody was virtuous and violent about the criminality of stealing a host's liquor, and the news that there was something other to drink than the stuff in the pail was stimulating in itself. It was soon established that the early leavers were Alastair, the political pig; and somebody remembered that the insulted poet with the pale hair had offered to see Lily home.

'He's got my Isolabella in her car,' David gritted.

'She didny have her car,' Mackie thought. 'She disnae bring it tae parties in case she has a drink an' crashes it.'

'We'll comb the streets,' Fergie said firmly, from his position beside the pail. 'Split into four groups an' make for the car stops.'

'An' whoever gets him, bring him back an' we'll pummel him tae death!' David cried. Everybody wanted the Isolabella back, but hardly anybody except David had any serious idea of actually going to look for it. There was a lot of movement and quick swigs from the pail, and somebody threw open a window to look along the street. Paul the actor started to rummage under the furniture. Then Mackie looked foolish.

'Here, ah jist minded, David,' he said. 'Ah took it oot

the gramophone an' put it in the oven in case anybody fun' it.' David dashed to the oven and came back popeyed.

'It's gone!' he howled. Everybody got unrelaxed again. Paul stood up waving a bottle.

'Is this it?' he asked. 'It was under the bed.'

'It's that political pig,' Mackie insisted. 'He planked it there an' then didny get the chance tae luft it when he left.' David glared slit-eyed at Paul.

'Or maybe you planked it. Maybe you thought we thought we had drunk it!' Paul registered horrified innocence.

'I *found* it for you! I mean to say, I don't expect people to be grateful, but I mean to say!' David grabbed the bottle.

'Somebody planked it, some durty thief, an' you're gettin' nane ae it, anybody. Except me. Especially you,' he added to Paul.

'You couldn't *force* me to drink it,' Paul said.

'Och, gaun, David, force him,' Fergie cooed.

'Well, all right,' said Paul. 'For the sake of peace. The last thing I want to do is bear a grudge. And in any case, who's got my mouth organ?'

'*Ah've* got your mouth organ,' David said. 'You'll get it when ye leave.' Paul went into a frightful pet, but took a thimbleful of Isolabella from David before David could change his mind, and did his best to look suave again. The bottle was passed round for everybody to admire the sugar-crusted twig inside it.

'It's a bloody Wop swindle,' Mackie gloomed. 'Takin' up space that should haud good alcohol. Who wahnts tae drink a flamin' tree?'

After the Isolabella was drunk the party started to peter out, but when I said I was going to telephone the hospital, everybody trooped out to find a phone box with me. The hospital was shirty in the extreme at being rung after midnight, but told me I had become the father of a son at twenty minutes to twelve.

236

'He made it for my birthday!' I said, baffled and trying to think how I should feel apart from relieved that Anna was fine.

'Well, there's nae drink left for toasts,' David said, grinning stupidly and thumping me on the back.

'Naw,' Mackie added, 'an' if there had been, Link would have feenished it bi noo. He's still in the hoose. Ah'm gaun back quick – he'll be in ma bed, ah'm tellin' ye. Ah'll kill him if he is.'

The Link Who Was Rarely Missing

Link didn't actually get Mackie's bed. He was too gentle and unaggressive for that. He slept in the chair. His system was to drop in on his acquaintances in the late evening when he was evicted from his digs, which was constantly, and sit by the fire until his hosts were dropping with sleep.

'Don't worry about me,' he would say. 'Just go to bed and I'll sit here and think for a while.' It was always too late at night by that time to order him out into the streets and he ended up with a share of the blankets and a shakedown. He turned up at our place a few weeks after the baby was born, and won Anna over easily by cooing over the infant and lifting it up with skilful hands more adroitly than most nurses. He was good at things like that. There was nothing we could do but feed him, at least.

'Oh, don't cook anything for me!' he cried in his jolly high-pitched pipe. 'Or would you like me to cook a special dish for you? I'll bake something fast if you've got some flour. A souffle thing.'

'Do you like baking?' Anna asked him, with the joy of enthusiast meeting enthusiast. 'This oven's a bit precarious for souffles.'

'I've done them over damp wood,' he said confidently. 'I was a chef in a hotel in Nice for a while . . .' and the terrible, disquieting thing about Link was that although he was a skilful liar – in fact, he would tell lies when the truth was actually more convenient, just to keep in trim – his wildest fantasies were quite likely to be true. After he made the souffle, Anna looked at him in sorrow and declared that she was going to give up baking altogether. He was certainly one of the best cooks in the business. He had an artistic feeling and passion for food.

'Oh,' he said. 'I've brought you something – just a wee thing to celebrate the baby.' He dug in his coat pocket and pulled out two china saucers with Japanese designs. 'Just wee things,' he repeated, 'but you could use them for ashtrays or something.'

'They're beautiful,' Anna said, fingering them gently. 'I'll put them against the wall.'

'What's this?' he said in surprise. 'Oh, it's a pawn ticket. Would you like it, Cliff?' He peered amiably at me. 'It's a watch. I bought the pawn ticket from a friend to get him out of, hee hee, a temporary embarrassment, but I never use a watch – they won't work on my wrist.'

I didn't own a watch.

'I'll buy it from you,' I said. 'Is it a good watch?'

'Oh, yes – gold, seventeen jewels. But you can have the ticket for nothing. A small return for your hospitality.'

'But you must need the money,' Anna said, stung to sympathy. Link waved the suggestion away, and I took the ticket and redeemed the watch next day for two pounds. It was as good as Link had promised.

He got into the habit of dropping in on us, but never actually stayed overnight. He always had a collection of incredible reminiscences, and usually a bundle of pawn tickets in his coat pocket, which intrigued me, and he was usually moving into or out of a new job; shop manager

238

one week, dock labourer the next.

'Of course, my landlady doesn't know I'm a dock labourer,' he explained. 'She's a dearie, but she thinks I'm a Naval officer supervising repairs of destroyers at the docks. It makes her happier.'

'What does she say when you come home in dirty dungarees?' I asked him sceptically.

'She thinks I'm far too conscientious, hee hee hee! Anyway, I've been in the Navy – no, I told you, of course. I was in the Army. What's the difference?'

When David came to visit us and inspect the baby, he brought Mackie with him. They had delayed the visit till Mackie's education grant instalment became due, so that they might buy a present for the child. David's eyes kept wandering to the two Japanese saucers on the wall.

'That's funny,' he said. 'Jo got two things like that in the Barras. Exactly like that.'

'These were a present,' Anna said. She got one of them down and stroked the surface. 'Link gave them to me.'

'Link!' Mackie echoed. 'He must have lufted them fae Jo.' We looked staggered.

'There's nae doubt,' David said firmly. 'If Link had anything tae dae wi' them at a', they *must* be stolen property. It's against his principles tae acquire anythin' honestly.'

'It's a wonder he gave you them,' Mackie said. 'Likely he couldny get anythin' on them in the pawn.'

'Funnily enough,' I said uneasily. 'He gave me a pawn ticket as well. For a watch.' I held out my wrist to display it.

'God!' Mackie yelled. 'Ah knew Link must have took it! The night ae the party! Ah bought it wi' ma gratuity!'

But the whole thing was a mere misunderstanding, of course. I mean, Link had a smooth explanation for it, with pile upon pile of circumstantial detail to give it force. He had pawned the watch *for* Mackie, he recalled. Or he thought that was it. He couldn't remember exactly when he had given Mackie the money he had got from the pawnshop, but he was sure Mackie hadn't wanted to see the watch again. The impressive thing about Link was that the next time I saw him, he was having a pint in the State Bar, where the art school students gathered at that time, and he was having it with Mackie. They were clearly the best of friends. It was hard to be angry with Link. He was so good at explaining things, and he was too funny to be lightly driven from society. One night he came to visit us while we were out, and Fergie was baby-sitting. Browsing through our book shelves he opened one book, and found three pound notes tucked inside it. I had put them there months before for a bill, or something, and had forgotten them completely. He waited till we got home so that he could display his find. He couldn't do anything else but display it, as Fergie had seen him finding it.

'As a matter of fact,' he said humbly, 'I just dropped in wondering if you might be able to advance me ten bob, Cliff. I have an appointment tomorrow with an industrialist who might offer me an important post, hee hee hee, and I might want to buy him a drink.'

Naturally I lent him the ten shillings without hesitation: I didn't expect to get it back, so I didn't lose any illusions.

His landlady at the time was a young woman, with a large husband who drank and beat her from time to time, and Link adopted the role of protector of the downtrodden and gave her legal advice and comforted her in his persuasive way. I remember this mainly because there was another transaction involving a watch, and this time David was nearly caught like me. The husband, whom everybody expected to bash Link, accepted him instead as a useful intermediary when he wasn't talking to his wife. When he finally left his wife and went to England, Link stayed on, being pampered and having the time of his life.

His story was that the husband, who was acquainted with the Art School and State Bar circle, had gone for good, and Link was now helping poor Nora to settle up her affairs and investigate the chances of divorce. One of the perks was a nice gold wristwatch formerly worn by the husband, but which Nora had kept – 'Because it actually belonged to her father,' Link explained. 'And she forced me to accept it because she was so grateful for my help.'

So he pawned it at once, and sold the ticket to David. David was wearing the watch in the back room of the State Bar one night when Nora's husband arrived and joined the party.

'Well, it cost me three quid tae get it fae the pawn,' he told me defensively. 'Did you ever get your two quid back for that other watch? Nut on your life. Ah jist decided tae save unpleasantness, so ah drank a' night like this,' and he pantomimed a man drinking with his hand pulled right inside his sleeve.

To look at Link superficially, you would never take him for a man likely to impress or dazzle. He stands about five feet three and tends to shuffle in his walk, possibly through wearing so many shoes borrowed from larger men. Meticulous and almost ladylike in many things, he isn't always impressively clean, and he changes so often from shaving clean to wearing a beard that the average state of his face is half-stubbled. But once something presses the spring that makes him work, he does dazzle by the sheer garrulous boldness of his words. When the Nora episode was beginning to look uncomfortable – Nora's husband might have been turning ugly at last towards Link, or Nora might have started thinking of him as a future husband – he landed lucky as usual, because another of the art students let out that his parents were going on holiday for a month and leaving him alone. Link was sitting on his doorstep when he got home that night, with his few belongings and some bits of bric-a-brac from Nora's house in a suitcase bearing Mackie's initials. Len, the rash-speaking student, saw that he was hooked, and since he hated cooking in any case, Link moved in with him for the month.

Some time during that month, while Len was out studying, Link took a tour through the wardrobes in the house, and found to his joy an ancient formal suit with a claw-hammer coat, a top hat and a black walking-stick with a silver knob, the long-disused property of Len's father. It suggested all sorts of possibilities that he hadn't fully worked out, but rather than pawn it straight away, he put it on, with the trouser-cuffs turned up inside and pinned to keep them from trailing behind him, and he went for a stroll along Sauchiehall Street. Link always had the self-esteem to carry an outfit like that.

Somewhere near the Regal his heart leapt when he saw two girls approaching and recognized one of them as his constant companion of some months back, who had decided to see through him and had thrown him over without a shilling. He must have looked like something out for his Hallowe'en, but with Link you could never tell, and the girls took him in popeyed.

'Fancy running into you of all people, Joan!' he piped. 'Times have changed, eh?'

Inclined to laugh at first, Joan heard the note of smug malice in his voice and saw the well-fed look on his face, and suspected that she might have acted hastily.

'Whit's the fancy dress fur?' she asked, but politely.

'Hee hee hee! I've just been to a board meeting,' Link giggled. 'My uncle left me the shares in his company when he died. Can you imagine me doing my big tycoon at a board meeting?'

They could easily imagine it. Joan was now frantic with regret and remorse, and Link followed straight through with a gesture at a great vulgar Buick that was standing at the pavement.

'I'm just waiting for one of my co-directors,' he cackled. 'The meeting ended early, so we thought we would take a wee run out to the Buchanan Arms and maybe stay there for dinner, or go round to Helensburgh. Would you care to join us?'

'Oh yes, Link!' Joan was totally conquered.

Link stepped over to the Buick and found to his joy that the rear door was unlocked. He swept it open.

'Hop in and wait out of the cold,' he invited them. 'I'm just making a few purchases, and I'll be right back.'

The girls hopped in, in a daze, and Link nipped up the nearest close, found a way out into Holland Street, and continued his stroll.

But occasionally he found small-time casual trickery palling. There was an outbreak of high-toned amateur theatricalism in Glasgow around this time, all Strindberg and Stanislavsky stuff, and Link somehow got in tow with some group that was trying to resuscitate Chinese theatre ballet or something unlikely along these lines. With his passion for thinking big, he sold the director the idea of a big European tour, and started writing to mayors and burgomasters all over the Continent fixing dates. After all, that's how big impresarios get where they are too, and anybody can write a convincing letter, but especially Link.

As a preliminary to the tour, he arranged a mass buffet lunch in one of the new foreign restaurants that had opened in recent years; canapes, sausages on sticks, petits fours and lashings of drink for about a hundred guests, including a pile of town councillors, some of the eminent Glaswegians whose eminence has been gained by getting on to every committee they can capture, and various other big fish, including police officials, who approved of cultural efforts and a spot of free drink. The assembly passed off splendidly, with goodwill speeches and blurts of dedicated flam and the merry gurgle of a hundred throats downing champagne and whisky and Martinis. Before it quite had time to wind up and disperse, Link buttonholed the restaurant manager and muttered persuasively to him:

'About the bill . . . You wouldn't be presenting a bill in the ordinary way for a function like this, of course.'

The manager's blood drained from his face and his hands groped for support, or a weapon.

'I mean,' said Link, 'although I'm the organizer, I have nothing to do with the cash side, of course. But you've got nothing to worry about. A splendid piece of catering, I must congratulate you.'

'Thank you, sir,' said the manager, waiting desperately for the next line.

'And of course, with all these important people – police, magistrates, and so on, it's a tremendous help to your prestige and your future business,' Link said blandly. 'Worth thousands of pounds in goodwill and advertising. And I may say they've all appreciated your efforts very much indeed. I think you can call it a big success.'

He was meticulous about getting away before the last of the eminent guests, and took reasonable precautions about not eating in that particular restaurant until it changed hands, which it did about a year later – probably by coincidence.

Link has disappeared recently. The story is that he is managing a factory, or a transport company, somewhere in the south of England, and either possibility is even probable. So I have never been able to check with him about what happened to the Chinese theatre-ballet-mime-posture tour of Europe. I have the impression that it never quite happened.

Who, the Drummer?

'The first time I met Alfred Hitchcock,' I was saying, when an Armenian-American-Jew named Eddie Traubner looked round and said:

'Who dat?'

'Alfred Hitchcock,' I repeated.

'The drummer?'

'Oh.'

'It's a gag,' Eddie explained kindly. 'In Hollywood, every bum is a name-dropper – "De Mille was just sayin' ta me yestiddy, As I told Zukor last week, Funny thing happened to me over at Crosby's house last night," – you know the kinda thing, every deadbeat does it all the time. So you say, "The first time I met Alfred Hitchcock." So I use the gag that Sammy Cahn invented to douse all name-droppers. "Who, the drummer?"'

'Which Sammy Cahn?' I asked, injured. 'The drummer one?'

'You got it,' Eddie smiled happily. 'I think we'll get along.'

'Well, all right,' I insisted. 'But nevertheless, the first time I met Alfred Hitchcock, I did meet Alfred Hitchcock, and I have a case of crushed morale to prove it.'

It could have been just as horrible in Glasgow, but my meeting with Hitchcock in London was one of my proofs for some time that London was a hell of a place to be in, until I saw the joke, which took about half an hour.

After we had a child, I managed to lose a lot of the feeling that so many people have all the time, that today is just something that has to be put in for the sake of something better tomorrow. Tomorrow isn't any better than today. Today is as good as anything you're going to get.

'I'm worried about our marriage,' Anna said one spring afternoon when I had written my day's column in a hurry and nipped home to sit and look out of the window.

'So am I,' I said. I had seen the same picture the evening before. 'We may as well as face the facts, kid.'

'Yeah,' she said. 'Somewhere along the line, somewhere . . .'

'Somebody changed the points and we landed at Yoker Depot,' I said.

'Och, shut up when I'm being dramatic, you bowly-legged wee bachle,' she said. 'You never let me have a scene. It says in *Woman* this week that every marriage has its time of crisis. Why don't we have a crisis?'

'This is the crisis,' I said. 'I'm going to London next week.'

'Not on your life.'

'I am,' I tittered. 'It's business. You know every newspaper-man's wife has to get used to seeing her man shoot off to big assignments without her. Stand back because I'm about to shoot.'

The Kemsley newspaper chain, which owned the *Daily Record* at the time, had cooked up one of its beautiful plans – a series of staff training courses for its provincial employees. They were to be taken to London, bedded and boarded for a week and exposed to a daily programme of conferences and meetings with the big London experts. Nobody except Lord Kemsley and some of his lieutenants could see much profit in a week of conferences, but a week in London for nothing was fine with everybody, especially the people who wanted to look for other jobs in Fleet Street but couldn't spare the time or the money to go on their own steam. It was one of the pointless but agreeable things that used to happen all the time in the newspaper business, and which are beginning to disappear nowadays since times are tough and big business has moved in. My turn had just come up for a visit to London. Anna looked suddenly horror-stricken.

'Your shoes!' she said. 'It's too late to get them mended.'

'I'll keep my feet out of sight,' I said. 'As long as the rain keeps off I'm all right.'

The rain kept off most of the time, and my only difficulty with my down-at-heel shoes was that I had to polish them with a hankie because I didn't have the nerve to put them outside my bedroom door at nights for the hotel staff to sneer at. It was my coat that irritated me when I met Hitchcock.

An old Glasgow friend John Lees was working in the London office and knew I was interested in show business and food, so he gave me an invitation to a reception in the

Dorchester to meet Hitchcock and Jane Wyman. I couldn't have been all that broke because I changed a five-pound note on the way so that I could pay the taxi, which just symbolizes my old trouble with money – clothes are nice, but I have to force myself to buy solid things like that because money in the hand for taxis and other stupidities is even nicer. I took the taxi partly for speed and partly because it looked like rain, and whatever happened I had no intention of putting my coat on. It looked all right turned outside in, folded carefully to hide the threadbare bits of the lining, and slung over my arm, with my good suit showing, but putting it on would have disqualified me for the Dorchester. I got there ten minutes early and sat boldly at a table in the lounge to write a quick letter home on Dorchester paper. Then I got up to look for the place where they were throwing the reception.

An interfering flunkey stopped me on the way and forced me down a side corridor to the cloakroom to deposit my coat. Several explanations of why I wanted to keep it in my hand failed to come to my lips as I stumbled through the carpet and plunked it carefully on the counter. I glared at the cloakroom man, ready for a fight, but he just took the bundle and vanished with it.

Hitchcock was very pleasant, and Jane Wyman was even more so as well as being prettier. After three gins I was once more the suave man-about-town. I passed from impressing Jane Wyman with my charm to getting acquainted with Stephen Watts, a London columnist I had always admired. He was friendly and witty and as elegant as hell, and when we had milked the reception for what it was worth we strolled out, two intellectual sophisticates together. I tried to get ahead of him to the cloakroom, or hang back and let him get there first, but it was impossible to do either without fainting or assuming the mannerisms of a lunatic, so we got there together.

The foul cloakroom attendant bounced round dangling a frightsomely correct black town coat to fit on to Watts, who kept on chatting lightly as the swine disappeared and came back holding my dingy brown bundle. Then, with enormous panache, he grabbed a key fold of it and shook the whole thing out, shredded lining and torn pockets and everything, and started stuffing me into it. It could happen just as easily in Glasgow, I expect, but it *feels* worse in London. I met Watts years later in the Corn Exchange in Glasgow, and he honestly seemed to have no recollection of the incident.

'Hitchcock should have seen it,' he told me. 'He could have made something of it. He would have noticed it, too.'

But the reason I was trying to tell this dull anecdote to Eddie Traubner was the end of a long chain of events that had started back in my BBC novitiate. One of the keenest *Canny Reid* fans was a BBC arranger named Ian Gourlay, and when *Canny Reid* was finished I started writing lyrics to the heap of tunes he had lying in his house. A long time afterwards Robert Wilson bought one of our songs, a harmless little number called 'Faraway Isle', and we considered ourselves arrived professional songwriters.

Another long time afterwards I found myself having a whisky breakfast in the Central hotel as one of the guests of an odd American act by the name of Sugar Chile Robinson. The whisky breakfast was the brilliant idea of his press agent, an expatriate American called Ernie Anderson, a sad-faced citizen with no visible roots and a tattoo on his right shoulder blade.

'Glasgow is the greatest,' he told me glibly. 'I'm coming back next month with the Andrews Sisters. Will you be here?'

'Sure,' I said, falling naturally into my horrible fake American. 'Why'ntcha get them to sing my song? It ud be a sensation.'

'Gimme a copy,' he said. 'You never know.' He was always earnest, but he had a slow strange smile, like a Mona Lisa with astigmatism and a heavy growth.

A fortnight later I started to be haunted by cryptic trunk telephone calls which kept missing me. I didn't connect them with anything, but they began to worry me. They arrived at the office five minutes before I got in, or at my mother's house a week after I had been there. I developed the sensations of a persecution maniac, and they came to a head one day when I was having a morning coffee with Tommy Morgan, Glasgow's greatest and most characteristic comic. I was trying to write some gags for him, and he gave me a lift to the foot of my street on his way home for lunch. I met Anna tottering down the street pale with concern.

'Clifford's disappeared,' she gasped. Clifford was two years old by this time.

'He can't be far away,' I said stupidly.

'He's been away for hours,' she said, frantic. 'He was playing in the garden, and the next minute he had vanished. That was at eleven o'clock.' It was one o'clock now, I sent Anna home in case he wandered back, and started to search the district in the helpless undirected way that is all you can do in such situations. There was no trace of him anywhere. The lunchtime traffic hurtled along Great Western Road in both directions at hideous speed, and the river Kelvin bubbled brown and horrible beneath it.

'He'll no be far away,' a points policeman told me, and I realized how stupid the phrase sounded. I called the police station with a long description and got a lot of sympathy in return but no help. On one of my returns to the house, Anna remembered that there had been a personal trunk call for me to the house next door, but nobody knew any details.

At a quarter past two, a neighbour walking along Great Western Road noticed a group of small children clustered round the closed door of a big shop about five blocks from our house. He was about to pass when he thought he recognized one of the children, and when he went over, he discovered that Clifford was standing right at the shop door posting a small black kitten through the letter box. The kitten kept crawling back out, and Clifford kept putting it gently but firmly back in, out of the cold. At half past two the telephone next door rang again, and our helpful neighbour called me in to get a hold of these mysterious callers at last.

It was Ernie Anderson.

'Hey, is there a song called the "Gathering of the Clans"?' he asked me. I didn't think there was.

'Well, there should be – there's a big thing in Edinboro next week called The Gathering of the Clans, and the Andrew Sisters want to sing a song about it.'

'Well, there's no such song,' I said. 'But just a minute. I'll write one and post it to you tomorrow.'

'That's what I thought you would say,' he said. 'I don't want to rush you – any time tomorrow a.m. will do.'

I left the scene of family reunion and went to see Ian Gourlay, and on the following morning we made a demonstration record of the song and sent it to London with the music. It made a good publicity thing for the Andrews Sisters, and although they never actually got the length of singing it in Glasgow, their manager, Lou Levy, who was also a music publisher, took it for publication. The Keynotes made a gramophone record of it, and before we knew where we were it was selling 500 copies a week. At about a farthing a copy, we were practically ready to retire, if we didn't have to eat and live in houses.

'You're really gonna go places, Cliff,' Lou told me during one of the long midnight sessions in the Central Hotel, where I spent practically all my time while the Andrews Sisters were appearing at the Empire. He was short and tough, with a quiet implacable face and attractive New York East Side accent, so low in timbre that it cracked. I went to Arran that year for my summer holidays.

When Howard Keel (the drummer) made his first visit to Glasgow, his manager Eddie Traubner came with him, bearing a letter of introduction and preceded by a long expensive cable from Lou asking me to show him the town. We took to each other at first sight.

250

'You're wastin' your time here,' he told me. 'With your talent you could be making real money in New York or Hollywood. Don't come to New York – it's lousy and cold in winter and stinkin' hot in summer and you need clothes for four seasons. In Hollywood you can wear the same clothes all the year round. It saves money.'

'What talent?' I said, seizing on the inessentials. 'You haven't seen me doing anything.'

'I'm a business manager,' he said. 'My hunches have never been wrong yet.' He had hired a Vauxhall, and I drove him out to Drymen in it one sunny afternoon.

'I think you could change out of first gear now,' he said pleasantly. 'We're goin' downhill.'

'See?' I said. 'I can't even drive.'

'You can drive all right. You should be writin' for television.'

'For money?'

'Lousy rich on your standards.'

'Rich is nice,' I said, remembering about the gears. 'Lousy rich especially.'

'I'll send you some scripts some clients of mine are making an' see if you can write a coupla story lines for them. I'll airmail them from New York before I go through to the coast.'

'Goody goody,' I said. But he did send the scripts. Only I somehow never managed to produce the right story lines, and the television series quietly died in any case. One of his latest letters promised a new series. 'If you can come through with some stories,' he wrote coldly, 'I'll bring you out here and you will start at a minimum of 350 dollars a week.'

I never met an offer like this less than halfway. For the next three weeks I spent most of my time pacing up and down just inside my front door with my bags packed and an airline timetable in my hand. Fortunately, there were a couple of unforeseen hitches, or I might have abandoned my birthplace and got corrupted with all that materialism they eat in California.

After all, I have sometimes asked myself, can you keep a grasp of the essential things of life and remain true to yourself in a faraway country with monotonous months of sunshine and 350 dollars a week? Too damned true you can. Especially a *minimum* of 350 dollars a week.

Hark at Sonny Boy, Mammy Mine

On a coach tour of Northern Ireland in the winter of 1950, I was thrown into a choking paroxysm by the sight of a theatre bill in some small lost town on the coast whose name I have forgotten, but which ran to a music hall. The top of the bill that week was Danny McCafferty – Ulster's Greatest Al Jolson!

What in God's name can you do with a country that actually has a classification of singers like that? But I don't know that I had any right to be laughing. It's funny enough to visualize straight-faced Ulstermen streaming in their thousands every night into village music schools to get lessons in pronouncing Mammy on one knee; but if such a thing had ever happened in Ulster it would have happened in Glasgow too. In fact, no study of Glasgow's folk culture can be adequate without dragging in such oddities as the Jolson Influence. That was my first visit to Northern Ireland, and it only served to confirm the Irishness, or the Celticness of Glasgow, which isn't a mere matter of religion at all.

We don't want to get this Jolson thing out of proportion, but it's intriguing, all the same. Back in 1928, when Jolson smote Glasgow with 'Sonny Boy', voice and everything, of course, *everybody* was singing Jolson songs, suddenly. But the first singing movie was an event of such size that the same thing was doubtless happening in Tokyo and Bootle. It was the postwar Jolson revival that really belted Glasgow in its big, warm, scruffy heart. Having missed the original Jolson mania – 'The Jazz Singer' and the 'Singing Fool' hadn't found their way out through the circuits to Scoat's Pictures by the time I left Gallowgate, and I never caught up with them at all – I viewed the revival coldly because it can't be denied that Jolson's art *is* scruffy. He sang with the same terrifying unrestraint as the drunk buskers of Glasgow who ram a sob into every single syllable of 'Ra Rose Av Tralee' on a Saturday night, and if they aren't scruffy, nobody is.

Anna and I were travelling home on a late tram from a visit to my mother's when the conductor came upstairs to change the destination boards, and he got on the chat about 'The Jolson Story'.

'Take it away—droon it,' I said derisively.

'Naw, honest,' he insisted. 'Ah said the same thing when the wife tried tae drag me. But nae kiddin', it's a terrific pitcher, ye got tae hand it tae auld Al. Bit ae a tear-jerker as well, of course – tuggin' at the auld heart-strings, ye know the kinda tripe – but it's rerr, honest. Ah've seen it twice – nae kiddin', it's that kinda pitcher. You wait.'

Finally it came round to the Salon in Hillhead, so we had to see it. We had tickets. The Salon itself is one of the oddities of Glasgow, especially odd in a district with so much aggressive gentility and bourgeois pretentions as Hillhead. It's a small, long, thin cinema still outside the big circuits, and it competes by running not-too-new films carefully chosen, and by selling them either wholesale or retail. It's the only picture house I ever met where if you buy six tickets at once you get a forty per cent discount. So we couldn't avoid seeing the Jolson film, and to my chagrin I enjoyed it as much as the tram conductor. The Jolson style was still scruffy, but it evoked an instant response, probably helped by Larry Parks, who acts better than I remember Jolson doing.

About a year later an acquaintance interested in amateur tennis asked me to a big tennis dance where I was supposed to be doing some kind of compère act that never emerged very clearly, but towards the end of the evening I found myself standing aimlessly on the platform when the band broke into a Jolson selection, and fighting uselessly against an inner compulsion I was suddenly pasting the slats out of 'April Showers'.

Not that anybody objected. Before the end of the chorus there were thirty or forty couples clustered round the platform; not to listen. The men wanted to do a Jolson too. It still remains as a disquieting memory: two score people in their good suits going down on one knee in unrehearsed synchrony and waving their arms and howling in the accents of an American Mammy-singer they had never seen. It never happened with Rudy Vallee or Crosby or Sinatra; or with anybody, in fact, except Will Fyfe, and that only in his one fabulous song 'I Belong to Glasgow'.

What did Jolson have for Glasgow? Because this wasn't a freak incident. During all those years of the early 'fifties, one tipsy traveller on the top deck of a Glasgow tram who started wailing a Jolson song would provoke twenty other Jolsons to join in, and each one convinced that he was the most authentic Al.

At a summer show in the Pavilion in Renfield Street, during one of those foul-ups that happen in the best theatre, a young extra leapt into the breach by running on front-cloth and doing a spontaneous seven-minute Jolson act. Obeying every tradition of show business, it brought the house down, and was kept in the show. It was a sensation, and the boy, dizzy with delight, realized he was set for life. Six weeks later he did the same act on the other side of Scotland and died a lingering death. Nobody wanted to know about 'Sonny Boy'.

Doctor Crock, the Cockney mad musician who plays

three-week dance dates at the Glasgow Playhouse to enormous business several times a year, has been travelling a singer-impersonator in his company for several years. When the singer fell ill and didn't appear two years ago, over four hundred people turned up unasked to audition for his job. All except three were Jolson singers, and did nothing else.

Maybe the answer to the mystery is racial. Jolson was a Jew, and there are a lot of emotional similarities between Jews and Celts: they are both practical and mystical peoples. They have the same matter-of-fact insistence on identity, and the same consciousness of minority that makes them both sentimental and arrogant; and their humour has the same mixture of coarse breadth and intellectual subtlety. And Glasgow's taste in entertainment has always included a shameless passion for real, hundred per cent ham; big, raw splashes of quick emotionalism. Maybe no community can achieve any support for the higher forms of art if it doesn't start off with a widespread lust for sheer low expression. On top of all the Jolson enthusiasm Glasgow managed to keep a symphony orchestra well supported during all the years in which Edinburgh somehow couldn't manage to get one going at all.

There was a time when I realized thankfully that I had evolved past my native city's crude old tastes in the popular arts – red-nosed comics in stage kilts and gruesome imitation Scotch songs. The comedy of the future was going to be the slick, sharp stuff of Bob Hope and Jack Benny. I felt a terrible impatience with the Glasgow pros who refused to recognize that the day for their stuff was long gone, and went on and on cheating the public. I mention this merely to show how easy it is to dismiss a whole native culture. One summer evening during the war, when the Glasgow pubs took a half-holiday every Thursday to conserve their supplies, I joined the small trek over the city boundary looking for a county hostelry that was still open. I landed in the first pub outside Glasgow on the way to London from Tollcross, and found a free-and-easy ready to start in the back room. Lanarkshire actually allowed people deliberately to sing in pubs.

The free-and-easy mustn't be pictured as a bright, sunny Viennese garden business. The back room was about the size of a small bedroom, all painted dark brown and containing some worn benches, a couple of tired tables and a frightened looking piano in which fully half of the keys produced nothing more than a thud of agony in place of a note. But a man turned up with an accordion.

There was no organization. A middle-aged dearie with a ginny smile, who was a regular habitué, did take some kind of control and insisted loudly that everybody – absolutely everybody – had to favour the company. People bought their own drinks, or bought drinks in private groups. I drank a beer quickly and listened in horrid fascination for 'Suvla Bay' to emerge, and by God, it did, first time; like sitting in a time machine and shooting straight back to Gallowgate.

'Come on, Sarah!' the customers cried. 'Give us yer masterpiece!'

The old dearie waved a deprecating hand, then said:

'Aye, all right – it'll gi'e the resta ye time tae get ready fur ye turn.' She took a calm sip from her glass, and without getting up, threw out one hand to rest it on the window sill, leaned sideways, fixed her eye on a spot high up on the opposite wall, and loosed a wavy but knife-edged soprano:

> 'Scotsa-landza,
> Scotsa-landza,
> Scotlandza aye sae braw . . .'

When she finished she shook her hand before her to dismiss the applause, and wiped an alcoholic tear impatiently away with the other hand. I stared and listened perfectly rapt, wanting at the same time to hoot with laughter and cheer and pat her on the head. It was a genuinely frightful performance. And I cheered more loudly than any. When my turn came I truly wanted to escape, but you can't escape. I stood up and turned up my collar to indicate that I was at a street corner, and quavered high up in my nose:

'Faraway in thaaaa Hielan's
There standzaaaaa wee hoose
An' it stands aaaaaat the breist o-o-o-o the brac—'

It was impossible to go wrong with 'Granny's Hielan' Hame'. As I hit the last tearful note the dearie launched herself at me and pounded me on the shoulders.

'Thanks, son!' she babbled. 'Ye broat the tears tae ma eyes!' And in fact, some colourless liquid was trickling down her cheeks. The accordionist gave me the Glasgow nod and said gravely:

'At's a rerr voice ye goat, rerr, Mac. Ye should gerrit trained.' They floored me. Didn't they realize they had been hearing a burlesque? No, they didn't, because there are some things so far-fetched in themselves that you can't burlesque them. Under false pretences, I was in, and I never really got out again.

It's all very well to lift a pained eyebrow when some drunk monster wails: 'For ra blood leaps in my veins When I hear the bagpipe's strains, Scotland, Dear auld Scotland, Forever!' giving five extra bars to the high note in the last word. But despite yourself, the blood *does* leap What's the theatrical moment that paralyses Glasgow with delight? It's that fearful moment that happens inexorably several times a year in, say, the Empress, or the Pavilion, or the Metropole. The tenor, as Prince Charlie, has just finished 'Over the Sea to Skye'; or maybe 'MacGregor, Despite Them, Shall Flourish Forever'! or in recent years, quite probably 'Scotland the Brave'. And as he lingers, with right arm outflung, there's a muffled shift expectantly in its seats; and then, yes, no, no, it's on the stage – no – it's coming from behind – yes! It is! It's a whole pipe band in full shriek tramping in from the lobby and splitting into three and swaggering down the aisles to the stage with a noise enough to crack your skull asunder.

Yes, it's the HLI! Or the Sutherlands. Or the Glesca Polis. It's the baun! Hurray! Hooch! We-e-e-ell! And if it's a big show, there's a winding road leading down a ramp from the backcloth of the glen, and the pipers will vanish momentarily and reappear marching down it; and if you're lucky, once they've lined up down both sides of the stage, a shepherd in a bum-bee tartan plaid will appear on the road and follow them down, with a pipe in one hand and a cromag in the other, and behind him, not one, but two, real collie dugs! Why in heaven's name two collie dugs? Don't ask stupid questions – cheer, clap, hooch! This is the greatest show on earth! But even a stranger, a foreigner, an Englishman even, will not ask the question because the infection of the excitement is irresistible. Nobody doubts for a second that it's corn. But corn is the stuff you can get your teeth into.

Glasgow does well for theatres for its million people. The old Queens unhappily burned down a few years ago, where Doris Droy and the late, beloved Sam Murray used to put on the roughest, bawdiest, longest-running panto-mimes in the world. The jokes at the Queens cut straight to the bone, and apart from reading the title, there was never any point in trying to connect the sketches with the story of the pantomime because the storyline usually sank without trace in the first seven minutes. Alien visitors of an anthropological turn used to make a point of joining the mobs of rumbustious Glaswegians and thoughtful students of Glasgow lore in the trek to the Queens panto every year, but they will trek no more.

At the other end of the list, the Theatre Royal which housed legit and opera and ballet, has been turned into a television studio. This still leaves the King's for pre-

London tours of new plays, opera, ballet and musicals. The other first-class legitimate house, the Alhambra, has gone entirely musical in the past few years. It usually houses musicals and spectaculars at the winter end of the year and occupies the summer profitably with the impressive Five Past Eight shows, one of the astonishing theatrical phenomena of postwar Scotland.

There are two shows of the same name, one in Edinburgh and one in Glasgow, running simultaneously and then shuffling round performers in alternate years. They change their programmes every week, and the shows are staged with an extravagance equal or superior to anything to be found in London. They have brought completely new audiences to the live theatre – the country bodies who swarm into Five Past Eight from coaches in organized parties from all over the hinterland of the West of Scotland, and the well-doing Glasgow middle classes who always thought music hall was really a bit vulgar, but realize it must be all right if it's in the Alhambra. The shows are really very good, of course.

They accommodate some of the younger comic stars thrown up in Glasgow since the war – and with very few exceptions, a Scots comic means a Glasgow comic. Professional funny men in Scotland are either born in Glasgow or nurtured by Glasgow. Typical is Jimmie Logan, a handsome, relaxed young man with a lot of sex appeal, who was born in the theatre and brought up as a working member of the improbable Logan family of Glasgow, who until they broke up a few years ago ran their own gallus family show in the Metropole for years on end to an audience of fanatical loyalty and enthusiasm.

Another is Rikki Fulton, who started a theatrical career as an actor in the BBC Children's Hour and turned comic almost by accident. Another is Stanley Baxter, an even rarer bird who rose to meteoric stardom as a straight actor in the Glasgow Citizen's Theatre. A skinny, thoughtful youth with an intelligent ugly face, he had become an actor of real talent before he was shrewdly lured away to the comic stage.

This fairly rare theatrical event actually happened to another Citizen's actor, Duncan Macrae, who now splits his time between comedy and legit and takes his fans with him from one to the other.

Many of the well-kempt citizens who go religiously to the Five Past Eight shows are descended directly from the faithful clientele of two repertory companies, the Wilson Barrett players and the Citizen's Theatre. The Barrett company actually occupied the same theatre, the Alhambra, for many years, until recently their support dwindled away. This is a pity, because a city can always do with plenty of repertory. But the regular Barrett audiences were a rather unvigorous mob, theatrically. They included a large ballast of pleasant women with good manners who seemed to get as much of a kick out of recognizing the cast familiarly and referring to them by their Christian names as out of the plays themselves. One night, after a lengthy absence, I was sitting in the front stalls watching a prodigiously good-looking young actor in the company going through such a hellish series of postures to indicate suppressed passion that I failed to repress a happy spontaneous giggle. I was shushed quite murderously by four ladies in front of me, and if I had been really strong-minded I would have stopped giggling and booed instead, in the interests of good theatre. I'm glad I didn't, though. Although I hate bad acting I can never help feeling sympathetic towards people on a stage because it's such a vulnerable place to be.

The shushing ladies probably moved over to the Citizen's Theatre when the Wilson Barrett company vanished. The Citizen's was launched towards the end of the war with tremendous enthusiasm to bring Glasgow the best of theatre on a relatively non-commercial basis, and it has done a lot of excellent work since. It started out in the only available theatre, the Athenaeum, which is a department of the Royal Academy of Music and is all right for amateur productions. Later it moved to the

Princess's Theatre, the old home of traditional pantomime in Gorbals on the south side of the Clyde, which
takes it out of the main show business centre of the city.
Because of this, and other reasons, it has had its ups and
downs. It is having one of its downs as I write this, but will
survive, I feel sure.

The Citizen's suffered too from the shushing ladies,
who find some kind of compensation in talking about
actors by their first names and feeling that they are a part
of the Theatre. They should be encouraged, of course, but
a real theatre is always in some danger if it depends on the
massed forces of respectability. You can't be vigorous,
especially in the theatre, if you're not at least a little bit
scruffy.

The Metropole and the Empress are still the homes of
solid proletarian entertainment, but supreme in the field is
the Pavilion, and supreme in the Pavilion is Tommy
Morgan, who has been running his own show for six
months every summer for nineteen years, which must be
some kind of record in world theatre. Big and coarse and
shrewd and aggressive and warm-hearted, Tommy Morgan
is dangerously near to being a living symbol of the spirit
of Glasgow.

Thomas Morgan, Esq.

'Glasgow?' he said to me a few weeks ago. 'Glasgow?
Look at it! A durty stinkin' dump. Who the hell could
love a place like this?'

261

'The people are all right,' I said, unperturbed.

'A shower a neds. Gimme Majorca! The sunshine! Oooh!' He stood up and pushed his hands above his head yearningly. 'Sunshine, for the love a God!' Then he laughed hoarsely at himself and sat down. 'Ah've got a dampt cheek, tae grumble.'

Tommy Morgan was born in Bridgeton. His father was a leather worker, thinker and Socialist, who was victimized after a threatened strike and never got back into the leather industry. Tommy grew up as a result closely acquainted with poverty and sometimes actual hunger, but it never affected him except to convince him that regular meals were a good thing and being short of money was bad. On the stage, his mastery of Glasgow's tough, wry humour hasn't any element of mimicry, it's simply the natural expression of his background and temperament. He is also known to the customers by his nickname of Clairty. It sounds silly, but this stems from the times in his childhood when his mother used to throw up the window and shout at him in the street, and her words were always prefaced by "clare tae goodness!' As a boy, he went indiscriminately to Catholic and Protestant schools, a practically impossible state of affairs in Glasgow. He used to run away from home simply for the sake of a change, and sleep out in closes or convenient brickyards. In the first world war he ran off to the army three times while under age, and he had the uniforms of three different regiments to choose from when he wanted to impress his girl friends. On one occasion his family went to see him off tearfully at Central Station and found him boiling a kettle for tea when they got back home to Bridgeton. He had jumped the train and got home before them.

'Ach, tae hell,' he said. 'This is nae weather fur sodgerin'.'

Morgan is not a character comedian. He just plays himself on stage, except that he usually appears once in each of his shows in dame, as Big Beenie, a ripe overblown female greeted with hysterical delight by the hardbitten, fastidious audiences at the Pavilion. Beenie also is Glasgow; occasionally pathetic but tough and resilient and nobody's mug. She wears magnificent tarty outfits and carries huge rococo handbags, and the fact that she always sports thick brown woollen stockings and zip-up houseboots doesn't appear to matter. She lives in a lusty hunt for a man but determined not to give an inch.

'Hauns aff!' she is fond of saying to fruity citizens in grey wigs and monocles on park benches. 'You know ma price – the ring on the finger. Allow Big Beenie!'

Allow Big Beenie? It's hard to translate. It means something like: No bad for Big Beenie; or, Big Beenie's the boy; or, There's nae flies on Big Beenie, eh? But as with any great comic, a reading of the script gives almost nothing of Morgan himself. The first time I took Ernie Anderson to watch the Morgan show, since as an American he wanted to take in all the local culture, he kept leaning on my shoulder and wheezing:

'My Gahd, this guy's killin' me an' I haven't understood one damn word yet!'

Morgan's script conferences, which I have attended often, usually collapse into reminiscences of show business, impossible stories that have to be believed.

'This joke sounds like Bret Harte,' he'll say. 'Did ye never see Bret Harte? My Goad, whit an artist. Talk aboot your script comics? In the auld days at the Princess's, Bret used tae say tae his straight man two seconds before the curtain went up: "A new act – ah'm a plumber an' you're a polisman. Right, we're on!"'

One of his stories always gave a thrill of pure horror and delight. A song-and-dance man he knew in Shettleston had just got his first professional booking, and at once bought himself a camel coat and a cigar holder. His mother was overcome with pride, and begged him to come to a party where she could show him off – none of her friends had ever met a real actor. George left the theatre in his fancy coat, carefully overlooking some of the grease paint on his face, and got to the party where he expected to be lionized. It was in a single-end in Shettleston Road, and about twenty women were jammed in the little room.

Instead of being surrounded and adored, he was accosted by his mother at once.

'You must listen tae this, George – this lassie should be on the stage. She's a rerr singer – writes a' her ain songs, tae. Come on, Myra, let George hear ye.'

George saw at once that he had been trapped, and by his own mother. Myra went frenziedly shy in the presence of the real actor, and the company had to beg her to perform before she would even consider it.

'All right,' she said sullenly. 'But ah'm too shy. Ah'll sing as long as naebody looks at me.'

With his scalp prickling, George watched her squeezing into a corner and standing with her face to the wall to begin her performance. Her friends listened entranced, and kept nudging George to remind him how good Myra was. The song she was singing was a pathetic ballad, and at first she seemed to be trying for a suitable key, until George realized that it just had no tune at all. It had no rhymes either, or scansion, and it went on and on and on through woe and disaster until a rain of nudges warned him Myra was coming to the climax. Her voice quavered up and up to the last thrilling line:

> 'And then she drew
> A ra-a-a-a-azor
> Across her throat!'

Popular taste in Glasgow begins round this level and ascends by minute gradations to Shakespeare, who is quite kindly regarded on Clydeside. It must have been at a gathering very similar, in the crowded steamy yellow gaslight of a back kitchen in Bridgeton, that Tommy Morgan took his biggest step towards going pro. It was just after the first war, and the booze was flying fast, when somebody threw up the window for more air and the clear passionate tremolo of a back-court busker floated up from the darkness.

'Bring the puir man up an' gi'e him a drink!' somebody suggested. The poor man was delighted to join the party and perform again out of the cold. His name was Tommy Yorke, and Morgan, who had brought him up from the back court, instantly proposed a stage partnership with him. They have been together ever since, and when the customers in the twenties weren't in the mood for Morgan's jokes, they could be battered into a response unfailingly by a solo from Yorkie of the number that had pierced the back-court air of Bridgeton. It was 'The Rose of No Man's Land'.

In a city where everybody sings, the standards are bound to vary – there must be some pretty shoogly tenors among the Italian peasantry, in spite of the legends – but the best do come to the top. Probably the best vindication of Glasgow's popular taste since the war has been the emergence of a young Paisley forester, Kenneth McKellar, as the singing darling of all classes from the shushing ladies to the Presley-bred goonagers. McKellar's success story is almost drab in its inevitability. He had a voice, so he left the Forestry Commission, where he was doing all right, and took up serious music study in London, sang some roles in opera and was well received, came back to Scotland to make a living on the stage.

With no crafty ballyhoo to speak of, he made a good mark singing in odd concerts. His predecessor Robert Wilson, who is still packing them in after a very long career indeed, encouraged the new arrival and the BBC gave him a quiet little series and in a few weeks the public was clamouring for more. McKellar has also been conscripted into the Five Past Eight shows. He is a burly young man with an honest Scots face, a quite startling purity of tone and an intelligent sensibility not common among singers, and the fact that he is now a sensation in Glasgow merely shows that the city knows the best when it hears it.

But Glasgow's taste is as fickle and ridiculous and as servile to ballyhoo as anybody else's, and the Empire Theatre is a shrine to its wildest excesses. It's there that Glasgow jammed the seats and the lobby and the streets all round to worship Danny Kaye, and stayed away in vast numbers to ignore Frank Sinatra. I thought Danny Kaye gave a great show, personally, and it's nice to see a good act appreciated. But in this branch of entertainment, nothing succeeds like success and an orgy of frenetical advance publicity, and it's doubtful if any performer coming to Glasgow will ever get the preliminary build-up that Danny Kaye had. Hope Street was jammed with thousands of fans to see him arriving, the mounties were out, the Glasgow Police pipe band played him from the train to the hotel, and the reporters arriving for his press reception were checked on a list by a kind of security guard from Val Parnell's office. Nobody could follow that. It's trite to say that times have changed, but they have, all the same. Old-style variety has been knocked sideways by the gramophone boom, and practically nobody but a recording singer ever tops the bill at the Empire at this point in history. And it only takes a string of non-hit records to topple last week's star. When Sinatra arrived in the long procession of American names, he was singing just as expertly as he ever did, but a new generation of teenagers thought of him as one of the old guard, and stayed at home to listen to their records of Frankie Laine. If Sinatra had returned in 1957, they might have had to call out the mounties again to hold back the fans.

I have never thought it tragic that most of the top-of-the-bill variety stars in Glasgow recently were Americans. A good American act is better than a bad British act, and as long as singers top the bills, the Americans are likely to be better because most British pop singers are pallid imitations of Americans. The art of Johnny Rae makes me squirm, but at least it's his own. Anyway, Glasgow has always liked Americans and American jokes, beginning

266

with Jolson or long before. Even before the postwar boom in emigration, it would have been hard to throw a stone in Argyle Street without bouncing it off somebody who either had cousins or brothers in America or who had lived in America himself at some time. Glaswegians were always great travellers, and especially to America and Canada, and there is clearly something in the American tempo of humour and music that jibes with the emotional rhythm of the Glaswegian. The Glaswegian takes to American humour more easily than to English, in fact, because his own jokes are brash and acid and informal, and classless. Of course it's pathetic to see young Glaswegians elevating any trashy American idea to the status of a cult merely because it's American, but they'll probably grow out of that, as their fathers did, and not all American ideas are trashy.

The underlying sympathy between Glasgow and America is not mere theorizing. On the face of it, Glasgow is a dirty, grubby city that nobody would choose to visit deliberately. But people do. During the war, American servicemen who had been stationed in Glasgow sometimes travelled from the south of England to spend a week-end leave in the city, and they did it for more than one reason. They liked the feeling of the place. Today, Glasgow stands above Edinburgh and third in the whole of Britain among the most-visited towns by tourists of all races.

The American theatricals who get a chance to walk round the city without the mounties usually react favourably to it. Archie Robbins, an extremely gifted comic who put in a week at the Empire, looked down West Nile Street the day he arrived and said:

'It's like Pittsburg!'

'What, horrible?' I asked him.

'No, no – well, horrible too, sure, but homey. Kind of rock bottom honest-to-God.'

'You can say that again,' I said.

'No thanks,' he said. 'I just said it. If they don't lynch

267

me here I think I'll like it. I like it anywhere they don't lynch me, of course. I hate getting lynched.'

They didn't lynch him, and he liked Glasgow. 'The food!' he told me next day. 'What wonderful food you get here. And it's cheap, too. I'm going to eat every day this week.'

The biggest American performer, in point of pure size, to visit Glasgow in recent years was Burl Ives, who was crushing the scales at an even twenty-one stone when he arrived. He was probably the city's most fervent admirer although the audiences he drew at the Empire were just fair. The city, and the country, exercised a baleful fascination over him. He bought a kilt, a terrible size of a thing which, when propped upright on the floor provided a reasonable toy fort for my two children to play inside; and a chanter on which he practised in preparation for playing the full stands of bagpipes.

'Ah, Glasgy, Glasgy!' he would cry in that voice rich yet reedy.

'Glasgow,' I used to correct him. 'Either Glesca, or Glasgow. If you say Glasgy, people will take you for a stage Scotchman playing in Edinburgh.'

'Glasgy, Glasgy!' he would cry again, and work his chin so that the top tuft of his beard stood out horizontally. 'Whether it's authentic or not, I've been thinking about it as Glasgy for too long to change now. Let me hear the "Carnwath Mill" again.'

So I would sing the 'Carnwath Mill' again while he plunked his guitar tentatively and hummed a harmony. I had been an admirer of Ives's work for many years since seeing him in feature parts in a few cowboy films, and since he came to Glasgow with Ernie Anderson, I found myself elected as a condensed guide to Glasgow folklore and music. The city stimulated Ives, and he was always a character who ate, drank and lived with a titanic appetite. A folk-singer about thirty years before folk-singing became a mass cult, he has a genuinely incalculable repertory of songs, and following his visits to Glasgow, a

268

fair selection of Glasgow's among them. His idea of a good time was to do two shows and then hole up somewhere with a few acquaintances and a case of whisky and go on singing for fun until four or five in the morning.

'What was that one again?' he would sigh, leaning back and shutting his eyes,

> 'Murder, Murder, Polis,
> Three Sterrs up . . .'

On his second visit to the city he had already worked another ancient local jingle into his act, the one that goes:

> 'Three craws
> Sat upon a wa',
> Sat upon a wa',
> Sat upon a wa',
> Three craws
> Sat upon a wa',
> On a cold and frosty mornin'.'

It was a riot.

During one of these sma'-oors song-fests, I remember, he kept coming back pleadingly to a little quatrain, very sweet and melancholy, that was new to me and which he had picked up somewhere near Edinburgh:

> 'Welcome the rose, both red and white
> Welcome the flower of my heart's delight
> The spirit rejoiceth from the spleen
> Welcome in Scotland, to be queen.'

'You take the bass, Cliff,' he kept saying. 'You try the alto, Peter. Softly, now!' And dutifully, with the second bottle of whisky halfway down, we would gently croon in three-part harmony. He had changed into his kilt to get the right atmosphere, and was sitting in that, about two acres of white shirt, and his stocking soles. Ernie had already telephoned for a taxi for me, since I wanted to get home before five. Chorus after chorus went by, and then the taxi company telephoned to say that their driver had radioed them from his cab to say that no customer had appeared yet.

'Tell them to wait another ten minutes, Laddie,' Burl murmured. 'Now, then, very softly: "Welcome the rose . . ."'

At last, swaying slightly from music and lack of sleep, I went down to a dark, totally deserted Hope Street and found the resigned taxi driver still waiting. As I was climbing in, there was a commotion behind me and Burl appeared on the pavement, with his guitar, and still in stocking soles.

'Just once more,' he whispered resonantly. 'Can you sing, cabby?'

'Anythin' you say,' the driver said co-operatively.

'Right, take the alto. "Welcome the rose, both red and white . . ."'

With a tolerant smile, the taxi driver sang da-da-dum in something like harmony. At the end of one chorus I said to him clearly:

'This man is a dangerous maniac. Drive gently away.'

He started up and rolled slowly down Hope Street. Burl gesticulated wildly and galloped alongside, twanging his guitar, and I finally rolled the window down, leaned out and joined him in the last chorus until the taxi left him behind. He was a true glutton.

The most surprising thing about his act at the Empire wasn't a folk-song at all, but a music-hall chorus Ian Gourlay and I had written for Tommy Morgan. Burl begged for the loan of it. Ian arranged it for the Empire orchestra, and it came in as the finish to his act with colossal panache as 'an old traditional ditty kindly lent to me by that celebrated scholar and folk-student, Mr Tommy Morgan.' And the song was:

'I'm glad that I was born in Glasgow,
I'm glad that Glasgow's my home town—'

That's another thing, by the way. This song isn't the only one we had written about Glasgow, and even apart from the classic Will Fyfe song, there are many many more. There must be something strongly-flavoured and unique in a city that evokes songs to it, as Glasgow and London and Paris do. I never heard of a crop of songs about Manchester or Birmingham, though there might be some without my knowledge. There are almost no songs even about Edinburgh, and the only one I've heard of that city written in modern times I wrote myself at the request of a singer, and it wasn't the least bit easy to write. The reason may be that Edinburgh takes pride in the beauty of the city, with good reason, and ties it up with a noble history and a well-grounded feeling of good manners and good breeding and social superiority; while Glasgow's pride centres on the opposites; on a rejection of social superiority and on an unhygienic aggressive warmth of character, which are more real ideas. I like Edinburgh, and I have never found it as cool and withdrawn as many Glaswegians accuse it of being. You can have a whale of a time in Edinburgh. But there is some truth all the same in the old legend that breeding in Edinburgh means good form, whereas in Glasgow it means good fun.

One of the other likeable Americans who wandered into Glasgow for an Empire stint was the singer Don Cornell. Most of these visitors put up at the Central Station Hotel, and by this time the lobby and the corridors were old familiar places to me. Don came with his pianist and his manager Mannie Greenfield, a heavily-built New Yorker with a bass baritone drawl and the look of one of the innocent gangsters you find in Runyon. He had brought a scribbled note of introduction from my American publisher Lou Levy, who had never actually published anything for me after his first enthusiasm. But we still exchanged friendly letters, and technically I was entitled to call him my American publisher when I wanted to make some kind of impression. I went over to the hotel and found the latest American trio relaxing in their suite. Mannie was padding about looking reflective and business-like.

'Lou tole us aboutcha,' he said. 'Dis is great, meet'n' ya.' Honestly, he spoke like that; a nice, plain guy. 'What gives wid de business in town, Cliff? You t'ink wuh gonna do okay in Glaz-gow?'

'You've got some ugly competition,' I said warily.

'Go on out'n moider 'em, Mannie,' Don Cornell said cheerfully. 'Isn' 'at what I pay ya fur? Shoodem, or sumpn.' Mannie gave a happy explosive laugh in his chest.

'I caint,' he said, 'Dey impounded my wadda pistol at the Customs. Who's de opposition anyway?'

'It's a new act called Billy Graham,' I said. Don leapt to his feet waving his arms and grinning.

'Unfair practices, that's what,' he shouted.

'Don' kid yaself boy,' said Mannie. 'Dis guy Graham's real box-office. I just hope he draws a different class a audience from us, is all.'

'So do I,' I said. 'I'll tell you tomorrow because I'm going to his show tonight.' Whatever else it was, the Billy Graham visit to Glasgow was a show that couldn't be overlooked.

Billies and Dans

It wouldn't be easy to say whether things like the Billy Graham crusade came under the heading of religion or entertainment. I didn't rate it very highly as either, but there's no doubt it was a roaring success at the turnstiles. It arrived with the backing of a sizeable section of the Protestant churches in Glasgow. The Catholic Church treated it with a dignified apathy, logically enough. But with twelve or fifteen thousand cramming into the Kelvin Hall every night for six weeks to see Billy Graham, it's fair to suspect that a sprinkling of good Catholics slipped in out of curiosity.

The old clash of Catholic and Protestant was kept pretty quiet during that period, probably because people were actually talking about religion, and the religious war in Glasgow has practically nothing to do with religion. It's the same kind of thing as group hatred anywhere else. You're either a durty Orangeman or a Papish bastard. It's much more subtle than anti-Semitism, and it must be understood that most people in Glasgow don't spend much time thinking about it at all from one year's end to another. But it's there, and even the most impartial Glaswegian is likely to have some feelings based on religion in this restricted sense.

I don't like the Catholic Church myself, on the whole. A religion based on authority and infallibility seems silly to me, as a philosophical idea, although its strength as an institution in the political sense must command respect. Obviously it has something that a lot of people want, and along with its gory history and its fondness for bigotry and repression (the Protestant church in Scotland has a fair amount of blood on its historical hands too) it obviously has spread a lot of Christian charity and goodwill towards men in the bygoing.

In Glasgow, it represents a very large minority population group which has a history of social under privilege. The bulk of Glasgow's Catholics are descended from Irish immigrants as I am myself. They fled from Irish unemployment and famines and were accepted as a new lower class in Glasgow, and you can still see it. Whatever the situation is elsewhere, there's nothing chic about Glasgow Catholicism. It's the religion of the lower classes, however obsolete the description may sound. The Catholics have a bigger proportion of poor people than the Protestants. The average child in a Glasgow Catholic school looks less kempt than the average child in a Glasgow Protestant school. Absenteeism is commoner among Catholic children than among Protestants. On the average, Glasgow Catholics probably grow up more ignorant educationally than Glasgow Protestants.

There are no published statistics covering such facts. There's a lot of exaggerated conjecture instead. Alarmed Protestants, the brooding kind, are perpetually afraid of the Roman peril because the Catholic birthrate, as a result of Rome's rigorous attitude to contraception, is higher than the Protestant. It is also a fact that people lower down the educational ladder usually reproduce faster in any case. Protestants in Glasgow suspect that the Catholic Church doesn't want its adherents too highly educated. Well, the Church is more concerned with good Catholics than with breeding successful businessmen or eggheads.

On the other hand, you can disprove any generalization about Glasgow Catholics by choosing examples. A rough Protestant school is just as rough as a rough Catholic school. The crack Catholic schools, St Aloysius for example, do just as well in external examinations as the crack Protestant schools like Hutcheson's Grammar. Most of the Protestants who make the generalizations reject the exceptions, if they have heard of them.

Still, most of the smartish businessmen's bars in the city contain fewer Catholics at lunch time than Protestants – a lot fewer than the relative population figures justify. And it isn't because Catholics are more temperance-minded than Protestants. There are too few Catholics in the newspaper industry in Glasgow, for instance. Freemasonry is strong among the printing craftsmen, of course, but even in the editorial departments the proportion of Catholics is fairly tiny. It's hard to say that there is any kind of bar against them, because there are notable exceptions. But Protestants tend to mix with Protestants, and to employ Protestants rather than Catholics, other things being even roughly equal. The average Glaswegian isn't bigoted, but he's aware of the fact of religion in this restricted sense. The difficulty is that many Protestants make assumptions about all individual Catholics on the basis of some generalized hostility to the Catholic idea. And Catholics are fairly active assumers too, when the situation arises.

The whole thing is a fearful tangle and it will never be sorted out. The old radical Socialists were convinced that the spread of enlightenment and social justice would render such religious differences irrelevant, and there is a certain degree of truth in that. But in some corners of civic affairs, the present-day Labour Party is in danger of compromise with the Catholic Church itself.

Glasgow's Catholic vote has always been a fairly solid left-wing vote, naturally enough, since Labour speaks for the under-privileged masses. But the Labour Party in Glasgow today is so concerned with keeping the Catholic vote solid that in some places it works more hand-in-glove with the parish priest than you would expect in a party that wants to unite all men regardless of race, creed or colour. There's a faint Tammany Hall tinkle about it, but that's partly because the Labour Party, membership of which was once an act of faith and even of sacrifice, has been a great bandwagon since the war. The quality of Labour representation in Glasgow Town Council is not what it was, but the opposition, Tory or Moderate or Progressive or whatever municipal Tories are calling themselves this year, is certainly no better. Municipal politics everywhere have passed their age of glorious strife over principles since the old disputed Socialist principles have become respectable and been adopted by everybody.

But religion never really loses its fire in Glasgow. And there is absolutely no possibility of expressing the mildest opinion on it, or even relating facts about it, with any hope of being understood by any large group of Glaswegians. A few years ago I wrote a newspaper piece saying that I disapproved of guns being issued to police and special constables in Ulster on the Eire border. I protested out of pure goodwill towards Ulstermen, Eireann, Fenian

275

and Orangemen alike, from a reasonable conviction that if you give people guns, other people are liable to get shot; but among several letters I got after the piece was published, one fairly typical specimen warned me that the writer had finally pinpointed me – I was 'nothing but a bloody Fenian'. There's nothing apathetic about that.

Naturally, I took my own prejudices with me to the Kelvin Hall to see the Billy Graham crusade. Religion is fine, although I don't have what most people call a religion; but I never liked the kind of religion that depended on a spellbinder backed by a thousand-voice choir. You get religion, if it's worth anything, sitting alone and wrestling with yourself, or God, or the Devil, without musical interruptions, and every day for life if necessary. Still, if Billy Graham could help people to be at peace with themselves, good luck to him.

It wasn't easy to get a ticket. I went to an upstairs office in Sauchiehall Street where the advance headquarters of the Crusade had been established, and found it teeming with folk. An American girl thought carefully when I asked for two press tickets for the opening night.

'Your office has already had tickets allocated,' she said, after consulting a chart.

'I know,' I said, 'I want two more.'

'I don't know,' she said. 'We have to be careful. There are so many tickets out it's quite obvious a lot of people have gotten press tickets who aren't *bona fide* journalists.'

'Well, I am.'

'Oh, I realize that. I'll let you have two tickets. But the situation is that some people who have gotten tickets without being *bona fide* are just going to get found out when they arrive at the Kelvin Hall.'

'Will you turn them out?' I asked.

'Well,' she scribbled a name on two tickets, 'they have no right to be there.'

I had bought an old car that winter, the first one we had owned. We were living just north of the University from Kelvin Hall, but we took the car in case there was a rush for buses after the meeting. As it was, there were so many cars that Kelvin Way was being used as an official park, and we had to leave the car not much more than halfway to the hall. The block of press seats was right down at the front and to one side of the centre stage, which was six or eight feet high. The rest of the seats rose in tiers up from there. The counsellors, local volunteers recruited by the Billy Graham committee, sat along the front row wearing badges for easy identification. Three of them just beside us looked like a family group, mother, daughter and son. The son, a boy of about eighteen, had a glazed stare and a loose lower jaw.

There was a big press turnout. A fat middle-aged woman in purple, wearing a lot of make-up and strong perfume, appeared among the press seats and sat beside us on the seat we were holding for the *News of the World* man, who shrugged and found a seat farther back. In a few minutes she saw somebody getting up from a counsellor's seat, and immediately changed to that. She had her handbag open, and was eating chocolates from it. After a few more moves she landed in one of the front-row press seats, and sat eating chocolates and staring hungrily up at the platform. As time went on, a group of Glasgow clergymen appeared and took their places on the stage behind the speaker's podium.

There were preliminaries, words, music from the massed choir. Billy Graham came forward, wearing a lapel microphone to give him freedom of movement. Tall, clean-cut, wavy hair, pale blue eyes, square jaw jutting. He spoke quietly, conversationally.

Some people thought this was emotionalism. It was not emotionalism, he said. It was the word of God. He was prepared to prove . . . he went on, gently, in that clear, slightly monotonous, attractive American accent. But whether it was emotionalism or not, pretty soon he got to the arm-waving bits, the rising cadences, the sudden silences, the stern pointing finger. His illustrations and analogies were on the simple side. Theologically you could have driven a bus through his argument. The two things that puzzled me were that so many Scottish ministers with good divinity degrees were sitting behind him apparently approving of this ramshackle theology; and that far from feeling the unwilling emotional response I had feared in myself, I kept waiting for him to get properly worked up and shifting in my seat for comfort.

After the sermon, the routine was to ask listeners to come forward and publicly to accept Jesus Christ. There was no response at all. I felt myself growing sorry and embarrassed for Graham. The organ played low, sugary music and he kept on quietly insistently inviting his hearers to come down to the platform.

'Just stand up quietly without disturbing anyone and come forward. Come forward and accept your Saviour. Quietly, quickly, come now, come forward, come down here now, quietly, quickly . . .'

Far away up one of the sloping aisles two people appeared moving down to the platform. They were wearing counsellor's badges. Other figures joined behind them. More people got up. About twelve rows up, I saw a young woman muttering to a child of six or seven and pushing him gently into the aisle from her seat. Finally he came forward while she sat and smiled at his retreating figure. A fat boy of twelve in steel-rimmed spectacles and wearing a school blazer, stumbled down one of the aisles sobbing, tears pouring down his face. At my side, my wife gasped and said quite loudly:

'That's disgraceful!'

I shushed her gently. She was seething, though normally the mildest and most unaggressive of girls. It must have been some kind of feral outbreak of the mother instinct. We left about then, got to the car before the crowds came, and drove as if pursued by demons to the Empire to catch the last half of the Don Cornell bill. There was a young comedian on-stage when we got in, cracking a slightly blue joke. This appealed to us as a clean, wholesome way to be spending a Monday evening.

278

The *Daily Record* at that time had the reasonable idea of running two stories on the Billy Graham opening; one by an enthusiast and one by me. A page was mathematically halved and we took a half each. The page provoked a startling amount of mail. When columnists say they have been inundated with letters, they usually mean they had six letters. But this time there was a real flood. Nearly all were stimulated by my own half of the page. A few were letters of congratulation, the great majority angry. A small number of the letters from Graham defenders were unpleasant. One was an attack on my wife for being out with me at the Billy Graham meeting instead of being at home doing housework and watching her own children. A pleasant little woman called on me at the office to heap me with bitter reproach, but she was out of breath after climbing the stairs to my room, and I was so polite and helpful about finding her a chair and letting her get her breath back that the feet were cawed from her wrath before she started. When I showed her downstairs later she was saying: 'Well, you're quite right to say what you think, of course – no use thinking one thing and saying another, that's just a Pharisee trick.'

My mother, whose Christian conviction may have mellowed, but has never wavered, got a bad jolt when she read the article, but she declared stoutly to the neighbours that at least her son didn't disguise what he thought. She even started to enjoy the excitement. She had her own reservations about Billy Graham too, partly based on a feeling that there was something inappropriate in a man of God getting a hundred pounds a week.

But what did Graham do to Glasgow? On the face of it, he was a prodigious success. The Kelvin Hall was packed nightly for six weeks, and thousands of his hearers came forward to declare themselves; not only from Glasgow – people came in busloads and even special trains from all over the lowlands and highlands.

The excitement lingered on after he had left. The ministers and other church people who had invited him,

279

and who formed the crusade committee, followed up with more evangelist services of their own. The atmosphere suggested that the Protestant churches had found the answer to spreading Catholicism. Unfortunately, it is a fact that many of the young people crowding the evangelist services were not converts to the Protestant Church, but old members of various churches trying a new tack. A lot of the preaching was to the converted. The figures published some time later of non-churchgoers who had been brought into churches by the Graham crusade were pathetically small. Most of those who had come forward to 'accept Christ' were already churchgoing Christians. A church committee formed the theory that the apparent success of Graham was caused by the lack of drama in the lives of most people, and by the lack of chances to do something histrionic in public. The committee was dead right, of course. Everybody wants to be an actor in some way.

In fact, many men invent gods because a god is the only audience a man can be sure will always see the joke, always recognize the noble performance overlooked by the world, always applaud and always reward.

But after all these slaps at Billy Graham and evangelism – and in retrospect, my suspicions of Billy Graham and his methods have mellowed into active nausea – it is still apparent that the Protestant churches have got a tighter grip on Glasgow. The agnosticism automatically embraced by intelligent young people twenty years ago is much less favoured than it was. And religion has become news again, which has its own effect. Popular newspapers take it for granted that the majority of readers are convinced Christians. Obeying the formula of popular newspapers, they write for the majority, and create the assumption that everybody is a convinced Christian. Thus, by adopting an assumption, you tend to turn it into a reality.

The Church of Scotland is now tinkering with some pretty Romish ideas in the cause of Protestant church unity – bishops, and now lenten fasts, according to

George MacLeod, the Moderator of the General Assembly. As a totally lapsed Presbyterian, I suppose I have no right to complain about this, although I would like to. But I don't see it coming to anything. Scotland, and Glasgow in particular, is too fond of a good-going argument to go for a religion of authority. I predict that if the Church of Scotland embraces bishops and lent and other Catholic practices in the hope of unifying the Protestant churches, the first result will be an enthusiastic breakaway church thirled to the old ways. It will be the Auld Lichters and the New Lichters again.

It always will be. Apart from the mere matter of doctrinal conviction, the Glaswegian will never feel happy about agreeing with everybody else, even with everybody else in Glasgow. Every so often he gets the feeling that he would rather argue than eat.

What's all the fuss about unity, anyway? It's true that we're a' Jock Tamson's bairns, and no man is an island. But every man has to be his own little plot on the maine and grow his spiritual crops or weeds his own way. *Quot homines*, as they say, *tot sententiae*. And in Glasgow, that amounts to roughly 1,050,000 *sententiae* according to the last census.

Small Change, Big Change

The pattern of life in a city is changing furtively all the time, but even if nothing in the city changed, it would be changed because the eye that sees it is changing all the time. That is a safe enough banality, but what alarmed me sometimes was that it wasn't necèssary to wait for old age to be confronted with change and decay and renewal. After twenty-five, everything accelerated, and especially the changes. By that age, you have made acquaintances in the rangy age-group covered simply by the word adult, and grown to regard them as contemporaries, until you realize abruptly that they are quite grey, or white, or dead. The great, the indestructible John Bell was dead; too young, but not young, and dead. Where would there be another monument to honesty and zest to fill that huge fat grinning place?

Those clothes-baskets on two-inch wheels that house-wives trailed clattering behind them to the steamie have vanished in time – but how recently they were bits of the furniture of Glasgow. The steamie was the great place for gossip and steam and clothes-washing and the basis of music-hall sketches, and even it itself is losing its importance.

The GOC buses that roared out to the East along Gallowgate were gone from the earth almost before I was able to read GOC. But the red boy bus I owned as an infant was automatically a GOC bus. The GOC was the only kind of red bus that existed. And the yellow trams and the blue trams and the red trams – when did they all turn green? Was it fifteen years ago, or only ten? The colour used to tell the route until somebody thought of putting numbers on them instead and painting them all the same colour.

Then they took away the trams from the hill in West Nile Street – every north-and-south street in the centre of the city is a hill up from the river – and they put the trolleybuses on instead, and tore up the granite setts and laid the street smooth with tarmac. It looks better. Broader. But when was it they stopped the trace-horses? They used to stand beside the Post Office in West Nile Street; great, magnificent Clydesdales, handled by desperate scruffy Victorian street arabs, and hitch on to the carts going up the hill to Buchanan Street station to help the shaft horses to pull. It looked so hard that everybody felt sorry for the horses, but they made a brave sight, and the mad trace-boys would mount them and gallop them insanely back down to the Post Office.

Then they put the three-wheel mechanical horses on trace-duty – an odd sight, a horse pulling a cart and a motor-tank arrangement pulling the horse. And now the mechanical horse does the job without horses at all. But this wasn't in the dim Victorian past – it was when I was a reporter working in West Nile Street and feeling myself a grown man; feeling older than I do today, in fact.

I used to think that it was time they relieved horses of hard pulling like that. Now they have, and it feels strange and disquieting to see it.

It creeps up quietly. When we went for walks on summer evenings, sometimes in a crowd or sometimes in couples, we often walked up through Springboig where the houses suddenly stopped and there were only fields and a stray cottage all the way to the Edinburgh Road, and farms beyond to the hamlet of Swinton. The biggest sign of habitation on the way was the building in the Jewish cemetery, which stood at the edge of an open field in a square divided by a brick wall from farmland. But that was just before I was married. Now my sister Johanne lives there, in a flat at the other end of the field. You would hardly notice the Jewish cemetery among the three-storey buildings and four-storey buildings that pile and zigzag out past the horizon, past the Edinburgh Road.

Hope Street looked different, although it wasn't much changed. But I had been working in it for so long that I could hardly ever manage to see it again as I had seen it when it was new to me. The *Record* office wasn't any longer a frontage of windows with printing machines visible in the basement. It was three-dimensional, with all the corridors and staircases clearly laid out. Looking at the Central Hotel I could see the lobby and the lounge and the tables in the Malmaison restaurant, with the sense of wonder and exploration gone forever. But that had all happened gradually too.

One physical change was the new restaurant across the street. I remember watching the frontage being built, slender vertical aerofoil sections of polished timber recalling pictures of Swedish exhibitions, with decorative pictured glass panels, vast tall panes set between them and sloping outwards to the top. It was at the time when architects and decorators were trying to abandon the square and rectangle and shape things as trapezia or rhombi, with no right angles. The new place was a quality restaurant, with a huge cold table at the entrance of the dining room and a Continental head waiter and an impressive doorman. Too rich for my pocket, I regretted. I had just started writing a column, and feeling vaguely discontented that I wasn't suddenly famous and accepted, and rich, as I had once thought columnists naturally were.

Then I was walking down Hope Street last year with Ronald McIntosh, an old colleague from my West Nile Street days who was visiting us for a week from London, and he noticed the new restaurant.

'Very good place,' I agreed. 'I don't usually eat there.' And as I said the very words, the doorman leaned out from the doorway and waved a salute and shouted, 'Good morning, Mr Hanley.'

'You stage-managed that whole conversation, you sod,' Ronald said.

'Simple explanation,' I said. 'The doorman's a nice man, that's all.'

How long had it taken to get to the condition where high-class doormen greet you by name? Impossible to tell, because these foolish things happen not with a bang but in a trickle.

Now I knew all the newspaper people in Glasgow, and as I had for a time written a holiday column every week, I knew all the travel agents and airline people too. It took time to get to know them. There was always a shifting group of people from the *Record* office who sporadically went for a drink before lunch to the Corn Exchange across in Gordon Street, and there was a similarly shifting group of travel people who went to the same place at the same time. All managerial and executive specimens, or writers with local names. Some members of the travel group sometimes mixed with the newspaper group, and some of the newspaper people with the travel group.

I can remember recognizing both groups, and not being a member of either, and I can remember later being a member of both. What I can't remember is the transition, the graduation. From wondering how long it took to be known, I got hellos from a third of the people I passed in the city, but I didn't feel any different.

But it was pleasant to be well supplied with familiar faces, to find friendly company in every corner. The Corn Exchange was the great place for gathering of spirits whose work had elastic hours and expenses. Even this situation was changing and reforming all the time, however. Individuals would drop out and go elsewhere, and disappear forever, or drop back in again after a few weeks of self-denial. You meet too many pals in the Corn, they would say, 'so I'm moving to another pub where I can get one drink and get out quick.' Then others would say the same thing, until the other pub became just as dangerously social, and they would drift back one by one seeking the safety of solitary drinking that doesn't really exist.

But there was a period, spread over a couple of years, during which the sessions in the Corn Exchange bloomed and proliferated without inhibition. It may have derived from a post-rationing compulsion to live high and fast. The group at the bar would start with two members, and snowball into seven, or eight, or twelve, and every man satisfied that if he had been given a drink, he couldn't leave without standing a round. It's hard to see how anybody got any work done at all, but during that time the travel business went through its biggest expansion in history and I myself was writing more stuff than I have ever written since, and getting more applause from my readers.

Sometimes the whole mob would still be in the middle of a drink and a discussion when chucking-out time came at half-past two in the afternoon. More often it would start to dwindle at two as drinkers decided they would have to eat something to see them through the day, leaving a diehard group of three or four wondering what to do next. It was so easy to keep on sitting, at the corner table at the window behind the door. The Corn Exchange was a beautifully old-fashioned pub, described on the door as Gentlemen's Lounge; a big, roomy room with a long bar at the far end and little tables, all dark polished wood and panelling, and a monstrous open fire in winter, with the drinks served by good-natured waitresses of middle age or at least mature years.

What the diehards would usually decide to do was take a taxi to Ferrari's for lunch – the cheap lunch at 6/6d, we assured one another. The group would probably be drawn from a regular coterie of Rene Meier, the Swissair manager; a young, roly-poly fellow with black-black eyebrows and a perpetual bubbling smile; Tommy Stevenson, a hard-working travel agent who must have been catching up at other times of the day; and another couple of newspaper people and myself.

The cheap lunch in Ferrari's was a paltry form of self-deception. The food in Ferrari's is so good, and the service is so insinuating, that it always seems a pity not to try something adventurous. And since the taxi landed us there before the bar closed, it was foolish not to order a bottle of wine, or a round of liqueurs, or both, before it closed. Somehow the afternoon would glide away with talk and eating. I recall one day when three of us hoisted ourselves from the lunch table and with no excuse at all went to find a club to relax in for half an hour over coffee. We found ourselves inevitably relaxing over brandy, and when we decided that it was definitely time to call a halt, we wandered out to discover that the pubs had just opened for the evening. From that point sanity was lost entirely. We marched into the handiest pub and ordered a bottle of champagne and Imperial Stout, standing in the sawdust at the counter. Champagne, in a pub? It was a glorious, an historic twist, although it kept slipping away from moment to moment.

But it was a whole time that was slipping away. There comes a point, at least it should come, when it no longer seems alluring to drop into a haze three days a week. Old cliques are crumbling away all the time with old habits.

So Strange a Thing to Die

All these newspaper cliques, for instance, are changed to hell; not only because people move about in the newspaper industry, or get older themselves, but because the industry is changing. Glasgow was always a reading kind of place, and well endowed with newspapers.

D. C. Thomson, the shellback paper tycoon of Dundee, has offices and plant for the pawky, kailyaird-type *Sunday Post* in the north of the city, the curious village of Port Dundas. There is also the *Glasgow Weekly News*, which was once a pawky kind of creature too, but which has sprouted pin-ups and sweater girls and gone over to the show-businessy, cartoony, titillating end of journalism in recent years to keep up with the English Joneses like *Reveille*.

Beaverbrook has another of his glass palaces in Albion

Street, just along from George Square and the City Chambers, where the *Express* and the *Sunday Express* produce Scottish editions, and there's an evening paper too, the *Citizen*.

There were four papers produced in Hope Street; the *Daily Record*, the *Noon Record*, the *Evening News* and the *Sunday Mail*. They were owned, when I joined the *Record*, by Lord Kemsley, that pious collector of newspapers whose simple faith always rested on Decency and Respect for Private Grief. Buchanan Street contains the offices of the Outram Group, which publishes the quality though stodgy *Glasgow Herald*; another morning paper of the popular type aimed at middle-class women readers, the *Bulletin*; and the *Evening Times*.

At the end of 1954, Lord Kemsley sold the majority holding in his Glasgow newspapers to the London *Daily Mirror* Group. The news was received with cynical amusement by the staffs of the papers. Things might have been worse. At the same time, the Kemsley group brusquely closed down two old newspapers in Manchester and jolted large numbers of people out of jobs that had looked secure for life. The Glasgow papers were at least still running, and now being run by a newspaper outfit that had always been brilliantly successful, and given to paying high wages. The *Daily Record* has always described itself as Scotland's National Newspaper, but it has never been actually owned by Scotsmen, even in the old days when it was called the Ha'penny Liar. In newspapers, as in anything else, workers never really liked absentee landlords, and there were few people in Hope Street who shed any tears for the fall of the Kemsley empire with its benevolent but parsimonious paternalism and its atmosphere of fuddy-duddyism.

All the same, the change of ownership didn't turn out completely rosy. The new owners wanted to take a firm grip and remould everything. The *Daily Record* started to look more like a local edition of the *Daily Mirror*. Readers complained, but the circulation went up. I didn't like it myself. Suddenly I was nobody again. There's nothing so fragile as a reputation.

A few people started to drift away from Hope Street. The old days were decidedly gone. There was a new air of tension in all the newspaper offices in the city. It's harder and harder to make a profit from newspapers today, and there's less and less room in the business for leisure and eccentricity.

Still, people insist on surviving. Months came and went. We brought in 1957 with a bang. Hogmanay parties don't have as much surprise in Hillhead as they do in the East End, where nearly anybody is liable to knock on the door throughout the night with no introduction other than a half-bottle of whisky. In Hillhead, people are more chary of strangers, and the strangers are charier of them. But we spilled in and out of neighbours' houses and our own, and passed the night with many an optimistic howl. I hadn't thought much of 1956, personally.

In the middle of January, Anna and I were going to Scandinavian Airlines annual party, which was always a jolly affair, and this year, to make it jollier, I had agreed to put on a funny turn with the manager, Charlie Bennett. We were going to wear ponchos and sombreros and stroll among the guests during supper playing guitars and singing Spanish songs; to help to create a Scandinavian atmosphere, I think it was.

By this time, all our old baby-sitters had started having babies, so I asked a girl in the *Evening News* features department to help us out, and she innocently agreed. Her name was Deirdre. She was about twenty, and just started as a contributor to the woman's pages. While I was speaking to her my name was called on the public address system, and I lifted her telephone to find myself speaking to Ernie Anderson. He was in London.

'I'm bringing Eddie Condon to Glasgow tomorrow morning,' he said, 'with the object, among other things, of finally destroying you. You'll get Condon on the front page of tomorrow's *Record*, naturally.'

'Printed in blood,' I said.

'Well, I'm not arguing about the colour of the ink, just so it's the main story, that's all. Can you meet the overnight train, and if we're not on that, can you meet the first plane at Renfrew? But we'll be on the train, I think I've got him beaten into submission. Humphrey Lyttleton'll be there too.'

'I have heard of him,' I admitted.

'Well, just be there, Hanley,' Ernie said. 'There's another guy I want you to meet. You can make money out of him.'

'If it's more than two shillings, I'll be there,' I promised.

'How are things on the *Record*?'

'I'll tell you tomorrow,' I said.

Things were slightly nonsensical at that moment. I had just been interviewing an eighteen-year-old glass grader who, according to a reader's letter, was the spit and image of the late James Dean. He had come into the office and we had taken pictures of him in his James Dean set. He was an inoffensive, clean youngster and wanted to be a film actor too, but he had absolutely no idea, and he didn't look very much like James Dean either, except for the haircut and the leather jacket. He made me realize how detached I had become from the job I was supposed to be doing. After all, there's nothing wrong with a story like that in a popular daily – it's harmless and even interesting, in a harmless sort of way. But I had been reacting so much against trivialities like the James Dean cult that I was beginning to get actively against them instead of seeing them clearly and tolerantly. Anyway, I left the telephone and went back to the desk to hear the reactions to the photograph. One of the unexpected effects of the new regime was that the office proliferated bosses, deputy bosses, temporary bosses and assistant bosses, and one of them was reading my caption.

'The picture's great,' he said. 'But it's going at the top of the page – we'll need a lot more stuff underneath it than that.'

290

'How much?' I asked him. 'Four inches? Eight inches? Twelve inches?' I was anxious to get it finished and go home.

'For God's sake,' he said, 'you're not a sausage machine.'

I had known him for years and years.

'I am a sausage machine,' I said impatiently, 'and just tell me the length of sausage you want. Then I'll know.'

'Listen!' he snapped, 'we've got to get *excited* about this!'

'For how many inches?' I asked him. He picked up some other papers, moved around a little, and shot off to an editorial conference. There were lots of conferences at that time. I found the sub-editor who was making up the page and checked on the length of the caption, and wrote it. The sub-editor looked at the picture.

'Do you think that's much like James Dean?' he asked derisively.

'Same number of heads,' I pointed out. He wasn't too interested. Suddenly a crop of rumours had sprung up in the office about the future of the *Evening News*. The newspaper industry produces more rumours in modern times than it does newspapers. Some people had stories that the two rival evening papers, the *Citizen* and the *Times*, were going to amalgamate to fight the *News*. In fact, the *Times* had the largest circulation of the three, but it was known as a fact in the city that none of the three was making a profit at all.

Other people had the *Evening News* buying over the *Times*. Or the *Times* buying the *News*. Or the *News* buying the *Citizen*. Everybody was sure that something funny was going on. But one had heard rumours before. I was slightly worried, because if nothing happened soon, I was likely to be offered a job with the *Times* and become a somebody again. I took Deirdre home with me for tea, and practised three or four, or four and half, chords on the guitar for the party.

We were at the party, which started with stand-up

cocktails, when we bumped into a friend from the *Evening Citizen*. He looked serious, considering he was drinking a big whisky for nothing.

'Terrible about the *News*,' he said.

'What it?' he said.

'Have you honestly not heard? It's closing down at eleven o'clock tomorrow morning. Honestly, it's official this time.'

A few minutes later we met Eric de Banzie, for many many years the gossip columnist of the *Evening News*. He was not happy. Evidently the story was official after all.

'The chances are,' I tried to tell him, 'that the *Evening Times* will invite you over, to attract your regular readers to the *Times*.' He wondered.

The nuisance about being faced with a major crisis is that there are always so many things going on at the same time, so that you can't get time to concentrate. I still had my guitar and my four chords, and Charlie Bennet was waiting for us to go on.

'Go on, snigger "Pagliacci",' Anna said unfeelingly. We went into the buffet and started yelling 'Cielito Lindo'. The soberer guests threw pennies, which we picked up. Some of the others shouted for 'Granada', so we gave them the first two bars before going back to 'Cielito Lindo'.

'We were great,' Charlie told me. 'With broken hearts,' I said. The news about the *News* was not heartbreaking, of course. It produced an apprehensive excitement that wasn't entirely unpleasant. It was a piece of Glasgow history, after all; something to be experienced and remembered – a disaster like a train wreck, or a sensation like a bullfight. You don't want such a thing to happen, but if it does happen, and since it is happening, you want to be there at the time. When we got home a little after midnight, our baby-sitter was eager to know how the guitar entertainment had gone over.

'Just a minute, but,' I said guiltily. 'The crash has arrived. The *Evening News* is closing down tomorrow morning.'

'Oh,' she said. 'I wonder if I'll have to go back home to Carnoustie. Oh, listen – I have an article going in tomorrow. Do you think it'll be published all right? Then I would have a piece by me in the very last edition. That's ghoulish, isn't it?'

'Well, it would always be a souvenir,' I said.

'Not many people can say they were on a paper that died. I'll bet some people have been in journalism for fifty years without being on a paper that died.'

'You can save it up for your memoirs,' I said.

'But tell me about the performance – was it a riot? I wonder if I should give notice to my landlady – if I don't have any money I wouldn't want to pay a week's rent in lieu of notice if I had to go back home. But I might get another job later, and I might not get such a good place the next time if I give it up.'

'You could store your bits of furniture here in case you come back,' I suggested.

'You could even have a free bed for a while,' Anna pointed out.

'It's exciting, isn't it?' Deirdre said. 'I mean, it's horrible, but it's exciting. I mean, it's not like being sacked all by yourself.'

It was horrible, but it was exciting. The newsvendors had always shouted: 'Tie-new-cirra*zen*' in Glasgow for as long as anybody could remember. It was as homely and changeless as the cry of Coal, or Eglinton Coal Bricquettes – never just Coal Bricquettes, always Eglinton Coal Bricquettes. Now they would have to shout '*Times and Citizen*', with a gap in the middle where the *News* used to be.

The *Evening News* was a good paper, although it had for years been lowest of the three in circulation. It had a quality and a bite to it against the greyish look of the *Times* and the sprawling shapelessness of the big-sized *Citizen*. It was the paper most read in the centre of the city, and its circulation was actually rising at the time although like the two others it was making an annual loss.

Next morning I called at the Central Hotel on my way to the office to see if Ernie and the visiting jazz-men had arrived. I met the television writer of the *Evening News* in the lobby and learned that they hadn't.

'They're flying, then,' I said. 'We may as well go over to the office and phone BEA for the arrival time.'

He looked pale and worried, like many people that morning. 'I imagine they'll spread the sackings over the three staffs,' he said hopefully. 'They wouldn't just turf out everybody in the *News*.'

'They can't, surely,' I agreed. 'We should be as much involved in the *Record* as the *News* is.' We went across the street to the office to telephone BEA. The muffled bump and hum of the machines was still there. Along the corridor on the editorial floor, people were standing in twos and threes, and walking in and out of rooms off the corridor. There had never been so much standing about. People would go into one room to talk to the occupant and wander out and go into the next room to say the same things over again. Unexpected combinations of writers and reporters and sub-editors gathered in knots and rearranged themselves in other knots to pick over the same few facts.

'They'll make an official announcement at noon.'

'No, half-past two.'

'Do we get any compensation?'

'Sure, a free copy of the last edition.'

'But what happens to the serial? The poor bloody public will die of suspense.'

'It's the first time I ever saw a ship deserting the sinking rats.'

'The sods could have saved the *News* if they had tried.'

'They're no' interested.'

'What in God's name's to become of Juliet?' (Juliet Jones, the strip serial.)

'What's to become of my poor building society?'

According to BEA, Eddie Condon and Ernie were due

at the hotel any second, so we went back to meet them. They arrived a few minutes later. I recognized Ernie's pale morose face, the thick glasses, the delighted sad smile.

'This is Eddie Condon, himself. I told you we would catch the night train, didn't I?'

'I believed you,' I said. Eddie Condon, short, about the same size as myself, looked somewhat like James Cagney, walked back on his heels with stiff legs and appeared to have been drinking. He narrowed his eyes to look at me.

'Your face is familiar,' he muttered. 'I think that parole board made a bad mistake.'

'You got here just in time,' I told Ernie, 'to see the *Evening News* dying. They're closing it today.'

'My timing was always good,' he said blandly. 'Come on, you'll have to meet Dick Gehman, he's a rich writer – he'll give you a hundred dollars for some dope on the Glasgow gangs.'

'In advance?'

Ernie grinned. 'What do you take him for, a Glaswegian?'

'Actually, I'm looking for a job as a chauffeur.'

'Provide your own Caddy?'

There was an unorganized drift to the hotel dining room for breakfast. It was full of milling musicians talking and eating. It would have been a jolly party on some other day. A group collected in one of the bedrooms later, musicians and reporters. Condon, peering at a wisp of fog outside and murmuring, 'Let's not overdo this sunshine, now.' Dick Gehman, the rich writer, tapping at a little portable typewriter on a table beside the washbasin. People sitting on the two beds asking one another what was happening next. Humphrey Lyttelton explaining with beautiful courtesy what jazz meant, to a young, brainless reporter. As time went on, I left with Gehman and a trumpeter called Davison to demonstrate an ordinary Glasgow pub, down Hope Street.

'What a country!' said Gehman, 'What a wonderful country. Everybody's so *polite*!'

'One hears conflicting reports,' I said.

'One is wrong,' Davison insisted. 'Honestly, I forgot people could be so nice.'

'Come on up and see the *Evening News* dying,' I said. Gehman came. Nothing had changed in the office. People were still moving about in the wrong places, like strangers in a new ship trying to get to know the geography of the place. I introduced Gehman to some acquaintances, who received him amiably enough without actually seeing him. Towards half-past two, a drift began across the open editorial floor where Jackie Robertson, the editor of the *News*, had appeared, his bulky height visible above the moving coteries. When a crowd had collected he started to speak.

'These are bitter moments . . . The *Evening News* will not publish after today. We have fought a good fight, and we have succeeded in making the *News* the best evening paper in Britain. We are going down fighting. I am grateful to you all for the wonderful job you have done. Some of us will be retained in this office, others will not.' He was in an emotional condition. The news editor of the *News* uttered a few sentences in reply. Always given to clipped, consciously chosen phrases, his voice too wavered. It was a violently emotional moment. It was after this I noticed what was different about the office. The hum and thump of the machines was gone. Nothing was being printed.

Outside, in the streets, it would have been hard to tell that anything was different. Only the newsvendors seemed to know. One of them shouted wryly at me: 'Souvenir edition!', waving the very last *Evening News* in the air. It was worse the next day. There was a silence in the office like an official holiday. Great areas were dark, places in which lights always burned from eight in the morning till after midnight; and where the darkness was, there were no people. By ten o'clock, people began to wander into the office to gather in knots again. The Day After The Bomb, with survivors crawling out of holes in the ground to find the town vanished, empty spaces and silence. I went upstairs to the artists' room.

'It's funny how everybody feels together,' I said vaguely. 'Except for one crumb who deserves to be nameless, the victims and the survivors are one big affectionate family.'

'You're right,' Eric Clarke said at once. 'I've discovered I liked the people that worked here – even the sods I hated.' Suddenly Eric's name was called on the public address, and he had to run into another room to answer the telephone. He came back hugging himself and giggling.

'You've got a new job!' we said spontaneously.

'No, it's better than that,' he choked. 'It was a guy trying to sell me a Goggomobil. Today!'

'In the altered economic circumstances,' I remarked, 'I fear I shall be compelled to call in my notes of hand.'

'That's right,' Eric said. 'You owe Molly Kelly ten bob and she's just been sacked.'

The *Evening News* is not the first paper to die in Glasgow, and it may not be the last, but so far it's the biggest. A newspaper is not only a piece of business property, it's a piece of society, a bit of the furniture of a city, as well as being a society in itself. When it dies, a small world is dispersed. I kept having to stop myself from saying things like: 'The lights have gone out all over Europe, and We have seen the end of an era.' We had, all the same.

297

Small Change, No Change

After tea-time one night I found myself intoning:

> 'Engine engine number nine,
> Ran alang a bogie line.'

My son fastened on me at once and demanded to know the rest.

'Have you never heard that?' I was puzzled. 'Engine engine number nine, ran alang a bogie line. Pea shoot, you're oot, engine engine number nine.'

'Again!' he shouted. My daughter was listening fascinated.

'Do another one,' she told me. It was one of those idyllic family moments when I wasn't shouting at them.

'Have you never heard that?' I hooted. 'Paddy on the railroad pickin' up stanes, alang came an engine an' broke Paddy's banes. Oh, said Paddy, that's no ferr. Oh, said the engine, you shouldny be therr.'

'That's the best,' Jane said. 'Sing it properly,' She pronounced 'properly' very properly, with an affected liquid 'r'.

'This is terrible,' I said to Anna. 'These kids are being dragged up totally ignorant of their heritage of scruffy folklore.'

'You'd better watch,' she said. 'Their teacher'll hate that.'

'Teachers ignorant of folklore next?' I said meanly. 'Here's one. Ah had a sausage, a bonny Hielan' sausage, ah put it in the oven for ma tea. When ah went tae the loabby, tae meet ma Uncle Boabby, the sausage ran efter me'.'

'But even I've never heard that,' Anna pointed out.

'You were raised in a cultural desert,' I said. 'Every child should live in Gallowgate. What in heaven's name are we doing in Hillheid? Look at it. Pathetic snobberies, fatuous presumptions and bad manners.'

'We'll move to Gallowgate.'

'Not if you dragged me kicking and screaming.' I said. 'Let the scruff live in Gallowgate, and to hell with them.'

'Do the sausage song again,' Clifford broke in.

'But you see what happens,' I said. 'The kids are growing up déraciné, or something. They don't even know how to play moshie.'

'Teach them then.'

'I don't know how to play moshie either. I'll buy them a peerie instead. But it's all wrong. This place is a barren village without blood or tradition.'

However, the next afternoon Jane came home from school singing:

'Born in a tenement in Gorbals Cross
Of all the teddy boys he was the boss
He had a razor six feet wide,
Killed a' the folk, an' threw them in the Clyde'.

'Where do they get that stuff?' I asked Anna.

'It's folklore,' she said.

'I know,' I said. 'It's great.'

But what does anybody know about children, and the world they live in? When my mother came out to the house that week she said:

'You don't remember anything about Gallowgate – you were only five when we left it.'

'Six,' I said. 'And I remember practically nothing in my life *except* Gallowgate. It seemed to last for centuries. Remember how much broken pastry we used to get for a

299

penny in McKean's? And a pound of midget tomatoes for tuppence in Glass's?'

'You don't mind Glass's,' she said thunderstruck. 'He's just a wee blether Anna.'

'Ha'penny plates a pea brac in the Bungalow,' I recited. 'Sugar pigs in Convery's.'

'That's right,' my mother admitted. 'You'd have thought you were too young to mind.'

So what did Hillhead look like today to a child of six? Nobody could tell but a child of six, who couldn't tell. And after all it wasn't so far from Gallowgate. I was looking at it from the window, and what suddenly bewildered me was: How and why did the whole thing arise in the first place? Byres Road – a hundred years ago it had byres in it, and at the bottom end there was an inn where club outings used to gallop in brakes from Glasgow for gluttonous roast goose dinners on a Sunday. You can understand that – byres and inns. People have to eat. But what did they go and build tenements and closes for?

I don't mean that I object to the tenements and the closes. I ask myself the question in pure scientific curiosity. Why should a million people all gather together and put up four-storey-buildings and streets among them, and pends and back courts, and decide to live the rest of their lives in this pile of stone? And why should anybody sane want to come and join them in it?

And having done that, why should they start finding affection for the heap, and giving it names and reputations as if it were a juju, and inventing jokes about it and writing songs about it, and carrying on as if it was something ancient and permanent and pre-ordained and the best thing of its kind in human history? It baffles me utterly, and the answers, the crisp fourth-hand answers in sociology do nothing but pile more mystery on top of the original mystery. The real answer is somewhere in the primitive magic we fancy we have left behind in the caves. That's what Glasgow is like. It isn't a place, it's a rite, and the motions are written somewhere in the blood. Half the time you would like to get rid of it altogether. But you can't live any kind of reasonable life without blood.

THE END

THE BIG WIND
by Beatrice Coogan

'The Ireland of 1840–1870 that Beatrice Coogan unveils in her magnificent novel is an Ireland that would be inconceivable to most Irishmen living in the Irish Republic today.

Then. ruthless landlords could throw the sick, the aged and the dying out of their homes; hundreds of thousands of men, women and children were allowed to die of hunger; a man could be sentenced to twenty years hard labour for stealing a loaf of bread to feed his children.

Mrs. Coogan catches all the horror, injustice and depravity of it and the blend of romance, action, compassion and cruelty woven around the lives of hundreds of people makes THE BIG WIND a towering novel and easily one of the best to emerge from Ireland in recent years'
Patrick Campbell, *Irish Echo*

'A work of major importance'
The Sunday Press, Dublin

0 552 08615 0   £3.25

ANOTHER STREET, ANOTHER DANCE
by Clifford Hanley

The long awaited, gutsy novel of Glasgow life by the author of DANCING IN THE STREETS.

In ANOTHER STREET, ANOTHER DANCE, Clifford Hanley returns to the warm, sprawling life of the old Glasgow tenements, the street games, the intellectual and political ferment of the twenties and thirties, the hard times and the unquenchable energy that made the city sing.

Meg Macrae, an innocent girl from the Islands, has to learn to cope with the big city, and men, and children. In her triumph, she becomes one of the great heroines of our time, and her youngest son, Peter, is destined for glory.

ANOTHER STREET, ANOTHER DANCE sweeps through the troubled depression years, from Red Clyde-side to the Spanish Civil War, and on through the tumultuous events of the Second World War. Above all, it is a tale teeming with blazing characters, vibrant with colour and rich with life.

'His ear for Glasgow dialogue is as brilliant as ever . . . funny, entertaining, compassionate and, in its own thoroughly admirable way, wise'
Glasgow Herald

0 552 12455 9   £1.95

A SELECTED LIST OF FINE NOVELS
AVAILABLE FROM CORGI BOOKS

WHILE EVERY EFFORT IS MADE TO KEEP PRICES LOW, IT IS SOME-
TIMES NECESSARY TO INCREASE PRICES AT SHORT NOTICE. CORGI
BOOKS RESERVE THE RIGHT TO SHOW NEW RETAIL PRICES ON
COVERS WHICH MAY DIFFER FROM THOSE PREVIOUSLY ADVERTISED
IN THE TEXT OR ELSEWHERE.

THE PRICES SHOWN BELOW WERE CORRECT AT THE TIME OF GOING
TO PRESS (OCTOBER '84).

☐	10757 3	WITCH'S BLOOD	William Blain	£2.50
☐	08615 0	THE BIG WIND	Beatrice Coogan	£3.25
☐	12455 9	ANOTHER STREET, ANOTHER DANCE	Clifford Hamley	£1.95
☐	11872 9	MANGO WALK	Rhona Martin	£1.75
☐	07583 3	NO MEAN CITY	A. McArthur & H. Kingsley Long	£1.95
☐	08335 6	CUT AND RUN	Bill McGhee	£1.95
☐	11762 5	THE MANGAN INHERITANCE	Brian Moore	£1.95
☐	99048 5	THE SKATER'S WALTZ	Philip Norman	£2.50
☐	12437 0	McNALLY'S EMPIRE	Gertrude Schweitzer	£2.50
☐	10612 7	SIX WEEKS	Fred Mustard Stewart	£1.75
☐	12060 X	CENTURY	Fred Mustard Stewart	£1.95
☐	12434 6	ELLIS ISLAND	Fred Mustard Stewart	£1.95
☐	10565 1	TRINITY	Leon Uris	£2.95
☐	08866 8	QB VII	Leon Uris	£2.50
☐	08384 4	EXODUS	Leon Uris	£2.95
☐	08091 8	TOPAZ	Leon Uris	£2.50
☐	08385 2	MILA 18	Leon Uris	£2.50
☐	07300 8	ARMAGEDDON	Leon Uris	£2.95
☐	08521 9	THE ANGRY HILLS	Leon Uris	£1.95

*All these books are available at your book shop or newsagent, or can be ordered
direct from the publisher. Just tick the titles you want and fill in the form below.*

CORGI BOOKS, Cash Sales Department, P.O. Box 11, Falmouth, Cornwall.

Please send cheque or postal order, no currency.

Please allow cost of book(s) plus the following for postage and packing:

U.K. Customers—Allow 55p for the first book, 22p for the second book and 14p for
each additional book ordered, to a maximum charge of £1.75.

B.F.P.O. and Eire—Allow 55p for the first book, 22p for the second book plus 14p
per copy for the next seven books, thereafter 8p per book.

Overseas Customers—Allow £1.00 for the first book and 25p per copy for each
additional book.

NAME (Block Letters) . . . .

ADDRESS . . . .

. . . .